An Artist at War

The Journal of John Gaitha Browning

War and Southwest Series
Number 3

September 23, 1943

Dearest Mother,

Received your letter, in good time, for change. Also received V letters from Eliz. and Miss Florence.

Was very glad to hear that Miss Lizzie would be with you. For gosh sakes pay her anything she wants and have her any time, every day if possible. She will be more willing if she knows she can work any time she doesn't have work at home to do. You can afford to give her agood salary, if you will make a deal with her I will send her a check every month too, which should make the work attractive enough to keep her on it. I will be waiting to hear in your next letter, so tell me what kind of deal you have made with her etc. If you will send me her address I will make the deal myself; I believe I could make the best one, at least I bet she would be there regularly.

Was much amused at what you thought I ought to do after the war. Part of it is all right, and I appreciate your thinking of me. I want a good studio and home combined, and I will most likely keep on painting regardless. That happens to be what I really want to do, more than anything else. Yesterday I was reading a copy of the Post, and came acros a small story of a man in the Ozarks. He left and built up a successful business, but later found that he didn't want a successful business in the city, so he sold out and went back to the Ozarks and a sleepy little town, and has been perfectly happy for forty years. The thing ended up by saying "He found the way of life which has brought him true contentment and, unlike too many of us, has had the courage to live that life." I often wonder just where and how I could possibly be content to spend the rest of my life, but if I find the answer by golly I am going to have the courage to carry it through. If I never find anyone who has the courage to stick it out with me, well-- I've been doing pretty well by myself for some time. I often think of Mr. DeYoung, and how unhappy he has been with a family that continually naged him to quit his work and do something else. Just last week I got a letter from Kathryn Witherstine, of Provincetown Mass. and it seems the same situation is in their family. Don Witherstine has been an artist all his life, but now they want him to quit and move to New York and do something else, which was somewhat of a surprise to me for I had never seen a more understanding family than he had, they were all swell.

Everyone tells of the hard summer in Texas, but if you have had rain the situation should be better by now. We have had no more rain, but it is getting hotter by the day and if it keeps up it should be 200 in the shade by the middle of our summer here. Possibly even a rain will not cool things off too much, I noticed the last time it rained it was about as hot while the rain was falling.

Write soon,

All my love,

"Was much amused at what you thought I ought to do after the war. Part of it is all right, and I appreciate your thinking of me. I want a good studio and home combined, and I will most likely keep on painting regardless."

An Artist at War

The Journal of John Gaitha Browning

Edited by

Oleta Stewart Toliver

University of North Texas Press
Denton, Texas

First printed in 1994 in the United States of America

The paper in this book meets the minimum requirements of the American National Standard for Permanence of paper for Printed Library Materials, Z39.48.1984.

Jacket design by Aaron Pendland

Library of Congress Cataloging-in-Publication Data

Browning, John Gaitha, b. 1913.

An artist at war : the journal of John Gaitha Browning / edited by Oleta Stewart Toliver.

p. cm.—(War and the Southwest series ; no. 3)

Includes index.

ISBN 0-929398-76-9

1. Browning, John Gaitha. b. 1913—Diaries. 2. World War, 1939–1945—Campaigns—Pacific Area. 3. World War, 1939–1945—Personal narratives. American. 4. Soldiers—United States—Diaries. 5. United States. Army—Biography. I. Toliver, Oleta Stewart, 1928– . II. Title. III. Title: Journal of John Gaitha Browning. IV. Series.

D767.9.B76 1994

940.54'8173—dc20

[B]

94-20152

CIP

10 9 8 7 6 5 4 3 2 1

War and the Southwest Series

The University of North Texas Press has undertaken to publish a series of significant books about War and the Southwest. This broad category includes first-hand accounts of military experiences by men and women of the Southwest, histories of warfare involving the people of the Southwest, and analyses of military life in the Southwest itself. The Southwest is defined loosely as those states of the United States west of the Mississippi River and south of a line from San Francisco to St. Louis as well as the borderlands straddling the Mexico-United States boundary. The series will include works involving military life in peacetime in addition to books on warfare itself. It will range chronologically from the first contact between indigenous tribes and Europeans to the present. The series is based on the belief that warfare is an important if unfortunate fact of life in human history and that understanding war is a requirement for a full understanding of the American past.

Books in the Series

FOO—A Japanese-American Prisoner of the Rising Sun
Wen Bon: A Naval Air Intelligence Officer behind Japanese Lines in China

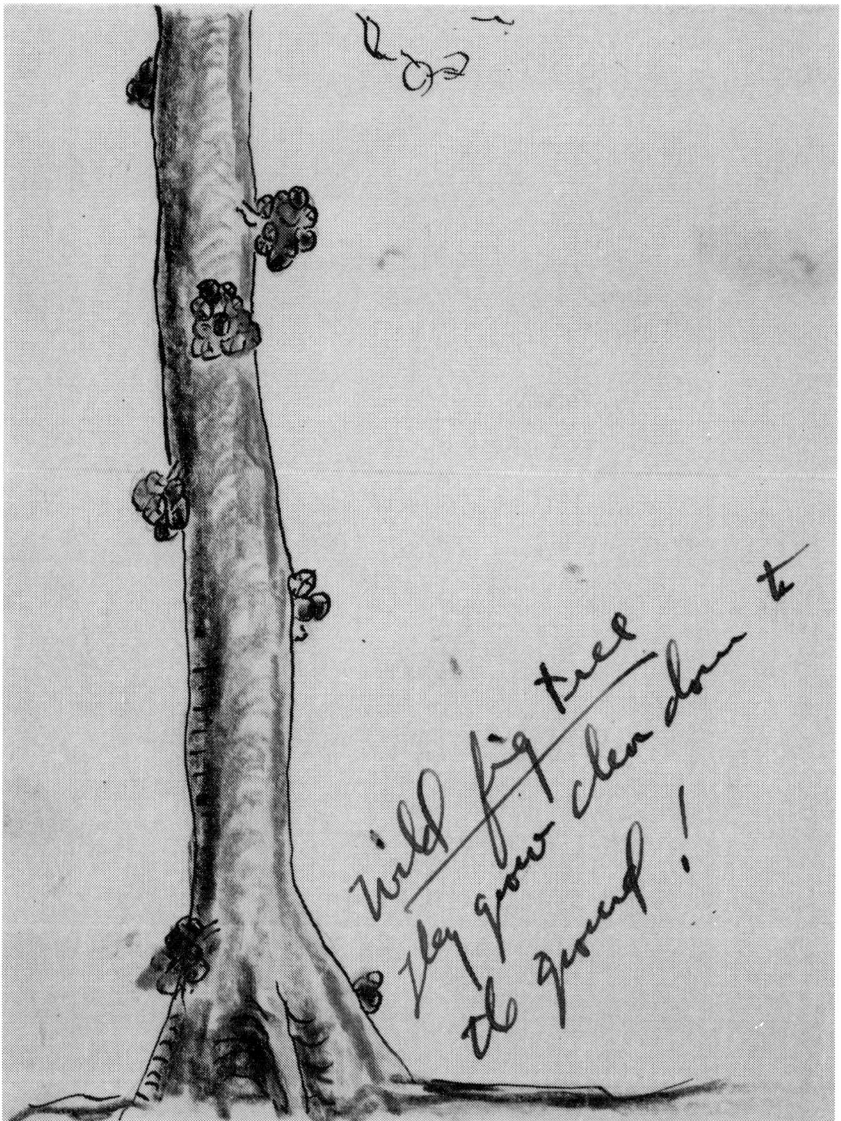

"Wild fig tree: They grow clear down to the ground!"

Dedication

To my father, Carl Otto Stewart (June 15, 1899, to October 20, 1992)—whose memoirs are written on the pages of my heart.

And to the parents of John Gaitha Browning—Claude L. and Addie Butler Browning. They would be proud of this journal's publication.

—Oleta Stewart Toliver

Contents

PART III: OCTOBER 30, 1944, TO JUNE 22, 1945

INTRODUCTION

John Gaitha Browning was born July 15, 1913, in Oxford, Mississippi, the son of Claude L. and Addie Butler Browning. His paternal grandparents were T. F. Browning and Bettie Collier Browning, residents of Lafayette County, Mississippi. The Claude Browning family moved to Brownwood, Texas, when Gaitha was six. One of his first memories is of the end of that long train ride across three states, as they arrived at their destination in a savage ice storm on March 22, 1919.

His pleasant childhood experiences were filled with loving family contacts with his unmarried aunts, Maude and Dot. His father spent long hours working in the Santa Fe Railroad Shop and had little time for the interests of a growing boy, but his mother placed the welfare and happiness of Gaitha and his sister, Elizabeth, above all else.

With her encouragement he joined a Boy Scout troop at an early age. The interests and activities which he shared here were to affect his life profoundly. His scoutmaster, Cliff Pouncey, was like a second father to the sensitive boy and developed his interest and knowledge in nature lore and in a study of the American Indian culture. His aptitude for the artistic was revealed in the Indian crafts at which he became so adept and in the piquant sketches with which he filled every scrap of paper. Learning to look for beauty and see the detail of everything that filled his world was to prepare him for a future of filling countless canvasses—not just with pictures, but with images so vividly produced that they became real.

His elementary years passed swiftly, and by the time he was in high school, the young Browning had acquired a wide reputation as an expert in Indian lore. He spent summers teaching Indian dancing, Indian crafts, and nature study in Boy Scout camps, not only in the Brownwood area, but in other states as well.

After graduating from Brownwood High School, he attended Howard Payne College (now University) for two years, acquiring typing and business organizational skills which were to serve him well throughout his future.

Although Gaitha was good at whatever studies he pursued, his soul yearned for the skills which would enable him to create and record beauty. During those years, Harry Anthony DeYoung[1] spent summers in San Antonio, where Gaitha went to study art with him. DeYoung recognized a creative brilliance in the youth and encouraged him to devote himself fulltime to his art.

Since boyhood, Gaitha had felt the insistent call of the vibrant beauty of New Mexico and Arizona, so he went to Gallup, New Mexico, and fell hopelessly in love with the country there. With sketchbooks filled to overflowing and an impatience to express in oil the excitement he felt, Gaitha opened his own studio in 1941, the year Pearl Harbor was bombed to bring the United States into World War II. Gaitha's devotion to his country overcame his devotion to his artist's palette, and on May 7, 1942, he entered the United States Army during the time a major buildup was being executed for landings on New Guinea and other South Pacific islands, with the eventual re-taking of the Philippines by the Allied Forces as the ultimate goal. On February 19, 1942, Japanese planes had bombed Darwin, Australia, and by August the Japanese Empire had reached its height and controlled the Gilbert, Marshall, Caroline and Mariana islands, stretching half-way across the Pacific.

The Allies began their first offensive action in the Pacific on August 7, 1942. U.S. Marines landed on Guadalcanal in the Solomon Islands. Bitter fighting continued for several months, while control of the island seesawed between Japanese and Allied troops. During August and September, the Australians defeated the Japanese on land for the first time in the war, beating them back at Milne Bay on the southeastern point of New Guinea. U.S. Army troops under Major General Alexander M. Patch finally cleared Guadalcanal in February of 1943.

Meanwhile, in the summer of 1942, Gaitha spent five days in an induction camp at Mineral Wells, Texas, before being sent to Camp Chaffey at Little Rock, Arkansas, for basic training. Private First Class John Gaitha Browning left Arkansas for Cape Cod, Massachusetts, and at Camp Edwards on Waquoit Island he became a part of the 592d Engineers' Amphibian Regiment.

His typing skills and his evident careful attention to detail earned him the post of headquarters company clerk of the Second Battalion. After his unit's training was complete, he spent a brief time at Camp Carrabelle, Florida. Then three companies shipped out to Fort Ord in San Francisco, California, where they were in February when ordered to board the U.S. Army Transport Willard A. Holbrook to be sent to an unknown destination in one of the theaters of war.

When the day of departure came in March, 1943, Browning decided to begin a journal of his experiences, with the hope that someday he would be able to read it and contemplate how his life was changed as a result of the war. With sketches and water-color renderings he planned to preserve the glimpses of goodness and beauty which he might chance to contact. His journal begins with a letter to his parents written in February of 1943 before he sailed in March.

I knew of John Gaitha Browning as a southwest artist, but until our accidental meeting in the spring of 1991, I had no idea of the breadth of his talent, the prolificness of his work, or the philosophy of living with which he lit up the world. Hundreds of his canvasses grace the walls of private collectors; no collection of southwest art of this century is complete without one of his works. No doubt his years of living among the Navajo, Zuni and Crow tribes contributed to his artistic understanding of the southwest.

The more research I did, the more famous I realized he was. Gaitha Browning paintings are recognized treasures, but the private journal Gaitha kept from the time of his entry into army life in 1942 throughout his travels in Australia, New Guinea, and the Philippines, until his return to civilian life, has up to now been an unrecognized treasure. A startlingly different view of a soldier's life during World War II unfolds with its pages.

Although Gaitha was involved in many battles, most of his attention in his writings is devoted to other servicemen, other peoples and cultures, and the natural beauty—or lack of it—in his surroundings. His desire was to record the good and beautiful, even when he had to search for it in the confusion and destruction of war. Gaitha's original intent was that his writings not be a record of "blood and guts." He maintained this determination throughout the journal and expressed it to me repeatedly as I worked on the project.

Gaitha was excited about the possibility of seeing his journal in print, and he also wanted us to work together on material about his post-war experiences as a Southwest artist. But heart surgery prior to our meeting had left him physically unable to spend long hours on the biographical projects. Heart failure caused his death on November 10, 1992. I completed work on the journal in a determined effort to carry out his wishes.

Although I have edited and amplified his actual journal with added information gleaned through research in his personal papers, taped interviews of his delightful storytelling sessions, and letters written to his friends and family (made available to me by his generosity), I have been careful to preserve the flavor of his artistic description.

His childhood and youthful contacts must have been sheltered and protected from confrontation with "man's inhumanity to man" because he entered the army with a fresh innocence and trust. His disappointment at the inherent lack of the "total goodness in man" comes from his introduction to the behavior of individuals who used their authority to promote their own selfish purposes, rather than for the good of the men under their command.

Almost tangibly I felt his revulsion for and his withdrawal from acts of machísmo. His concept of masculinity was derived from colonial times and his Old South heritage, when a MAN was characterized by his integrity of thought and action. Gaitha's mother must have helped him to develop this attitude, and Scout Master Cliff Pouncey must have done a great deal to reinforce it. Like his mother, Gaitha was always an inveterate reader, and his values—distilled from history readings—cannot be characterized as old-fashioned, for today they could serve well the man who follows them.

The racial views expressed in the journal reflect the prejudices of Gaitha's contemporaries, his Old South background, and his reactions to the wartime atmosphere. Although his parents left Mississippi when he was still a little child, he grew up in Texas with the values they brought with them—values which fortunately softened with experience and maturity. He came to respect both Hispanics and Blacks through contact with their handicrafts and artistic expression.

Reading the record of his continuing experiences, we see his growth toward tolerance and acceptance of his own and others' circumstances. He learns to circumvent the shattered relationships and traumas of battle; whether at the typewriter as a company clerk or at his artist's palette, whatever work he performed was done with careful attention to detail, flawless accuracy, and an incredible consistency in searching for—and finding—beauty in the midst of war and separation from his friends and family. Much of the beauty is expressed in his vivid descriptions of South Pacific wildlife, landscape, and folkways.

His is the story of a rare human being who made life better for all whom he touched. Gathering Gaitha's thoughts on paper has been a memorable adventure for me. While we worked together for the journal's publication, I learned to love this forceful artist, this gentle man, as the brother I always wanted.

Because many names are directly from his memory, some may be misspelled or incorrect. It is our hope that the reader will search for the greater truth expressed, rather than these inconsistencies.

—Oleta Stewart Toliver

NOTES

[1] Three of Harry Anthony DeYoung's better-known works hang at the Alamo in San Antonio, Texas.

February 15, 1943.

Dearest Mother and Dad,

Received your letter today, the one you wrote the day after we talked on the phone. I sure enjoyed it too, but just wish I could have been there to see you also.

We are still getting ready to leave, and still guessing where we will go. We just know that it isn't far, and isn't into any kind of action. As we are leaving a lot of the usual army dirty work is going on, for there are some people the officers don't want to take along and are using this as an excuse to get rid of them. Some just the opposite, who don't want to go themselves and others are determined to see that they do go. You wouldn't believe all the dirty things people can hatch up to get even with one another when they have the chance.

Today is beautiful and warm, in fact so warm that all the windows are open and you sure get hot in the sun. I noticed that the willows in town are budding, so guess Spring is on the way here.

Walked down to the postoffice and sent off a few rough sketches. They are mostly pictures I want to paint, but can't, so just plan them when I can get out and sketch, and maybe I will have time to work them up into real paintings when I get home. Am always getting ideas and wanting to paint, but feel that if I can do a little something I will be learning all the time, and what I learn will come in handy later.

I know that Tippy never did like for Pigtail to bother him, even when we first got him, and I am glad he can make Pigtail let him alone. Eliz told me how Micky will howl when Pigtail hollers "Call for Phillip Morris".

Hope you looked at the booklet on New Mexico houses, for sent it to you so you could see the nice designs. Those fireplaces sure suit me, I would give anything to have a studio with one, and will someday too. Until I can I will just keep sketching the interesting things wherever I go.

Don't be surprised if you stop hearing from me, for we may just up and leave tomorrow or Wed. but you know that I will write the first minute I can.

I love you lots,

Walter

"[S]ent off a few rough sketches. They are mostly pictures I want to paint, but can't, so just plan them when I can get out and sketch, and maybe I will have time to work them up into real paintings when I get home. Am always getting ideas and wanting to paint, but feel that if I can do a little something I will be learning all the time, and what I learn will come in handy later."

February 6, 1943
Fort Ord, California

Dearest Mother and Dad,

So glad to get your letter today, along with the one from Ella.[1] I always enjoy her letters and get a kick out of the funny, homey things she tells. I'm glad Roy[2] is doing so well that he wants to stay in, for it is his own doing; the army had nothing to do with it. Just yesterday—after they have had so much trouble with the men drinking—it was decided that if a man was just off without leave two or three days a month, there shouldn't be anything done about it—that maybe he deserved to get on a two or three day drunk once a month.

After that, I expect just anything, for you know when the men find they can get by with two days, they will take five just to see if they can get by with that. I still don't understand the army—as usual—and I still say it plays up the lowest instinct in everyone and gives them every chance to go down instead of up.

I probably won't write you tomorrow, for I will go in to Carmel Monday, and then will phone, although you will have talked to me long before you get this. I was to have gotten a pass today, but will have to wait until Monday or maybe Tuesday now. Reason: Well, my two friends here in the office found that I was to get a three-day pass this weekend, and as neither of them could get one, they both decided they would get twenty-four hour passes, one on Saturday and one on Sunday, which throws me two days later for my three days; for I can't go until they get back. But after all, it will work out better for me, as I have a cold, and it will be better—and probably well—by then.

It was right funny today. Three of us in here had terrible colds and were practically sick, and if we weren't a frowzy looking bunch! The hospital gave us some medicine to help the head colds, but we haven't done much today except just sit and look sleepy. I am just lucky in being here where I can do that if I don't feel well.

I'm going to take my small sketch box with me and do the old mission in Carmel. Three whole days will seem like ages after this stir, and by just going to Carmel I won't have that long hard bus trip like the one to Los Angeles.

I'm so sorry that Maude is still sick but am glad she can go to Dot's[3] and be quiet. I know you are not able to wait on anyone, and you shouldn't try. You will all do well to just stay well until the weather is better.

Lots of love,

Gaitha

PART I

March 17, 1943, to July 29, 1943

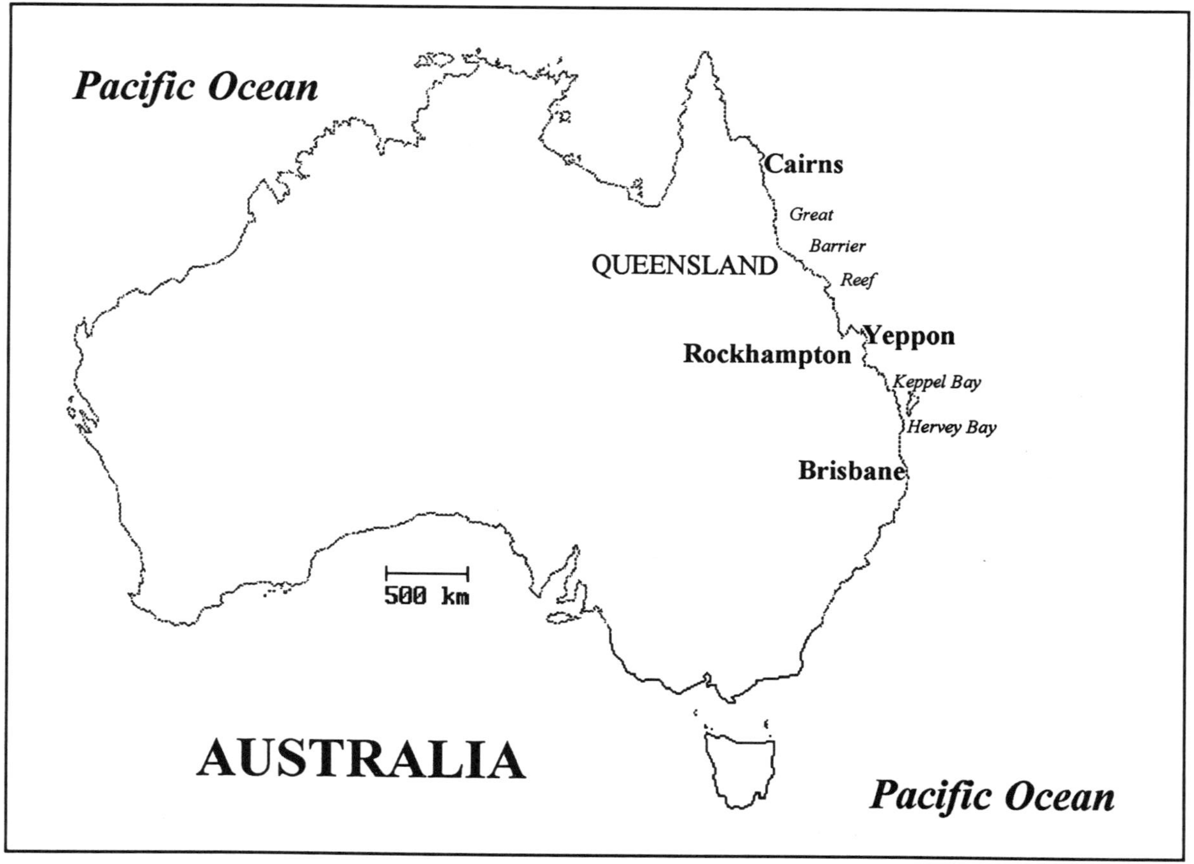
Pacific Ocean
Cairns
Great
Barrier
Reef
QUEENSLAND
Yeppon
Rockhampton
Keppel Bay
Hervey Bay
Brisbane
500 km
AUSTRALIA
Pacific Ocean

1 At Sea

March 17, 1943

We arrived at Oakland Bay on the night of February 17, 1943, to board the transport. The Oakland Bridge lights made a golden arch across the water, and reflections danced in bright streaks across the dark surface, making a striking farewell to tired Amphibians who had ridden all day on a crowded train. It was quite a trial, getting up the gangplank with the heavy equipment, barracks bag, rifle, typewriter, and sketch box, plus all the equipment we were wearing. Someone behind and above me dropped a rifle, and it hit my helmet with the loud sound of a baseball bat on a washpot, but did no damage. This and several later such incidents proved to me that a steel helmet is useful to ward off more things than bullets.

I went down the steps into the hold of the ship, two "floors" beneath the deck, where canvas bunks were crowded four deep in the hold. At once sizing up the situation, I took a top bunk under a light. Later I found this was a good idea, as you had the privilege of stepping in three faces on your way up. Besides having more head room and a light, the bunk had a metal ventilator above it with a lot of space on its flat top—also various pipes to tie things to.

We didn't leave the hold that night, and the boat stayed in dock until about seven o'clock the next morning, February 18, when we set sail for an unknown shore.[4] As for myself, there was a mixed feeling of regret, excitement, and helplessness as we sailed out under the Golden Gate Bridge. The fog diffused the red sunlight of morning and painted the rooftops in soft colors along the waterfront. Gulls wheeled about, and choppy greenish water came to the boat in great broken swells. It seemed pretty rough for the bay. Later in the day the water changed—became deeper in color and more blue—but still rolled and tossed, making hills and valleys of the world in which we sailed.

All day the gulls followed, and a silver blimp hovered overhead, back and forth, back and forth, watching for a shadow that might be a submarine lurking at this place where targets could be easily picked off as they left the West Coast ports.

Rough sea the first day out was unfortunate, as it gave many men an unpleasant start for the long voyage. Seasickness was in evidence everywhere. Men lay on deck rolling and vomiting; others managed to reach the washroom, only to splatter the floor. Some grabbed their steel helmets in emergency, and some were too sick and weak to leave their bunks. There was really nothing at all that could be done with a seasick man. He just resented any attention whatever and usually informed anyone who offered help that he preferred to die alone and to get the hell away from him. Luckily, I was not at all sick, although as the ship heaved and pitched, I did have the same feeling you get when going down in a fast elevator.

A little exploration showed that the ship was a large one, 538 feet long. Originally named the *President Taft*—one of the "Dollar Liners"—it had been built sometime after the Ark and remodeled in 1921. She had been a two-class tourist ship with a few first-class cabins and a large number of "tourist class" spaces, plus four cargo holds. Renamed the U.S. Army Transport *Willard A. Holbrook*, she had seen at least six trips in the recent months since Pearl Harbor—one to the hot spots of the Solomons. Geared for war, she was painted gray all over, with all doors and openings lightproofed, and she was armed to the teeth. With two five-inch guns, two three-inchers, six 20mm cannons, and twelve 50-calibre machine guns, she was prepared to give a nasty sting if attacked. Running at eighteen knots, she was much faster than a sub. The flying bridge had been enclosed and armored with inch-thick steel just in case something came along that couldn't be outrun. All the guns—with the exception of the 50s—were manned by navy gunners who seemed not much more than kids but were well trained and efficient.

We carried about three thousand men, which made the decks crowded to the point that if many went up at once, you had difficulty in finding even a spot large enough to sit down anywhere. What a contrast from her pleasure trip cargo days as the *President Taft*, when the craft never carried more than three to four hundred passengers.

We were crowded into the first three decks of the holds, while the lower space was filled with war goods, not the least of which was a large shipment of torpedoes! From the waterline, the ship was thirty-five feet deep, or as the sailors said, "She drew three feet of water" or something of the sort.

I was in Hold Number 3 on the forward deck and wondered which end of a ship sank first when hit in the middle—the idea being that if she were hit forward, I wouldn't have to worry about getting off anyway. We wore large cork life jackets at all times, and the dern things quickly became a nuisance, but could not be discarded for a minute. The sides of the decks fore and aft were fitted with large life rafts, and the small box rafts were stacked near the middle of the deck. Many lifeboats were amidship on the boat deck, hooked to their devits and ready to be lowered. Daily drills were held for the crews of these boats, as well as for us. About all three thousand men could do was stand on the deck ready to climb overboard, and I wondered what chance they all would have on a sinking ship.

After the first day, the water calmed. The gulls left us. The blimp left, and we were in the middle of an empty sea. Only a pair of gooney birds[5] remained, flying in tireless graceful circles just above the water, sometimes touching a wave with a wing tip, they flew so near. They kept it up hour after hour, day after day, and I wondered what they could gain and how they could hold out on such a strenuous schedule. Someone said they roosted on the ship's rigging at night, but I doubted it. Still, where could they go, and could they keep at their flying twenty-four hours a day?

As we neared the equator, the sea became calmer, smoother, and bluer, until on Sunday we were sailing through a gigantic circle of liquid lapis shot through with unearthly blues, greens, and violets—all blending into something too beautiful for a ship of war to swim into. The sky hung over it, paler—but as beautiful. Flying fish came out from time to time to plop back into the shining water like silver streaks. Once a school of tuna passed, merrily jumping out of the water in easy leaps.

At this stage of the voyage the moon rose full, behind fleecy tatters of clouds, a sight to stay on deck for, and many took advantage of the pageant. The deck was crowded with men on that silent ghost ship that showed no lights, no cigarettes—this was good submarine weather.

Our first "ship sighted" appeared as a tiny speck on the horizon. From the instant it was seen, the guns were manned, and glasses trained on it from the bridge. It never came close enough to offer a good view from our deck, but was supposed to have been a freighter. Later we sighted several ships and exchanged blinker signals with each of them. Had we met a cruiser or any type of enemy battleship, she could have easily run us down and outgunned us, possibly opening fire from eight or nine miles distance. We were a good target for any broken down Japanese battlewagon, but none appeared.

Possibly the food on the boat caused the most unfavorable comment I had heard since entering the army (and I had heard plenty). Feeding three thousand men was a problem, of course, in the limited galley of a ship built to carry no more than five hundred at most. As the long lines of men passed with large divided trays, the cooks threw on (and I mean THREW, because sometimes they missed) a spoonful of soggy oatmeal, a second spoonful of prunes or apricots, a slice of bread (and the longer we were out, the harder it got), perhaps a dash of jam or jelly, and two boiled eggs. Tea and coffee (what coffee!) and butter were on the table, along with a bowl of coarse sugar almost like rock salt. Day after day this was the breakfast menu.

At lunch time there was no meal in the dining hall, but in each company sandwiches were passed out, plus an apple or orange for each of us. Two slices of bread with a piece of cheese or bologna were sandwiches in name only.

Supper was almost as bad, usually stew or such, with little variation. Once we each got half a chicken and a very decent meal, but usually everyone was hungry when the day was done. This caused a lively "black market" to spring up.

The black market developed more in the spirit of fun than from any idea of gain. Every other day we got some Coca-Colas and maybe a candy bar, if we turned in an order beforehand. So on the in-between nights, the black market flourished best. An orange or apple brought as much as twenty-five cents, and prices rose with the ability of the seller to auction his wares. Once Lieutenant Mahoney gave me four or five candy bars of a kind I didn't like, so I had fun selling them on the black market at fifteen and twenty cents each. It broke the monotony of the day, and sometimes you were able to pick up something to eat that you wanted.

Card games flourished, and bills became worn as they changed hands day after day. In those crowded quarters little in the form of army training was introduced to interrupt the games.

On the morning of February 25, we crossed the equator, and our officers arranged for the traditional ceremony. Lieutenant Callaway called for me. When I went to the stateroom, he wanted me to help with the make-up of the principals in King Neptune's Court. We went down to the carpenter's shop where one of the ship's officers waited with an assortment of ridiculous costumes and a collection of greasepaint.

Lieutenant Callway was the Royal Baby, wearing diapers made from a sheet, a lace baby cap, and a large green butterfly painted on his ample stomach. Captain Gudgeon made a good and subtle Neptune, and Captain Shaul was a ruthless Royal Barber. The cast included a wife, and also a mistress for Neptune, a jester, and others.

Court convened on B deck aft, where a tank had been constructed of framework and heavy canvas. Neptune opened the court with a thump of his tridon and a wave of his long white whiskers. The fun was on, beginning with indignities on the colonel himself, who was led out blindfolded onto the raised square of the hold, clad only in his shorts. He was charged with issuing orders that no WAVE or WAC could come aboard the ship at any time. The barber proceeded to give him a Royal Shampoo by first covering his head with pancake batter, then breaking two eggs into the mess and rubbing it in well. Next he was given the Royal Zoot Suit to wear. This was a large rubber suit open only at the top and equipped with a drawstring. When the colonel was safely inside the suit, a large hose was suddenly dragged out, and the suit was filled with water until he was a large rubberball with hands and feet. The colonel was ordered to walk around, presenting an awkward and hilarious sight.

Others were brought out and charged with various crimes of a somewhat indecent nature and were given a real clipping with the barber clippers. Some culprits went away with paths cut to the scalp. Neither hair nor dignity was spared. Some men had their hind parts painted in designs with indelible inks. Afterwards, each man on the ship became a Shellback, and all were pronounced members of the Shellbacks forever.

The next day Shellback Certificates were given out, and I lettered those for our company. Trying to find a way to make a few of them more attractive, I worked the design over with ink and watercolors. To escape the crowd I worked up on the forbidden deck overlooking B deck aft and came into contact with practically all of the officers of the regiment. As I worked at my card table, one after another brought their certificates to be colored. At fifty cents a shot I made more than forty dollars in less than five days, finally getting so tired of painting mermaids and fishes that at last I threw up the job and delivered the last eight to the officers' rooms without collecting. I was glad to donate the four dollars they represented for freedom, because as long as I sat and worked, they kept bringing the things to me.

There was little chance to do sketching of any kind, but I did several fast watercolor impressions and some pencil sketches—all very sketchy. I made plans for a painting looking off starboard when Venus rose in the blue green sky of a very young tropic night, with soldiers and a large life raft silhouetted against it.

Only once in the ten-thousand-mile voyage did we sight land. A palm-fringed shore appeared far off to the south, but as soon as it was sighted, the ship veered off, and the land was soon lost beyond the horizon. The wonder of the trip was that it was made alone without convoy of any kind. Toward the end of the journey the sea again became heavy, but few men became seasick, as they had become used to the roll of the ship.

On March 7, late in the afternoon a ship was sighted. As it came nearer, we saw it was a destroyer flying the American flag. The *Holbrook* began exchanging blinker signals, and the two ships blinked furiously, probably making arrangements for the convoying of our ship during the night. No doubt enemy subs would be likely to haunt this sea lane, and the destroyer was sent to guard against harm to us.

Much faster than our ship, the destroyer began making trips across our bow, back and forth, out a mile and back across, on guard and clearing the way. We never identified the destroyer, and even the ship's officers, who were off duty and sitting around on deck, refused to comment when a ship of any kind was sighted. No one was admitted to the bridge at any time, and our colonel never had more than a few words with the ship's captain at any time. Apparently the whole voyage was made under sealed orders. The only time the guns were fired was when a barrel, which was thought to be a mine, was sighted. One of the three-inchers opened fire, along with two 20mm cannons. It was the policy to destroy anything that might be a mine if possible.

By morning the destroyer was gone, and we were entering some sort of port. It turned out to be Brisbane Harbor. There was a wait for the tide and then a twenty-six-mile sail to Brisbane, up the Brisbane River. While we were anchored in the harbor, several launches came and left passengers—some of them our officers who had been sent ahead on advance detail a month or more before. A large white ship sailed past with huge red crosses on it—an Australian hospital ship. We could see the nurses standing along the rail waving gayly as they sailed out of the harbor to some unknown destination without convoy. These ships traveled alone and brightly lighted.

Finally we heaved anchor and continued to Brisbane, getting into a fairly narrow channel, then dropped anchor again beside a U.S. Army warehouse and began to disembark.

As we stood on deck I got my first good look at Australian soil. There was a strange and subtle difference between this and the land I had left—an intangible difference—yet it was there. I was annoyed that I could not put it down in words.

2 Arrival In Australia

March 18, 1943

We marched off the boat much as we had come on, dropped our barracks bags in one of the warehouses, and marched through a part of the town to a tent camp built on one of Brisbane's best race tracks. (Racing was out for the duration.)

A group of pleasant folk, very like Americans, watched us march along the streets as they sat on their doorsteps in the afternoon of a warm day that felt like August to me, even if the date was March 18. Australian seasons are reversed from ours. We landed there in the same sort of season we have at the end of a long Texas summer. White summer clouds hung lazily in the blue sky, dust was rising, the sun was hot.

Strange—living in California and leaving it just as things were ready to burst into spring. When I had been in Monterey last, the willows were showing green buds. Eighteen days later we were landing in the late summer of Australia! "For the first time in my life," I thought, "I shall see no spring."

The ride up from Brisbane was on one of those Australian-English trains divided into compartments seating six. Each compartment had its own doors (one on each side of the car). Two long seats within the compartment faced each other, but were enclosed only as high as the back of the seats. The result was a chair car with no aisle up the middle as we know it. The ride was through little-used country with scattered pineapple patches and a few small fields of this and that. I was impressed by the sparse population—only seven million people on a continent of this size!

Once we stopped for a meal in a rather down-at-the-heels railroad station. Nothing seemed impressive, and things from Brisbane to Rockhampton moved in a slow tempo that we Americans had discarded a quarter of a century ago.

Suddenly I remembered that, in Texas, spring had officially arrived—an odd thought in the dirt and dust of our new camp near Rockhampton.

Gradually the place began taking shape as an army camp. Day after day groups worked on clearing the area of underbrush, dug company ice boxes in the hard clay, and constructed latrines. Finally the camp was nearing completion.

March 22, 1943

Today the word passed around that General Krueger would inspect camp. (I had heard of him before I got into the army when he reviewed troops at Camp Bowie in Brownwood, Texas.) I often wonder at the frenzied preparation when the visit of a big shot is in the offing. Each officer, from commander of camp to the least second louie, at once gets Saint Vitus's Dance and starts on some wild preparation of something that won't be seen anyway. The men are simply work crews boosting someone else along, and aren't supposed to stop and wonder why. Strangely enough, few do, and each day I am amazed at the thousands who flatfoot along without imagination or enthusiasm.

Major Cecil Bilger asked if I would teach him some outdoor pencil sketching techniques in my spare time, which gives me something to look forward to. Bilger is certainly a gentleman and has my respect, which is something that I can say for very few officers. He handles things in a quiet, efficient manner without bluster or hokum. Recently I learned that he is an expert taxidermist. He worked his way through college by practicing the art. It is good to find that he is somewhat of a naturalist and brings good nature books from town almost every trip. I am getting some knowledge of the things I am most interested in. It will be good to work with such a man as Bilger and a pleasure to teach him what little I know of pencil work.

Lieutenant Callaway, our battalion adjutant, has just suggested that I accompany a group on the truck to the beach for a swim. It is about four miles, so we rarely have time to walk the distance. The truck carries lifeguards to and from the beach for a swimming period at high tide each day. Today the tide was in full, and the water was fine. I usually get wet in the surf, then spend my time beachcombing, which isn't such a bad sport. There is something nice about the sun on your skin, the sound and sight of the surf, and the fascination of new shells and whatever else the tide throws up on the sand.

Lieutenant Callaway sees me writing this and says, "You can't write that."

"Why?" I ask, and he says, "Well, you can't take it into a combat zone when we go."

I just say "Okay," keep on writing, and let it go at that. All sorts of asinine "don'ts" are sent around that amount to nothing and generally turn out to be the whims of a petty officer in some position where he thinks he must issue nice sounding instructions in order to hold his job. Lieutenant Callaway's redeeming feature is his southern manner, which I am used to. Roly poly fat, he has the traditional fat man's easygoing nature. He is occasionally blunt about things, but rarely with malice.

News just came that the body of a sergeant who was missing has been found, washed up on the shore amidst the swamp and mangrove roots. The poor fellow disappeared while swimming and wasn't missed until the next day when his shorts, dog tags, money belt, etc., were found where he had undressed on the shore. Apparently he disappeared at the general swim period, but was not missed then. Old-time fishermen on the coast here say there are hundreds of tiger sharks off shore. One man said, "You wouldn't catch me in that water over my knees." Apparently the boy had been snapped up at a point where an inlet comes in toward the beach, making a channel of deeper water almost to the shore. The body was in bad shape, and only the torso—no arms or legs—remained. The rest had been torn off. The fellow's ten-thousand-mile trip was futile, and his chance to serve was lost. I felt badly to think he would not be here to finish the work with us, although I did not know him at all. I suppose the poor remains will be buried in Australia—the first casualty in the entire outfit, and so far from home. But he will be in a friendly country at least.

We are still looking for the general to come by, although it is now 3:00 p.m. Some of the officers had heard that General Krueger sometimes stopped in his tours over camps and asked soldiers (just common privates!) what they think of a camp, its officers, etc. This seems to alarm the officers no end. It would be very nice to have a talk with the general himself and have him really know the state of chaos here. Too much faith is put in a colonel's hands, because he is from West Point—that most overrated pile of rocks on the Hudson. Too often our West Pointers "overact" in order to hold up their reputations as such and make a generally miserable situation for the men under them.

We have seen a prime example under Lieutenant Colonel Neff, who is "building" tough men by having them out here without water (it is hauled in in cans), without bathing facilities, no laundry or place to do it, or a minute's free time. We can all do without these things when the time comes to do so, but to jump off the boat into it without reason is impossible and only builds bad feelings. Sometimes I wonder if such observations by me are just, even if true. I know they come from the bitter memories of earlier days in the army, when the injustice of this animal game was driven into me and forever prevents me from accepting it as anything but repulsive. But whereas there are few of my kind, there are hundreds who every day carry out the routine gleefully and are "good soldiers." Thank God I have been unable to become a "good soldier," but will leave it all with a free mind that can again turn to beautiful and constructive things and friends I once knew and loved.

I must send Pigtail[6] a cable on his birthday. Wish I could see that kid.

I hope to keep this writing up. Maybe it and my letters will tell a story later when it is of more interest than now. Now it may all seem dull and tiring, but later it will be history.

3 In Camp At Brisbane

March 23, 1943

The arrival of evening was accompanied by the bustle of trucks going into town for the first time, taking men on their first trip since coming into the camp. Today was payday, so most want to get in with their pay and blow it away as usual on a woman or liquor. Almost twenty of our company went, and that number will be allowed out each night.

Rockhampton, a typical town of Australia, closes up tight at 7:00 p.m., but I am sure the Australians, being human, will try to find some way of making liquor available after the curfew hour and thus boost business. They won't sit by for long and not see money going into their cash registers.

I didn't go in, because I will wait until the rush is over. I would like to get in to see what the place looks like, although I have been told it is pretty corny and dull.

This payday was the first in Australian money. Mine was a five pound note plus some change, or about eighteen dollars. We were paid five on the boat. From our camp pay, four dollars went for laundry, about eight for insurance, and twenty-five dollars allowance. The eighteen dollars was all that remained to spend. However that will be more than I will be able to spend here. Next payday, on April 1 or thereabouts, we will draw our extra ten percent overseas pay, which will help.

Captain Shaul called me today to come and get a small lizard. It turned out to be a pigmy iguana, about twelve inches long. I shook the small tree, and Sergeant McCleary caught Mr. Iguana neatly when he fell. He had a dark brown coat covered with circles of a lighter color. We tied him in front of the tent until most of the group had seen him, and then turned him loose. Several days before, we had seen a giant iguana three feet long at least, but he got away in a hurry.

I am getting the reputation of being a lover of the wild things, and people call me often to show me wildlife—a thing I appreciate. For without a love of nature the army would be intolerable for me. The captain said today he has learned which of the Australian parrots are the best talkers. We planned earlier to find out about them and get one, and I have promised to train it to swear like a sailor. After a stretch in this army, I am sure the parrot would be unfit for any other company.

I received my first letter today from Ella. She had sent it to Mother who had addressed it to me. Mother had written a note on the back of it saying she was worried about where I could be. The note was dated the day we sailed from San Francisco, February 28, 1943. I am sure she has been much more worried since, but I hope she has received some of my "V" mail by now. I do what I can to keep her from worrying, but because she is a mother, she just can't help but worry, I know. We arrived here on March 17, and I am sure she spent all the time between our sailing and when she received my cable wondering about me.

Sent Pigtail a cable for his birthday today. Just greetings and love and kisses. Cables are more or less "canned," so your expressions are limited.

Camp is rapidly nearing completion and a schedule of training starts tomorrow. One of the three of us will have to go out for half of each day for some of the work. Our colonel has ordered all clerks, etc., to do so. However, I won't mind so much, as this will be the first such training I have taken part in since the end of basic training in Arkansas the middle of last July. It will just be repetition of the old stuff, but in a new country.

Each company and our battalion office received a large box today from the Red Cross. A most complete assortment I must say! A radio-phonograph, a group of twelve-inch fifteen-minute transcriptions made by popular radio bands, dozens of books of every kind, and even a bunch of harmonicas. The companies also received an additional large box of athletic supplies of all kinds. I can see why everything is so scarce at home, for we are getting so much, and it makes you feel that there must be a lot of wonderful people behind you.

I'm anxious to see how the boys do on their first trip to town. If they are picked up by the MP's, they have been promised it will be their last trip for a long time. We will see.

March 24, 1943

Last night we had the usual "pay night" doings. Before dark I noticed several groups spreading blankets on the ground and gathering in tight circles. When dark came, the games continued, and candles were stuck in bottles for light as the cards fell, and wages changed hands.

Dotson[7] and I decided to try to get a much needed bath, so we got a five-gallon can of water from what was supposed to be the kitchen supply, along with one of those shower buckets made so that when you pull the lever, you get something resembling a shower. We found a tree to tie the bucket to, filled the bucket, undressed, and proceeded to soap and fight the mosquitoes all at once. In spite of my flying slaps and the soap suds, the mosquitoes bit me in several uncomfortable places, but the shower was a success, and we left feeling much better.

When we passed the card players, the blankets were scattered with poker chips, shillings, florins, half and one pound notes, as the players dealt and raked the chips here and there.

Here was Harold Emley—sheep shearer from Idaho, big and muscular, with the largest hands I have ever seen on a man—and Miller—skinny blonde, ex-hobo, fisherman, etc. He had his wife follow him about the U.S. as we moved across the continent. She was forty (Miller is twenty-four), common, bleached, hard—I wondered at his lack of taste in women. But the group around the cards couldn't by any stretch of imagination be called a select group.

Washenberger came up very drunk on Australian beer (which is stronger than any in America) and at once one of the unlucky players began to ask him for the loan of enough capital to get his pay back. The last I saw of them, the unlucky Washenberger was going off to get the money. Dotson and I left, and I lighted a candle by Dotson's bed. We began to enjoy a new book which had come in the box from the Red Cross. It was "boners," mostly gleaned from school examination papers and about the funniest thing we had seen in ages. While we were reading and roaring, Skorupski came in, and, in an excited wild manner, tried to borrow a pound in order to stay in the game. Neither of us consented, so out he went to try someone else.

About 1:00 a.m. the boys came back from town, and I waked up for a minute—but just for a minute—so I didn't hear any reports of the town.

This morning I learned that the place was "dead as hell" with "no liquor or women." One sergeant did get to some sort of a dance and remarked, "I almost had a tall gotch-eyed gal in the notion, but she learned I had to leave at eleven o'clock, and quit me right there for a 542d guy who had the whole night free."

According to him, "Those 542d sons of bitches live near town and get all the women." The same sort of complaint also came from the officers, who are accustomed to having a corner on all the loose women in a town. The 542d group moved in ahead of us, so this company seems to be behind in most of its usual business. All stores were closed by the time members of our bunch got to town, so their only pleasure was a shower and a meal at the Red Cross.

The company office has just phoned to ask if I want a pass tonight, but I refused. I want to visit the book shop, etc., so I'll wait until later to see Rockhampton. Whenever anyone phones and offers you a pass, you know passes are hard to give away. Usually you have to go down and raise hell for an hour before you get one.

I went to the beach again with the life guards. The sun was nice. I noticed that far out in the bay the deep water begins as suddenly as a knife cut—from the tan, sand-filled water to a deep green out near the islands. Each day I have been there, two friendly dogs greet us on the sand. They beg us to throw sticks into the surf and will dash into the biggest wave to get them, never tiring until we get weary of throwing. Australia has a great many dogs, and I have yet to see one that is not as friendly as the people themselves—a credit to both.

This afternoon we had quite a bit of work on clothing and cigarette rations for the battalion, ordering a ten-day supply of tobacco. I have been taking my allotment of cigarettes, just putting the cartons away with the hope of someday getting into territory where they will be trade money with the natives. The Australians surely like American cigarettes and ask for them often, but not in the manner of barter—they just want them as a gift.

We now have a new stalk of bananas in the top of the tent—very green. That is a good and safe place for them to ripen, out of reach.

Almost nightly we have a movie brought from America. The equipment is remarkably good, and the movie about as perfect as one in our own

American theaters, except for the delay in changing reels. The movies arrive regularly, and there seem to be plenty of "fans" in the army waiting for them.

After the shows as we lie in our cots, Clarence Estadt and I have long talks about this and that. He was co-owner and editor of a newspaper in a small Ohio town. There are five of us in the tent, but he and I do most of the talking—the others being mostly disinterested in conversation. I have found that there are few good conversationalists in the army. Most men know little to talk about once the subject is switched from women.

Estadt mentioned his resentment about conditions on the boat coming to Australia—especially about the poor food served the enlisted men in contrast with the luxurious meals served to the officers by trained Filipino waiters. It was true that many of the officers were ignorant of the sloppy mess we had day after day. Others didn't care, and still others felt there was nothing they could do about it.

We spoke of some of the poor examples of men we were forced to serve under, but we were thankful for being old enough to withstand the army desire to bend men into a G.I. mold. We have a couple of second lieutenants barely twenty years old, trying to fill an adult place over men twice their age. They will most certainly lose something very valuable in this all-too-short span of life allotted to us, and will most likely remain in the army after the war is over, for they will be fitted for no other place. We will have thousands with a "military spirit" who will be as useless to us in the coming work for a more liveable and beautiful world as are those left forever on our battlefields.

March 25, 1943

The day began as usual. In the office we have a Chinese and a Polish interpreter from our battalion. They are doing practice work by talking on the phone to another man of the same nationality. The Chinese is named Moy and seems very interesting. While he was not busy this morning, I had him write a short letter to Quirl[8] in Chinese characters. I typed it, and he translated it onto a sheet of "V" mail. I can imagine what Quirl will say when he opens it. There isn't a Chinaman within two hundred miles of

Brownwood, so he may never know what it is all about. Just in case we ever get together, I have the English version of the letter.

Dear Quirl,

We are still out in the wilderness, but are thankful that the camp is almost complete. Maybe we will get a chance to see outside the boundaries of the area. As Friend Moy is here, he is writing you, because I am sure you are tired of the letters in plain English that I send. Anyway, the Chinese will be just as understandable as my English.

Australia is very interesting, and I am learning some things about the birds and other wildlife. I find that my previous study of the wild things in America is a help even here. At least you have a vague idea of what a thing is.

Best wishes to all the gang,
Gaitha

When Moy wrote this in Chinese characters, he did so from left to right in the usual way, but I noticed that his own dairy is neatly written from right to left and from top to bottom, in the ancient Chinese form.

Still no information on laundry, so I proceeded to do my own, putting fatigue clothes in a tub with G.I. soap, a wicked yellow soap used throughout the army that will practically eat the skin right off your hands if you aren't careful. I boiled the dickens out of my clothes, and they were clean, but some white shorts and towels didn't look so good—at least not very white.

It is very nice to be in a job which gives me time to do necessary things. There is rarely a time that I cannot get off to the beach or do needed outside work. A smart private said the other day, "It looks like you've found a home in the army." Maybe I have. Anyway my job as clerk is much more pleasant than most of the other jobs in the company.

Moy is chattering into the phone and putting down queer Chinese characters. Charlie Wilson is writing a letter to his wife in New York. Mac is listening to the new radio with Lieutenant Callaway, and the bananas in the top of the tent are slowly turning golden yellow. All of us seem to have gotten some of the native spirit that makes you want to rest and rest and rest.

Tonight I am on duty in the headquarters tent. Charlie went to town, and Mac is out with the baseball team. A lot of the fellows are coming by to send cables home. We have been here since the 8th of the month now, and there has been opportunity since the first day to wire home. I wonder why all these fellows have neglected the folks at home so long.

People are enjoying our bananas. I can see right now where we will have to rap some knuckles.

March 26, 1943

Our "usual" day was relieved somewhat by the appearance of Joe E. Brown,[9] who is making a tour of camps in out-of-the-way places. He is traveling alone, and I imagine he will eventually work his way up to the front. Dressed in khaki shorts and big G.I. shoes, he gave a program consisting more than anything else of his famous mouth—but entertaining—and, I must say, he is certainly a sincere booster, making the trip at his own expense and on his own initiative.

Tonight I went to the movie, and at dusk, while I was waiting there, the nightly flight of huge fruit bats came over. Called "flying foxes," these gigantic bats travel in flights of thousands. They filled the sky to the horizon in both directions and passed for nearly thirty minutes. Since they measure some two feet across the wings, imagine what would happen if they descended on a nice orchard of ripe fruit!

As the moon is coming up late now, the stars are more easily seen, and the Southern Cross gleamed brightly as we left the movie area. Too bad that those at home are unable to see it, for it is an impressive constellation.

All my tent mates came in after the show, and we all turned in at about the same time. As usual we lay on our cots talking. Brownnel was in a good humor and recounted all the new jokes of the day. Martin,[10] as usual, never spoke a word during the whole time.

March 27, 1943

Early morning business slacked up, and a "bull session" is in progress among the officers in battalion headquarters. In such discussions interesting sidelights on character surface, and everyone surprises me with their frankness and lack of self-respect by talking of intimate affairs with all kinds of characters—mostly women. You learn what type of men you are among in a hurry.

Word has been sent out there will be no swimming at Keppel Sands. Reason—mostly unknown—but it is thought that the colonel became alarmed when someone was stung by a man-of-war. If so, the whole thing is very silly, for any beach anywhere in the world is likely to throw up an occasional stinging jellyfish. But—as we have learned—it doesn't take much to alarm our regimental headquarters. I just wonder what will happen when we get into battle.

Captain Gudgeon from Intelligence Headquarters has asked me about doing some work—sketching some beaches from the boats. It will be interesting if I can do what he has in mind. He also wanted me to go out and look at some machine gun emplacements, which I did. Lieutenant Coleman came by, and we went to plan the camouflage for the guns. The trip was worthwhile, for it was to a point on the coast I had not seen. The MGs protect our maintenance shop for boats, and the three of them are on a high point overlooking the sea.[11]

The water was unusually beautiful—a light blue green. In the distance the purple ridges of small islands showed where the Great Barrier Reef breaks away. The high rocky point had a number of wind-blown trees of small size—those fascinating ones found by every shore the world over, I suppose. Anyway, similar ones are in such far-separated places as California, Cape Cod, Australia, and Florida. The prevailing winds twist them from the time they are seedlings, and they gradually assume wizened, weird shapes. They are beautiful as they stand high and still defiant—though bent—looking over the blue of the sea.

An eagle soared slowly over the shallows near shore in search of food. What type of eagle, I do not know, but suppose it was most likely one of the fish eagles, or ospreys. A beautiful butterfly came by and made me want to start collecting, but what—just what—would a soldier do with a butterfly collection in Australia?

The gun emplacements turned out to be simple to camouflage, and we will begin tomorrow—at least someone will. I will offer what knowledge I can to the job. We will probably build a huge dummy rock for at least one of the guns, since it can be easily tied in with the other cliff rocks around.

March 28, 1943

Today is Sunday, and I planned to go to services, but was again on the camouflage work from 9:00 a.m. until noon. One gun was covered with a sand-colored net, and from several hundred feet away it blended in with the surroundings until it was difficult to see. The other gun will be covered with the "rock."

I saw some more large tropical butterflies and wished all over again that I could collect them, but I have hit upon a plan which will be the next best thing. I will get specimens when I can and make detailed drawings in ink and watercolor. These will be permanent and can be sent home in letters. Today there were several white and yellow butterflies around which were the fastest fliers I ever saw. They passed like bullets, and will, no doubt, be hard to catch.

Last night Dotson and I hunted the new shower which has water piped to it from the big tank on the hill. The shower is out in the woods between here and regimental headquarters area. It was plenty hard to locate in the dark. A pole frame supports four shower-heads. A few square feet of poles are laid together to form a "floor" underneath so you won't be standing in the mud. This completes the camp "shower room." However, it was at least wet and washed off the day's dust.

Dotson is always a good pal at the end of the day, and one of the few really sensible and frank people around. Having done a lot of college work in sociology, he is seldom fooled by people and surprises me often by his candid observations of them.

We wondered what we would find after the war when we return to America, and if we will be content to settle in one spot, but agreed that happiness is a transient thing, flitting in and out of every life. He being the only person who has any interest in such discussion of ideas, I often sit for hours talking with him. He is an orphan, who finished four years of college by his own efforts, working his way. Now twenty-five, he feels much as I do about the army and life in general.

Tonight Lieutenant Trundle was Officer of the Day, and I was Charge of Quarters. (Both C.Q. and O.D. must remain in battalion headquarters and carry out any business that comes up during the night.) Being one of the better of our officers, he wasn't afraid to talk about affairs, and I learned a great many things about people and doings in the outfit.

March 29, 1943

We practically completed the camouflage today, but find that there is no spray gun or camouflage paint in the regiment. We only have one captain, one tech sergeant, one staff sergeant, one sergeant, one T/4 sergeant, one T/5 corporal, and several privates—all of whom are supposed to be our Regimental Intelligence which includes camouflage work—but not one of them thought to bring any equipment from America.

Just what we will do, I don't know, but I suspect I will forget the whole thing if something doesn't improve, for it surely isn't up to Private Browning to work the thing out while the above array of rated men sit on their fannies.

March 30, 1943

No news, no nothing. I am disgusted!

4 A Trip To Town

March 31, 1943

Today is the 31st and Pigtail's birthday. He is six and will be a school boy next September. It simply can't be six years since he was a small red baby with a wrinkled face! I just hope all this we are now in will make a better world for him, for if it doesn't, it won't be much worthwhile.

We who are thirty have had a great share of what there is to be had in this race with time. If we go, and by our going somehow help to create something that can help those now six to know a better existence than we had, the whole thing is very much worthwhile.

I found that there was a chance to go to town this morning, so I got a pass and dressed. We were in a truck with one lieutenant riding in the cab and another in back with a sergeant and me. When we had gotten about five miles up the road, a jeep came roaring up. It contained Captain "Grandma" Page. He brought the news that we were in the wrong truck and would have to return and swap vehicles. The fact being that you have to look at the number to tell one truck from the other, I couldn't see any reason why ours should not continue on, but no! So the three of us in the back decided that rather than expose our poor seats to that five-mile pounding over the rough road, we would get out and wait.

We walked up the road in the pleasant morning. I was rewarded by the song of the same bird I had heard once before—seven notes more beautiful than a flute—and I wondered what type of bird could have such a voice.[12]

At the small railroad station we sat down where the camp road crossed the tracks and did not have to sit long until our truck came along. The driver said the other truck was supposed to haul rock, and that only Truck Number So-and-So could be used. At least twenty-five miles had been driven in a useless, senseless maneuver, and folks at home are struggling with "A" cards!

The town proved to be not unpleasant at all, and by the look and manner of it, once again I was swept back to my childhood days. I was more sure than ever I was correct in saying that Australia is the America of twenty-five years ago. The arrangement of the stores, the manner of the people, the furnishings of a hotel lobby all spoke of a past America.

We ate lunch at the Leichdheart Hotel, the best place in town. The dining rooms didn't open until 1:00 p.m., so we waited in the lobby where a large, old-fashioned ceiling fan stirred the air into a feeling of coolness. At 1:00 we entered the big dining room set with a number of large tables covered by white cloths hanging far down, as I remember them long ago. Each table seated eight people. We had six at ours—the four of us and two sergeants who were staying at the hotel on furloughs.

The sergeants put us wise to the customs of the people here. You pay for a meal and have the privilege of eating as much food as you wish for one price. You simply re-order whatever you want more of. We had roast mutton, salad, etc.—all very good. Old traditions still exist, and it was a pleasure to find a place where you ate, then went out at will and paid the clerk at the desk. You got no check, nor were you watched by a sharp-eyed cashier as you departed. In fact you were trusted implicitly, for no one even asked the number of meals for which you owed. We in the U.S. have taken a more grim view of things and somehow lost our trust in one another—even in so simple a thing as buying and eating a meal in a public place.

After lunch I went around town and looked for some books on Australia to send home. Although there were three bookshops, all of them were sold out of what I wanted, *Pacific Wonderland.* None of the dealers expected another edition of this splendid book, as paper is scarce. I found several pamphlets which were interesting, so I got them with the hope that Mother would enjoy knowing more of Australia.

I was in need of swim trunks, but found that none had been made here in a year. In fact, the stores looked bare of everything. All clothing is sold on a rationed basis, and you must have coupons to buy. (From letters, I gather something of the kind is happening at home, too.)

I was surprised that a milkshake was just about what you would get in the States and very good. On my way back to the truck I passed a fish store, and what should be in the window but some big crabs! I went in and found they were freshly cooked, as the woman was still taking them out of the pot, so I got the biggest one she had (and the biggest crab I ever saw in my life), weighing between five and six pounds. It cost five shillings, or about seventy-five cents.

The truck was loaded and ready to pull out, but we went by the MP Station to pick up three A.W.O.L.'s before leaving. Two of them had been gone for more than a week. They were brought out of the guard room looking very disheveled, bleary-eyed, and sorry. Their personal property was returned (except three bottles of liquor), and they got on the truck. One I knew slightly from having seen him from time to time in one of our companies. On his collar he had a large lipstick smear which he said he probably got "off that old gal I had down by the river last night." Another of the boys had a swollen eye and said, "Something must have bit me." I replied that the something most likely had five fingers.

The ride back was rough and dusty, but as it was fairly late in the afternoon, not so hot.

I invited the office gang to eat crab that night, but all refused except one—Charlie. He went to the mess hall and got some bread and butter, a hammer, and two canteen cups of cold chocolate, and we began cracking the giant crab. Meat from one claw half filled a mess kit, so when all the meat was taken out, it was as much as three people could eat. There were three of us, because Dotson came up in time.

He said he wanted to get in on another good meal, because he was on his way to the medics to see if he had the beginning of a fever.

April 1, 1943

Some of the boys caught a frilled lizard and brought him up here to me. The poor thing was terrified and had been tied by the neck after being beaten out of a tree. He was a splendid fellow thirty-one inches long. Once put on the ground he reared up on his hind feet, spread his ruff, opened his mouth wide, and ran at the nearest person—who happened to be a captain. The desired effect was obtained, for officers went in every direction.

I took the string off his neck and put him on the floor of the headquarters tent. I could see he was exhausted and probably injured by the rough treatment. He had summoned a last effort when he scared the crowd.

This morning he was dead, but I made sketches of him anyway, wondering as I did so how this strange reptile had remained as a remnant of that almost forgotten age when the world was full of giants many times his size, but very similar. Australia is full of strange animals that should have been extinct thousands of years ago by every rule of evolution.

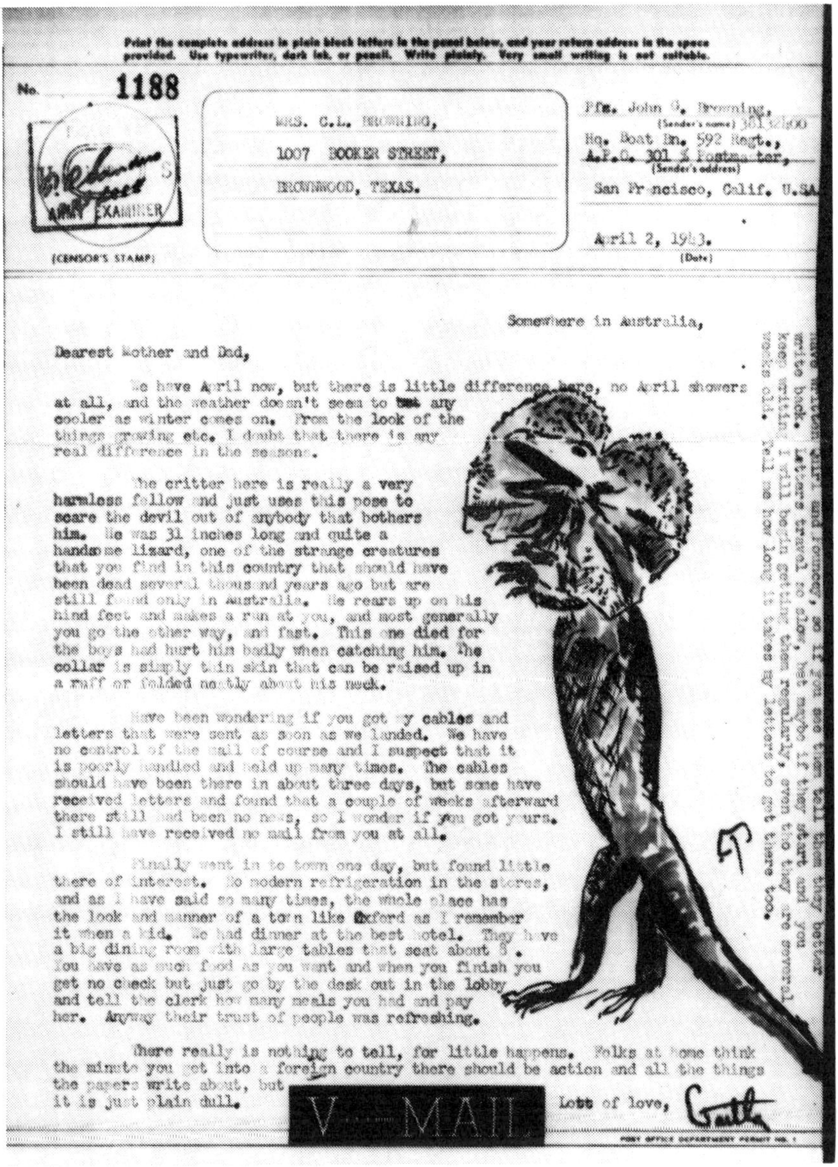

Print the complete address in plain block letters in the panel below, and your return address in the space provided. Use typewriter, dark ink, or pencil. Write plainly. Very small writing is not suitable.

No. 1188

ARMY EXAMINER

(CENSOR'S STAMP)

MRS. C.L. BROWNING,
1007 BOOKER STREET,
BROWNWOOD, TEXAS.

PFC. John G. Browning,
(Sender's name) 38132600
Hq. Boat Bn. 592 Regt.,
A.P.O. 301 % Postmaster,
(Sender's address)
San Francisco, Calif. U.SA.

April 2, 1943.
(Date)

Somewhere in Australia,

Dearest Mother and Dad,

We have April now, but there is little difference here, no April showers at all, and the weather doesn't seem to get any cooler as winter comes on. From the look of the things growing etc. I doubt that there is any real difference in the seasons.

The critter here is really a very harmless fellow and just uses this pose to scare the devil out of anybody that bothers him. He was 31 inches long and quite a handsome lizard, one of the strange creatures that you find in this country that should have been dead several thousand years ago but are still found only in Australia. He rears up on his hind feet and makes a run at you, and most generally you go the other way, and fast. This one died for the boys had hurt him badly when catching him. The collar is simply thin skin that can be raised up in a ruff or folded neatly about his neck.

Have been wondering if you got my cables and letters that were sent as soon as we landed. We have no control of the mail of course and I suspect that it is poorly handled and held up many times. The cables should have been there in about three days, but some have received letters and found that a couple of weeks afterward there still had been no news, so I wonder if you got yours. I still have received no mail from you at all.

Finally went in to town one day, but found little there of interest. No modern refrigeration in the stores, and as I have said so many times, the whole place has the look and manner of a town like Oxford as I remember it when a kid. We had dinner at the best hotel. They have a big dining room with large tables that seat about 8. You have as much food as you want and when you finish you get no check but just go by the desk out in the lobby and tell the clerk how many meals you had and pay her. Anyway their trust of people was refreshing.

There really is nothing to tell, for little happens. Folks at home think the minute you get into a foreign country there should be action and all the things the papers write about, but it is just plain dull.

Have written Girl and Rouncey, so if you see them tell them they better write back. Letters travel so slow, but maybe if they start and you keep writing I will begin getting them regularly, even tho they are several weeks old. Tell me how long it takes my letters to get there too.

Lots of love, Gaitha

V-MAIL

POST OFFICE DEPARTMENT PERMIT NO. 1

This is a new month, but somehow I don't find the challenge in it that usually comes with a new day, new week, or new month. It is just another in a long endless line of dates passing.

We had a new soldier move into our tent, and he at once took charge of all convenient places to put his things. He took up all the room I had, which was little enough at best. I made him move his stuff and told him to keep it moved if he wanted to even slightly get along with me, for he had his own space in the tent and would have to be satisfied with it. I am dern tired of trying to keep everyone around here in a good humor.

April 2, 1943

Some of the boys simply have the army licked! They are known as "eight balls" and don't intend to work—wonderful if you can do it. Nothing seems to make any impression on them. Each company tries to get rid of them, so they are swapped back and forth from company to company. One of these men is very adept with a slingshot and brings down various things which he knows I am interested in. (He got the frilled lizzard.) I had him lined up to get a parakeet out of the flock that feeds in the trees every morning, but I see from today's orders that "the hunter" has been transferred again.

Our company has lugged an old sewing machine fifteen thousand miles so far, and it still sews well. I will use it to make myself some swim trunks from a large thick bath towel I got at the PX. In an hour or so I could probably promote a hundred pairs of trunks in Brownwood, but that is just some ten thousand miles away.

One of our regimental officers has just come into the tent, and there is a discussion of a drawing going on. They have found a copy of *Esquire* and are trying to decide who the girl looks most like of the women they know, taking point by point from hair on down to toes.

A small circus has put up just outside our gate about a half-mile up the road. From what I saw yesterday it is a small one and pretty punk, but a lot of us are going tonight, just to be going. That corny circus will probably make more money in a couple of nights here than it has seen in a year!

April 3, 1943

The circus provided several laughs, even before we went. Regimental headquarters phoned our office and gave an order to put on extra guards for the gasoline supply dump at the motorpool, because the circus was here. Did they fear that the circus people would filch gas? Goodness no! A more comical reason, but a very true one. It seems that when the circus was located near the 542d area, a lot of five-gallon cans of gas disappeared. It was learned that the soldiers themselves were taking it to the circus. The area was very short of gas because of rationing, and it is seventy-five cents a gallon here now.

The news had gotten out that the favors of the trapeze girl could be bought for a five-gallon can of gas—a story that proved to be too, too true. She got quite a supply before the boys had their gas supply cut off. To forestall such a raid on our gasoline, the guard was posted. Money the soldiers had plenty of, but the gal was after gas! It was something money couldn't buy. To date, no stories have come out as to whether or not any of our men got any gas or the gal.

Charlie and I went to the "big top." It proved to be a one-ring show run by what appeared to be a family or two. No more than a dozen people actually did the whole show. The animals were well trained, and I was surprised at the acts they took part in. According to U.S. standards, the whole show was pretty ordinary. We are used to big spectacular shows carrying hundreds of people and having thousands of dollars to run on. Here there were two elephants—one a good sized tusker and one only a baby. The baby did unusually well, but stopped between each of his acts and squealed at the trainer as if protesting the whole affair. I am sure he was not afraid. It was mere protest from a spoiled child impudent enough to show off even in front of an audience.

The steel cage contained three lions, two cheetahs, and a collie dog. A fourth lion had apparently died recently, for one of the trucks parked out in front contained a green lion hide, which I had noticed earlier. Evidently the trainer knew his business, for he put his cats through the paces deftly and with a fine flair of showmanship.

Perhaps the star of the show was a boy who was probably eighteen—a fine looking fellow who seemed able to do anything and appeared in almost every act from tight-wire walking to rope spinning and trick horse-back riding. All in all, it was a very good evening, a change from the movie and camp. We ate bad peanuts and terrible, *terrible* Australian candy, which at its best is bad enough. The soldiers bought all the best seats out at five shillings each. Australians find the Yanks spend money in a way the Aussies are not used to.

Radio Tokyo announces that amphibious troops have moved into the South Pacific (that's us!) and wishes luck on their first mission. What gall! Those dirty little, yellow outfits will probably decide we don't need much luck to just kick hell out of them when we do get going. I never think much of this outfit until I hear something like that.

I need to send some washing in, but there are still no provisions for it. I will not wash unless I have to. So, since the officers were sending their laundry out this morning, I just put my laundry bag in the pile of bundles, and it was taken into the laundry. I may get hell when it turns up, but at least it will be clean by that time.

Got my first letter from home since being here! My sister Elizabeth wrote on March 13. She had received my cable on the same date. So had Mother, and both were much relieved to hear that I was at least on solid ground again, but they still did not know where I am. It was nice to hear news even as old as that. They had not had news of me for twenty-five days. By now, they have letters, I am sure, and know more about it all. The cable was three days going from Brisbane to Brownwood.

With a pair of good army binoculars I got my first good look at the little, green parrots that flock in the tops of the tall eucalyptus trees. With the naked eye they appear small and dull, but through the glasses they show up wonderfully. They are a beautiful green, much brighter on the head, with a sprinkle of yellow on the breast. This is all set off by a brilliant red beak and red underneath the wings. When they fly, they show the brilliant wine lining. Quite a showy little bird!

Early in the morning they flock by the hundreds in the big trees and sit eating, or rather hang and sit. Sometimes they are hanging head down, eating the buds high in the tops, perhaps seventy-five feet above the ground.

Through the glasses the trees look as though they have been grazed by cattle. I have heard of these little, green parrots being pests in farming country and can certainly see why.

An officers' party is taking place in town, and those who were going have just left here—most quite drunk already and disgusting. Major Bilger is still on a trip to Cairns, and I am sure his being gone has something to do with all of this. Here my old Victorian spirit is showing up again. I seem always to feel that way toward drunks and often wonder if I should. I ought to become used to drunks and every vice known to man after seeing them every day in the week. Maybe I adjust slowly, but it still disgusts me.

April 4, 1943

Today is Sunday, but few sing of it here. Things are much as usual. Business does slack up some though, and I found time today to remake my mosquito bar frame over my cot. We have had at least one case of malaria already, and I don't want to be the second. You can't keep some mosquitoes from biting you during the day, but a properly arranged net will certainly keep them off at night.

Found a different variety of parrot in the eucalyptus today with brilliant red-orange breast, black head and belly, and green back. It would be interesting to keep a cage of these colorful, though noisy, birds, but collecting them would be another matter! They fly like lightning and never come near the ground.

April 5, 1943

This morning I continued studying the little green parrots and still find only the two varieties. They are busy tree trimmers, and the small limbs fall regularly. Sometimes a small "bush" will come sailing down, and almost any time you can see fresh, green limb tips scattered over the ground. Sergeant Wilson noticed me watching the birds and volunteered this information: "I saw a whole cage of those parrots the other night at a whore house in Rockhampton. That woman has quite a collection of them!"

An interesting connection with this was that another fellow had told me the same thing earlier in the day, but had said "I saw a whole cage of them at the wash woman's house." Just who lied I don't know, but I suspect

Wilson would not have thought of concealing his whereabouts, being a person who considers himself a "tough" soldier. He's also dull enough to overlook the fact that boasting to show—or try to show—how "army" he is makes him much less a man.

April 6, 1943

Being in a blue mood, I decided not to try to keep up this diary—that the army just isn't worth the effort it takes to write about it. But today, I feel slightly better and think that even if it is of some small interest to a few close friends, it will be worthwhile. You can't get over to the folks back home the utter despair of it, even if you want to. They have fixed ideas of what the army is like, both at home and overseas, and really resent any change in these ideas. In a way they are wonderful darlings to refuse any but a pleasant romantic picture of army life in camp, or one of action or glory in battle. It is better that they cannot understand the dull boredom, underhanded administration, and the ignorance of officers as they press their "position" of rank and haggle over who outranks whom on the smallest excuse. It is best that the homefolks don't know about the forced association with many men who are so seldom born with a free soul or who are naturally good, clean fellows with faith in anything at all.

Plans for a night hike are in progress, but I am Charge of Quarters, so probably won't go. At present I am trying to grow two new toenails that came off recently as the result of a sixteen-mile hike in Fort Ord, California, that was practically made on the run. I came in fine shape, and the toenail problems didn't show up for several days. Then they turned blue and are now off. I guess they are supposed to finally grow back, but the process is surely slow.

Lieutenant Mahony has just come in. He is a swell guy—one of the best. A good athlete, he still keeps in condition by running each afternoon and is probably in better physical condition than anyone in the outfit. I can understand his disgust at "Grandma" Page for complaining about being stiff and sore after a few miles of walking.

I received three letters from Mother, one as recent as March 24, and it was sure good to hear from home. News only thirteen days old! All seemed to be well, and Mother was go glad to hear from me. However, the first letter she got was definitely not the first one I wrote. Mail across the sea now is very uncertain business and doesn't arrive in sequence. Also, I got a letter from Robert Smith.[13] He is in Australia or near. He had much the same trip as our men. I hope to locate him, for it would be wonderful to have a friend near.

My light keeps going out. It is a carbide contraption that takes spells about burning, must be fed water, and is generally temperamental.

April 7, 1943

We went out again on camouflage work, planning some more of the MG emplacements. We still have no materials to work with. I hope to get to town and try to find a few things.

Have gotten a pass tonight and will go in for the first time on the recreation truck that goes each night.

April 8, 1943

The morning after! Ye gods, what a night! To start the party off, the truck was more than an hour late starting to town, but finally we began the dusty, dirty ride of thirty miles to Rockhampton. Other trucks passed and showered us with new dust, and once, a major who had frustrated ambitions to be a traffic cop stopped us and said we were going over fifteen miles per hour, thus breaking the speed limit set by the colonel. The same major runs up and down the road each night doing this sort of thing, although his duties are those of Ordinance Officer, which certainly doesn't include traffic work.

We unloaded by the bridge,[14] and the fellows soon scattered. McCleary and I went immediately to the Red Cross and ordered a steak, iced tea, etc. Australians have good steaks, but they are poorly cut, and I often wonder if there are any first rate butchers in the whole country. Apparently, to them, meat is meat and is just whacked off any old way, with the result that, too often, it is coarse and stringy and very tough.

The American Red Cross pays some of the girls and women who serve in the restaurant. Others are volunteers, but all seem to be going about it cheerfully and doing a good job. Probably the girls like American soldiers. However, the one serving us said the Amphibians were the rudest group she had ever seen. Wondering why she would say this to us, we noticed that we both had on shirts with no Amphibian shoulder patches, and she at once jumped at the conclusion that we were from some other outfit. Usually the order to wear the distinguishing patches is strictly enforced, but we had gotten by somehow. We agreed with the girl and gave the Amphibians the devil and finished by saying we would hate to be any part of an outfit like that. The girl had really hit the thing squarely. I have never known a ruder group in my life, and they usually get that reputation quickly in any town.

As we finished the meal, one of the jeep drivers came up and began telling where he had found a place to buy liquor after hours. Mack[15] was interested at once, and off they went—to the black market.

I finished eating and wandered down the main street, wondering why I had really come to town. Of all the places that close up at dark, this is the worst. Absolutely nothing remains open that could be of interest. A few "milk bars" or ice cream stands and a couple of fruit stands. Another unit of the Red Cross was open across the street, but few men were there and little was going on.

Later I met Mack again carrying a bottle wrapped in paper. He was going into the Red Cross to check it in the check room there, for the MPs grab anything that looks like liquor. We met several of the boys, all with a couple of drinks under their belts, but not at all drunk, and we all went down to the dance hall of the town.

Two shillings admittance is charged, and the MP at the door looks you over good. Evidently the hall is more or less sponsored, or at least approved, by the army police and officers, for it was orderly and apparently O.K. The music was fairly good, and at least two of the fifty to seventy-five girls were good-looking. The rest looked like fugitives from a goon convention. I never learned how the place was run. Probably some of the dancers were paid for their work. (And it was work!) Several Aussie women soldiers were there in uniform too. I danced a couple of times, but mostly just watched the show. It was quite a show too! No Australian soldiers were there, and I didn't know if there simply were none in the neighborhood, or if they just didn't attend.

As it was nearing 11:00 p.m., we left, found a late milk bar open, got a milk shake, bought some fruit, and made for the bridge. Several of our boys had not returned, so we waited. Most were now full of black market whiskey and were talking loudly. Patrick Carey (an Irishman from New York's east side) and Stanley (ex-bum, etc.) were arguing about some trivial thing. Richard Bohigan came up and began trying to climb into the back of the truck. Pat, trying to be helpful, grabbed him by the foot that was sticking over the end gate and proceeded to tumble him in on his head on the metal floor of the truck.

Of course, Bohigan resented this treatment, and the two had to be separated and put in opposite ends of the truck. Pat sat down and got out his bottle, against the protests of several who thought he had had more than enough for one night. The bottle gurgled mightily.

Finally, all arrived, and we began the return trip. Most eventually passed out and fell into Stanley's lap. After thirty minutes or so, Stanley noticed that he was holding Pat and decided Pat should sit up. He proceeded to set him upright, but, of course, Pat was like a dish rag and just wouldn't stay put, flopping again, still dead out.

About this time the truck stopped, and the driver got out and walked unsteadily around the cab. My gosh! The driver was reeling too, drunk as a hoot owl! He took the notion into his dizzy brain that something was wrong with the truck and refused to drive it another yard, so there we sat.

Stanley again decided Pat was a burden and got up and tried to stand him on his feet. This aroused him some, at least to the extent that he knew he didn't want to stand up. He swung weakly at Stanley. They clinched, and in doing so leaned on the strap across the back of the truck, and both flipped over to the gravel below, hitting like two rocks. By the time we got off to see what was up, Stanley was up, but Pat was out cold with an ugly place on his head. He had hit square on the top of his head, taking the hair and skin off his scalp as neatly as any Indian ever scalped a pioneer. He was so completely knocked out that I feared he had broken his neck in the fall. Stanley stood over him, yelling at him to wake up.

A truck from Short Battalion stopped, but the lieutenant in charge refused to take Pat to the medics and left. Finally a truck came by that did take him on, but we had to force him into the truck, as he had revived and wanted to fight. Later the wrecker came and pulled us in while someone else got in the cab and steered the truck. Our driver was in back with us, screaming crazily at everyone, telling them they better swear there was something really wrong with the truck tomorrow, for he was sure he would be up for this. He wasn't too drunk to think of the fact that he might get a skinning later.

After reading over what I've just written, it sounds pretty crazy, but it is just what happened. Except being there, it was disgusting. I want someone to poke me right in the nose when I want to go in with that truck again!

5 In Camp at Easter

April 9, 1943

We're at camouflage work again. Company A has three MGs to be camouflaged, and the company commander came by to ask me to direct the work. It isn't difficult work, but so few of our officers or men seem to have any idea of it at all. With a good group of workers, we got along well with the project today. At least one of the jobs is the best I have worked at so far, possibly because I stuck with every phase of it clear through. I hate to leave a camouflage job and come back to find that some monstrosity has been constructed that wouldn't fool a one-eyed man who was five miles away.

Again the view was lovely from the point, but the water was rather dull and very choppy from the stiff wind. Possibly the wind accounted for the fact that hundreds of butterflies had collected on the sheltered side of the hill. They were very similar to our monarches, but of different colors—black with pale blue markings instead of the rich browns of the American Monarch. However, that ended the difference, for they fly the same, light the same, and hang by the dozens on the leaves of tall grass and low tree limbs. Being fully as hardy as our monarchs, they no doubt find places much like the "butterfly trees" of Carmel, California, to spend the winter.

Several dusky beauties of another variety sailed by. One was black velvet with sky blue circles on the lower wings.

I just received "V" letters from Elizabeth and Quirl, the first of the kind I have gotten. All seems to be well at home, which makes it easier for me here.

April 11, 1943

Sunday—and some time off for a hike around the beach. The tide was half in and had covered most of the interesting shore that is exposed at the lowest point. I did get a good look at the camouflage we have been doing. From a distance I found it O.K. in spots, but needing more work.

I received my first letter from Suzy,[16] and it made me happier than anything that has happened in a long time. She certainly wrote a sweet letter, as she usually does. That girl must have what it takes. She sure has stuck with that nursing job and will finish her training in September. After that, she seems undecided about what she will do, but has decided against joining the army nurses, and I am glad of that. The nurses' corps is probably much better than the army, but it would be hard even having to think of her in that. I am sure she will be very much needed at home now, as nurses and doctors are getting scarce. Sometimes I doubt that she ever sincerely wanted to be a nurse, but chose it as a means of being independent—something for security.

I was to have begun a series of charts on boats for Major Bilger, but found that there was no large paper available for the work. Our navigation headquarters is down at Kepple Sands, so I went with the major to plan the work. While waiting to find out about the paper, the major suggested that if I wanted to, I might go down to the beach for a couple of hours. I did!

I put my clothes on a rock and walked down the beach to the point. There is a lot of beach exposed when the tide is out. The sun was very nice, and this was the first time I had had a chance at a sun bath in several days.

There seemed to be very little in the way of new shells, etc., probably because the water is very shallow for several miles out, and little of the ocean floor is washed this far inland over the sand bars. I did get several interesting shells though, and sketched them on a letter to Suzy when I returned to camp.

After a couple of hours, we found that no paper could be obtained at once, so the major and I returned in the jeep. When the paper does come, I will spend a number of days down there working at leisure. The Major said, "When you get tired of working, go down to the beach and rest. There is no hurry about the work." A very unusual statement, for usually officers know so little about such work that it is expected you can turn it out like a mill.

My collection of "beachcomber's loot" attracted the attention of Lieutenant Jones, and I was surprised that he, too, was a beachcomber and had quite a collection of things which he showed me. I intend to keep hunting out those people interested in such things and get more interest up in hobbies.

Mack and I went over to the shower this afternoon, and our two prize A.W.O.L.s were there for a shower too, along with their guard carrying a loaded rifle. They have been "over the hill" about five times so far. As soon as they get out of the stockade when a sentence is up, they are off again, so now they are being kept in pup tents out toward the edge of the camp area awaiting another courtmartial.

They talk cheerfully and don't seem to be as bad as they are supposed to be—just a couple of men who can't like the army, or ever get in the frame of mind to stick it out either. It has been hard on them I know. I don't know what their background is, but it would be interesting to talk with them long enough to find out. The guard has to go with them with fixed bayonet everywhere they decide to go.

Later I passed them going to supper, and one was singing to the guard who was walking behind, "I don't want to walk without you, Baby!" One is the same fellow I mentioned earlier as having been in the guard room in town after a week's absence; we brought him back out to camp.

The Brigade Band is playing. It comes over about once a week for a concert before the movie, but I am again on duty, so will not be able to attend.

The A.P.O.[17] man will be out tomorrow night (our only chance to get money orders) so I will send a money order to Davis Floral at home and have flowers sent for Mothers' Day, and some wired to Suzy at Galveston. Mother appreciated hers so on her birthday that I want to send them now anytime I can. It is hard to find anything to do for those at home when you are this far away, but knowing the Davises personally, I just write them and they know what to do and what to send.

April 13, 1943

Captain Gudgeon came by and discussed camouflage work with me this morning. We planned to try a new spray gun and other things. Our executive officer suggested that if the captain wants me to direct his camouflage, he better do something about getting me a rating. The captain replied that if it were possible, he would like to have me on his staff. Of course, I would like the work, but you just can't depend on anything. Tomorrow they may stick someone into the place who has never done any of the work, for no reason other than that someone else happened along and said, "I want John Jones to be your camouflage man," and the captain wouldn't hesitate for a minute. None of the army officers seem to stand on any of their rights to choose their help, but if someone higher up has an idea, they simply follow, even to the extent of hampering progress, without ever going to the person and explaining that John Jones is simply no good at that particular job.

Major Bilger is acting as regimental commander in the absence of Colonel Neff, leaving no one in our office at the present to take his place. Things are pretty busy, but I went out again on the camouflage project, got the colors mixed, and the burlap garlands dipped in shades of green. They will be woven into the wire frames covering the guns that are up on the wooded slope, and will blend in with the surrounding bushes. Someday I hope to be able to go right through with these jobs and not be having to leave them and do the work here.

I heard from Robert Smith again. Evidently he is in New Guinea or the surrounding islands from his description of the natives. I hope to catch up with him someday.

I received a letter from Mother and one from Ella, or rather, Mother had written on the back of Ella's. It had been sent to her to forward to me. I was amused at Ella saying, "Roy wrote me that one fellow in the same outfit with him said he had three wives in different places." Dear Ella, she just doesn't know that only a few people are as upright and clean as she is, and that there are now probably hundreds of men who have married each time they go to a new place. A few may be caught, but many will not, and even the girls they marry will not be able to trace them when they leave.

April 15, 1943

I worked on my "desk" this morning and tried to get it a better height to draw on. (I'm not worried about it being the correct height to work on!) Our furniture is a joke, but out here even a small piece of good lumber is unobtainable. Nails are very scarce, so we use table legs sawed from saplings and try to find a box with which to make the top. After a few weeks, we usually have a lot of stuff built for our headquarters tent, a process that must be repeated each time we move.

There is much discussion going on about candidates for O.C.S.[18] as there is to be another school held soon—probably down at Brisbane. There is a lot of red tape to attending and much ado about selecting candidates, but usually it ends up the usual way. A couple of officers decide that maybe they better not send the full quota, but just two or three this time, etc. Then the two are chosen with the same idea—that two men can judge a dozen and tell exactly what they can do. Some fellows positively take a position of servitude that is ridiculous in order to try to win favor and get their O.C.S. papers through. They jump at the beck and call of every officer who might be able to push them in any way.

I am very glad I have no desire for a commission—at least that makes me free. The officers are quick to take advantage of those who are afraid of losing their ratings and can usually make them do anything with threats to reduce them.

Lately there has been a lot of talk from higher-ups about the conduct of the Amphibians in town—a problem that most everyone knew existed from the beginning. Last night all the men who were in town Monday or Tuesday were called up. Out came the general's car with several big bugs and a seven-year-old boy. It seems that either Monday or Tuesday a soldier had popped the kid in the eye. Otherwise the boy was not harmed, but the soldier got away so they were trying to identify the man who did it. Probably the soldier was drunk, and the kid had asked him for "some Yankee money" as they so often do. Instead of a dime, which would have tickled him to death, he got a sock in the eye. I know plenty of men who would pop their own old grandmother in the eye when they are drunk.

Captain Shaul asked me to go along on an inspection of the machine guns and camouflage. In talking about the work, I found that he felt that either the S-2 or regimental headquarters should get going and do the work or give the job to me. Major Bilger later said there should be a sergeant's rating for that kind of work. All of which sounds all right, but probably doesn't amount to anything.

All the recently camouflaged guns protect our maintenance shop and boat anchorage and are set on the long, high ridge overlooking the whole vicinity—dug in and sand-bagged. Now two other companies have their guns ready, and we will have to work on them. The captain and I went down below the guns at the bottom of the hill where boxes of ammunition and dynamite are stored. The road down is almost 45 degrees and has to be held in place by heavy wire mats in order to afford enough hold for the tires to climb it.

The tide was coming in on the long sandy beach in beautiful whispers—swish-out again, swish-out again—on the clean sand in long, white, young breakers. The tide was still out so far that the water was very shallow—swish, silence for a minute—swish, in comes the white roll broken here and there with another row of white breakers behind, like sheep chasing one another into land.

Up from the sand a ways, I see some strange trees of the pine family with long, hanging, fine, needle-like leaves of dull green—dusty green. Still farther up is a jungle growth of tall, deep green trees, vines and weeds with colorful butterflies hunting the fragrant blossoms of the vines. Above that, almost sheer rock and clay rise to the ridge and the guns. It is nice to get out and see a few things once in a while.

As we came back, Captain Shaul said he was to be assigned a Jeep, and that we would have to tear out and go exploring again. He hasn't forgotten the time we went up the swamp and now refers to me as a guy who likes to explore the country. He has discovered that there are a couple pairs of hip boots in the company, so now we plan to wade the swamp and see what is beyond the road and wall of vines and trees.

April 16, 1943

I received a letter from Mother and one from Ridgley.[19] Things at home are fine, or were on March 29. Ridgley has a new daughter and is very proud of her—says she is a regular Indian papoose with jet black hair. I sent a cable of congratulations to Marie and him and wrote them a letter. They are indeed swell friends, and I am proud of them. When I visited them last Christmas time, we all hoped for a daughter, for they already have Jim, who is five.

Our Number One Bad Boy and impudent officer, Captain Miller, pulled one too many stunts, and now there is an order transferring him out to another battalion. He and another captain took a Jeep from the motor pool against our adjutant's orders and without a dispatch slip. They bluffed the private on guard at the gate and went to town. Once before they both went in, got dead drunk, and had to be brought back by someone else.

April 18, 1943

It's Sunday again, and most of the morning was taken up with skinning and preparing to tan a seven-foot python. The Indian urge was too great. I proceeded to make snake leather, which was either a brave or foolish decision in view of the equipment on hand. Strong soap and salt were the only materials available, so I started out with them. No nails or tacks were to be had, so I whittled a canful of bamboo pegs which are as tough and hard as small nails. There is no lumber on which to stretch the skin, so a smooth gum tree will do, and the pegs will drive into it easily.

If it turns out well, people all over the U.S. will get bits of Australian python in their letters. Except for Major Bilger, I can't find anyone here who ever skinned a snake, much less tanned one's skin, and the whole thing is rather mysterious and fascinating to the men. "What will you use to tan it?" they ask, and a simple explanation like "just G.I. soap" is very unsatisfactory, for the operation is supposed to be very difficult.

April 19, 1943

I've found a copy of a letter sent in by a man long ago, when we were in camp at Waquoit Island, Cape Cod. A rare piece of humor, it was intended to be serious and was written by a dissatisfied fellow in our outfit. Knowing the situation thoroughly makes the letter even funnier. At the time we were having a lot of mutton in our rations, hence the mention that mutton makes his nose burn. Also he was having to do a lot of kitchen work, hence the kitchen makes his nose burn. A mental case—he really didn't belong in the Army, but was finally transferred to a medical outfit.

October 5, 1942

Subject: Transfer to Non-Combatant Unit

To: Commanding Officer, 592d Engineers' Amphibian Regiment, Camp Edwards, Massachusetts (Through Channels)

1. I believe that I should be placed in a non-combatant unit because of the following reasons:

a. I had a case of gonorrhea and have been cured of it. About two years later I went under an operation for fistula and after this operation, the doctor told me that I had a case of syphilis. I have been under treatment for this ailment; have been cured also.

b. Ever since I was a child, I have been bothered with burns in the nose and throat 'til up to the present time; and when there is a change in the weather, during the day and mostly at night, I get a very bad spell of coughing, which prevents me from getting the proper amount of sleep. The only way I get some sleep is from utter exhaustion from lack of sleep. I have been to a few doctors and a few hospitals in order to find out what is causing this condition, but they were unable to analyze the case. I have been under a tonsil operation—a lingual tonsil operation—and also an operation on the nose for deviated septum, which the doctors claimed were the causes of these burns on the nose and the throat, and causing a nervous disorder.

c. I also have had many scratch tests, but to no avail. Salt water also irritates this condition and makes it worse than usual, causing me to become allergic to salt water.

d. I have aches and pains in the body—very severe aches and pains—which are caused from sleeping in tents on account of the drafts that come from sleeping in tents. If I were able to sleep in a warmer place, such as in a barracks where drafts and cold winds would be stopped better, the condition would not prevail. Then again, these aches and pains in the body may be caused by my being a victim previously of gonorrhea and syphilis. This is another defect that makes it difficult for me to get the proper amount of sleep.

e. The doctors told me that I was allergic to two types of food, which are veal and lamb. Every time I enter a place where either lamb or veal or both are being cooked, the severe burning in my nose and throat occurs, only this time I get dizzy spells also.

f. Guard duty is another factor that creates a nervous condition, which reacts on my whole body in general, causing great discomfort and restlessness while I am on my feet.

g. Quite a few years ago, I woke up with a paralytic stroke on the right foot; which caused me so much pain if I walked on my whole foot that I was ordered to walk on the toes of the foot that was stricken in order to move about with any success. I went to the hospital for treatment. They massaged it for about four weeks, after which I was able to walk all right, but the pains still remained.

h. I applied for Government Insurance, but my application was rejected by the Veterans' Administration because of my formerly having syphilis. I do not believe that this is sufficient cause for my being rejected, as I have been given a cure for this ailment, and also, every soldier is entitled to Government Insurance.

i. In view of the reasons already mentioned, I believe I should be transferred to a non-combatant unit.

j. I would appreciate a reply to this letter as soon as possible, as I am anxious to receive word of this matter.

Apparently his worst fears were finally realized, for I have heard that he is in Australia with the medical unit to which he was transferred. I feel sorry for the outfit, not the soldier.

Some fairly late copies of American magazines arrived for some of our battalion office force, so we are having a field day. *Readers Digest*, *Life*, and *Esquire* look mighty good after some of these Australian attempts at publication. Really, Australian magazines are pitiful and a waste of paper. The American zip and fresh ideas are sadly missing.

Major Bilger is preparing to go on an eight-day experimental hike with some new jungle equipment, so we have been looking over the things in the jungle kit that we will eventually be issued when we go up to Guinea. The hammock is quite nifty and enables you to get off the ground and sleep in an enclosed bed with a nice mosquito net that zips shut tightly. No jungle bugs could get in that.

The python skin turned out very well and is about finished. I hope to get some alum in town for the next one, but don't intend to fool with any little old snake less than seven or eight feet long.

The day was somewhat different, as I got a chance to go to town about eight this morning. It was early, so the ride was less dusty than usual, and it was less rough than usual since I was sitting on a load of clothes that were to be salvaged (or swapped for new ones). There was plenty of time, because we weren't to leave until 4:00 p.m. I began by hunting a hardware store and looking for all the foolish, but necessary, things that I don't want to be caught in the wilderness without, such as string, a knife, etc. Since there were fishhooks, I got several dozen, just in case I need them or am able to trade them to the natives. Also, I got some big hanks of cord and some small rope, a large pair of cutting scissors, a small pair, and some sandpaper. At the 5 & 10 I bought some needles, thread, and such junk. Later at a leather and saddle shop, I found a very good sheath knife made by an Australian from an old bayonet—good steel.

When I went to the Red Cross Service Club for dinner, Lieutenant Mahony with whom I came, and Captain Page were there. We joined Lieutenant Sage and the warrant officer, Mr. Banks, and had a very enjoyable meal—then flipped coins to see who paid for it all. Captain Page lost, but the check for the six of us (another lieutenant came up later) was only about $1.75. Food is cheap, and the Red Cross is very reasonable with prices.

As I was going to the A.P.O. to mail some Australian books to Mother, Lieutenant Mahony asked me to get him a money order. Most everyone from majors to privates send money orders home, as none of us can spend what we get. There just isn't any way to spend much.

After lunch I ran into a couple of our boys who are in town on guard at some of the warehouses. They are having a holiday, since they are only on duty part time and can be around town when off. They will probably tell a lot of tall stories when they complete their week.

Tonight I am on duty again. Major Bilger received a copy of the Carmel, California, "Pine Cone" so I am enjoying that while G.I. takes a nap in my shirt. He is a very small kitten that happened in one day—the way kittens

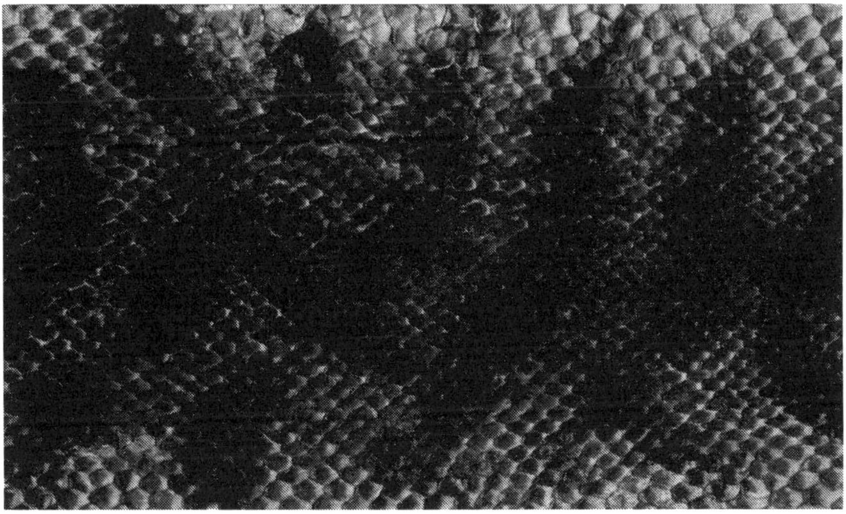

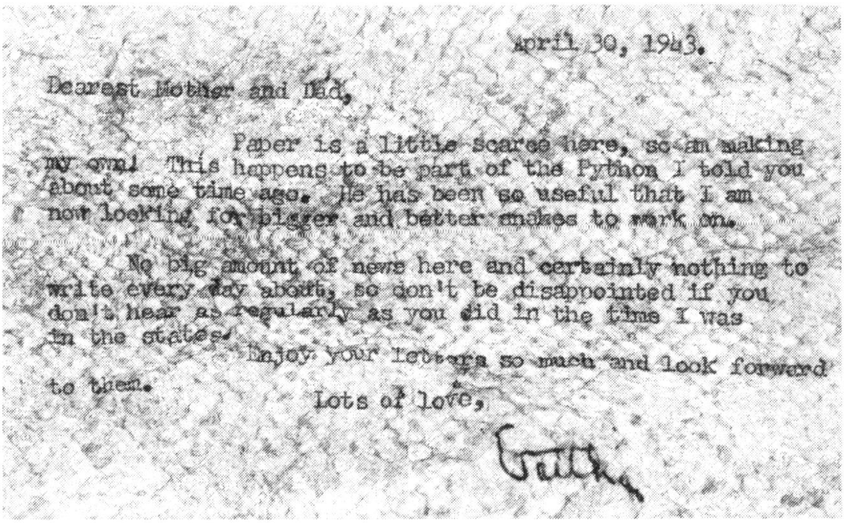

April 30, 1943.

Dearest Mother and Dad,

Paper is a little scarce here, so am making my own! This happens to be part of the Python I told you about some time ago. He has been so useful that I am now looking for bigger and better snakes to work on.

No big amount of news here and certainly nothing to write every day about, so don't be disappointed if you don't hear as regularly as you did in the time I was in the states.

Enjoy your letters so much and look forward to them.

Lots of love,

"Paper is a little scarce here, so am making my own! this happens to be part of the Python I told you about some time ago. He has been so useful that I am now looking for bigger and better snakes to work on."

do—and stayed. I wonder how he escapes the wheels of all the trucks and jeeps that go in and out all day. I fixed him a bed in a pigeon hole of the field desk in front of me, but he insists on climbing into my lap or into my shirt, where he lies like a tiny fur ball with a motor.

I got a small hammer in town, so I will proceed to pound some good Australian silver pieces into rings. They make clever ones, and when carefully worked, the lettering of the coin remains inside the ring. Some such handicraft seems to be going on in our office all the time, and I wonder what the very military and strict major of the Shore Battalion would think of our Boat Battalion Headquarters. If he had come in yesterday when McCleary was pounding out a ring, I was tanning the snake skin over the back of the adjutant's chair, and Charlie and the Jeep driver were in a game of cribbage! But Major Bilger doesn't mind, so we still have fun.

April 22, 1943

This morning we unpacked jungle rations, and Charlie and I are eating *only* this stuff for two days. Major Bilger asked me if I had rather eat it four days or share it with someone. I really didn't care about the number of days, but Charlie wanted to be a guinea pig too, so we will both take two days of it. Just an experiment—but someday we might have to depend on this ration when nothing else is available. Four days' rations only fill a box twelve by twelve inches. I wonder!

I cut the papaya I bought in town and lost all my friends when I gave them some of it. Most said it tasted terrible, and they would have to be starving before they would eat it. I didn't care much for it either. So far, most of the tropical fruits have been somewhat disappointing with the exception of bananas and pineapples.

We actually enjoyed the "canned" breakfast. That small box contains some very good food, and the best powdered milk I ever tasted—much better than our condensed milk. We had coffee (made from small packages of powder in hot water), cereal, milk, and crackers (glorified dog biscuits).

More camouflage work today for Company B, and I am still trying to get things done without any authority and little backing. I just hope to either be relieved of the job or given the job officially.

Good Friday services were held today, and I enjoyed them very much. Few men attended the Protestant service. I don't know what kind of crowd was present at the Catholic service, which was held at a different time. We have a great many Catholic boys from New York and the East.

There has been rain all day, off and on—our first full day of showers. While up on the point overlooking the sea, we saw two of our boats coming in from eighty miles down the coast. Our crews went down and brought them back. We spotted the boats when they were still two specks on the horizon. Through glasses they proved to be taking a heavy sea, and we knew the crews were tired and hungry and taking a beating. They were also probably very wet. The assault boats are not built for long trips and have no place to get out of the rain and weather. Later Major Shaul (who was with the boats) told us all about the trip. It was rough all right! The two boats had been shipped over from the States and assigned to us for training and use.

Received a letter from Elizabeth, written April 2. They had received a few letters from me. All seemed to be well except Mother. She has been under the weather, but nothing serious apparently.

Lunch wasn't so bad out of the small four days' supply box. We had ham loaf, crackers, milk, dried apricots, raisins, and a pound can of peanuts to nibble on through the day. There is also chewing gum and candy in the box.

April 24, 1943

Work again today, high above the green sea, and it was as beautiful as usual. In general, Australia has somewhat disappointed me. It simply doesn't measure up to anything we have in the States. But the sea is nice most any place, and here is no exception. The tall grass on the hill, on which butterflies sit and sip, has begun to bloom. This is the nearest thing I have seen to our yucca or bear grass, but doesn't have the impressive bunch of blossoms, just a pointed tip on the long white stalk down which the tiny blooms burst out.

The wind was strong, but we pulled off our shirts and worked in the sun. Everyone will be very brown after a time in the tropical climate.

I cut Cliff Pouncey a hat band from the tanned python skin. He will enjoy it more than anyone I know. I wrote Suzy a letter on the back of a piece the size of an envelope and gave several pieces to people who had wanted them.

Put a razor edge on my knife. It takes a good edge. Dull. Dull! Dull!! Ye gods! How dull!!! And the folks back home think we must be doing something exciting just because we are overseas.

Tomorrow is Easter Sunday, and we should have an especially good service, but what a difference between it and a year ago.

April 25, 1943

A beautiful bright Easter morning, but cool as the dickens. It makes you wonder if it really is true that Australia has little change from season to season. Everyone slept late and enjoyed a breakfast of sausage and eggs, which we don't get often. Fresh eggs seem to be scarce around here—hope the seagulls start laying soon. At 9 a.m. we had Easter services with the best attendance I have seen. The altar built from rustic logs under a small thatched shed was almost covered with bougainvillea and palm leaves. The bougainvillea blooms were in several shades from pink to purple.

Here was another Easter, and I was at least ten thousand miles from the service at the Shrine of the Ages on the rim of the Grand Canyon. Each year I have promised myself that I will attend services there, but find this time that more land and sea separates us than ever before.

DREAM, INCOMPLETE

Written by a soldier in Australia who again missed his goal:
to be at the "Shrine of the Ages" on Easter morning.

Once long ago I promised me
That Easter morn would find that sea
Of Canyon loveliness spread far below
As anthems rose. I did not go—
And time cut short those dreams
Not yet reality, of blue streams,
Distant sea, to visit when time came round;

Green hills, valleys in spring, a spot of ground.
Time turned to guns and ships and dreams were dead
As we marched off into reality instead,
With gods of war that strip all beauty bare
And toss aside her body with no care
That it should ever rise again to lead the way
Nor thought of need of her some distant day.

Easter Day, sound of morning born anew.
Far away my Canyon echoes too,
Not from bomb or gun or place
But age-old anthems sung again
As the Canyon's blue is shattered
By sunlight jewels scattered—
Brahman, Buddha, Zion, one by one
Their crests flash crimson in the sun
Like sacred candles lighted for the day.
Shrine of the Ages, that points the upward way
And knows with wisdom, old as time, all men's creeds
Loves each one; and then proceeds
On Easter morning to give an hour of serenity
And steal their hearts for all eternity.
J. G. B.

But someday I will be there, for the Canyon will be waiting, as magnetic and mysterious as ever.

6 A Visit To Yeppoon

April 26, 1943

Went to Yeppoon up the coast this afternoon, and the trip turned out to be quite pleasant. The ride was beautiful around the shore, and we saw some new country. There are many beautiful curving beaches between here and Yeppoon with the white surf rolling in endlessly. The small town itself is on one of these and has the best ocean bathing beach I have yet seen in Australia.

There was a good crowd, but not large enough to congest even that small town. A number of trucks from our and other units had brought soldiers for the afternoon. As usual with a crowd, we split up when we got off the truck, and three others and I went to the beach for a swim. The water was warm, and it was fine riding the big breakers as they rolled smoothly in over the clean sand. The boy who had done most of the stunts in the small circus was on the beach with his two elephants, selling rides to the soldiers and others. I talked with him for some time and learned they are not showing now at all, but are wintering along the coast. The army took all their help and may get this boy, the star performer, before long. Evidently it is all they can do to keep going, and no doubt the circus will fold up for the duration if the boy goes off.

Several of our men found dates and were sitting on the beach talking to the girls. After the swim we found a small "fish bar" and had fish, which doesn't sound so great, but turned out to be delicious—the most wonderful fish I ever ate. Fried in deep fat, rolled in some sort of batter, and fried golden brown, it was served with bread and butter and hot tea. A simple meal, but one of the best I have had.

A large crowd of civilians was taking advantage of the holiday, and all the stores were open for trade. Across from the main street an English flag was waving, and we discovered the place to be an English flying school. The cadets were mere boys—the youngest I have ever seen training in any place. I don't know the system of training the English and Aussies use, but I suppose these kids are to grow up into the Royal Air Force.

April 27, 1943

Because a big demonstration is being prepared for General Douglas MacArthur and his staff, there is a lot of coming and going and planning. The thing is to be held at or near the place we visited Easter Sunday, Yeppoon. Probably it will be held on one of the splendid beaches we saw, and our regiment has some part in it. There was a rehearsal of the demonstration this afternoon, and most went for a look. The actual program will be pretty airtight, and everyone will not be able to attend. Actually General MacArthur is not held in the esteem here that he is in the States. Most army people dislike him thoroughly in these parts, from all the reports we have had. The Australians simply refuse to swoon when he passes by. Most feel that he actually did no more in the Philippines campaign than a number of others, but hit the American public with a good press story right at the time when everyone was looking for a hero to publicize.

April 28, 1943

I left here for Rockhampton this morning, and when I arrived, went to the salvage depot maintained by the army. The depot is interesting, for it had not occurred to me that such a place existed. Every type of article the army ever had is somewhere to be found in that huge warehouse. Broken and worn-out things are brought in, and crews go to work to make them useful again, if possible. Cots were being repaired. Canvas covers were being sewed for them on a huge sewing machine. Tents were being mended and clothes sorted. Much of the stuff will again see service, and will be needed too—a fact I realize more than ever after making the crossing myself.

The sergeant had no paint sprayers, which is what I was after, but he told me that the Department of Interior had a couple. I went down there, and a pleasant old fellow at once offered to give me the spraying outfit if it could be used at all. It could, and was new, so I now have some way to paint my camouflage jobs. I never did find out exactly what this Department of the Interior is, but evidently it is in some way connected with the state of Queensland. The old man said he would just charge the sprayer off; it had been sent to them for an experiment.

May 3, 1943

A new month and there is talk of another move. An advanced detachment will leave tomorrow for the north. No doubt we will follow soon.

Yesterday I received a most satisfactory bunch of letters from home. Mrs. Stallings[20] gave me all the news of the Brownwood Art Association, which doesn't seem to be much these days, as everyone has gone in for war work in a big way. Ella writes from Mississippi that she enjoys hearing from Australia.

More camouflage work today, and the new sprayer works fine. It will enable me to do better work. The tide was out when we climbed the hill, but late in the afternoon when we prepared to leave, it was coming in—long curving white ridges far below, broken up and looking like white sheep running toward the shore, but never quite seeming to climb out of the sand. The tall grasses are still blooming, although things in general are beginning to get a little tired looking as if they were ready for Australia's winter.

Today Harry Chambers came up to the tent looking for someone and stopped to talk a while. Harry is unusual only in that he is one of the physically perfect of our thousand or so men—a distinction few men anywhere can claim. An attractive manner and perfect physique give him two strikes on anybody anywhere. This proves again that we are only human and not much removed from the day when the strong were the rulers men loved to follow.

I have noticed how easily these men gain what others work long and hard for, but many of them are unable to hold what they are given. A number—of the comparative few we have—got army ratings of sergeant or better early in the organization of the battalion, because they typified what we mortals want our leaders to look like. They looked good—as if they could do anything which needed to be done—so our officers chose them. Some have kept their positions and proved out but most, definitely, have not. Harry Chambers among them. So, they are privates again, and probably happier being so.

Once some time ago I had a chance to ask Harry how he lost his rating and got transferred to our company, and he told me quite frankly. It was a long story, but the gist of it was that he met a girl while on a twenty-four hour pass. He went with her to her apartment and was three days late coming back. From this and other stories I gather that he just can't resist any woman, nor they him, so he is continually getting in late, overstaying passes, etc.

Private Woods, once a staff sergeant and very much like Harry, lost his rating by being quick with his fists, not quick with the women. Since last July when I first knew him in this outfit, he has knocked down someone on the average of once a week, which included a captain who had to have a whole set of new teeth afterwards. Attractive and with a quick smile, Woods is not the person you would pick to run amuck, but he does, at the most inopportune times. Therefore, he cannot be trusted. In spite of all this, his fellow soldiers still admire him, for a number of times I have seen him the center of a group, talking happily or laughing with them as he did some camp work, his big shoulders bare and brown in the sun, with muscles running over his splendid body like mice caught under a fine grade of golden silk.

Kevin Coonerty personifies the opposite extreme, being small and skinny—a bag of bones—but well educated, quick in grasping what is to be done, a gentleman in every way and able to do anything the army requires. He is practically unnoticed among other privates, and I doubt that he will be noticed until he has worked long and hard. But when he does get his stripes, they will be his for the duration.

May 4, 1943

After writing about Robert Woods last night, I had him brought back to mind this morning when I brought in the report of his company to the office. I found his name on it—the only A.W.O.L. in the battalion at present. He went to town and failed to return. What a wonderful person he could be if he could balance up.[21]

Advanced detail has been moving all day; most seem glad to go, for it is "boresome" here. The Australian newspapers put out a regular "scare sheet" yesterday. Every headline was an adverse report, the papers were filled with stories of Japanese strength in our area. We all expect some sort of hell to break loose in the whole South Pacific area soon, for both sides are amassing strength. I just wish the African campaign[22] could end quickly and divert some strength to our area.

Most of those who were inducted with me at Brownwood are now in the middle of the African war and have been there for nearly a year. From reports I gather that we are merely holding here until something breaks—at least the latest reports make no claims beyond that.

Today is Tuesday and pass day. A number are planning to go to town tonight. There is no movie, so I probably will twiddle my thumbs for amusement.

Received a letter from Suzy. Her letters always cheer me up. She said a lot about living for today and quoted a very fine idea that she has pinned on her desk. "Too many of us are detoured from genuine living. We deposit our days in a bank of the future, and time destroys our investment." She seemed to think I might not be hopeless in that respect, and that maybe I am enjoying each day more than I ever have before. I am, and I do not plan to ever again deposit my days.

May 5, 1943

"The night was filled with music," and *what* music! Early in the evening most of the officers were drinking, and by 10 p.m. most were drunk. I left the office and then went to bed, only to be waked at midnight by the men coming in from town. Several drunks were in the next tent down the hill and kept up loud talking and yelling. Finally getting more or less used to the noise, I dozed off, but was awakened suddenly by Brownell in our tent. He was yelling at the top of his voice to the drunks to shut up. His bellow did no good whatsoever, but it did wake everyone around who was not already awake. About two a.m. things calmed down, and we went to sleep.

At 3:00 someone came in to wake Roth,[23] telling him he would have to get ready to go into town to replace a guard who had been removed from his post for drunkenness and put in the stockade. Oh beautiful night! Today everyone around has an awful headache from drinking, and most are grumpy as the devil. McCleary must have had quite a spree for he was in town all yesterday and last night. Today he looks something like a sick dog.

May 6, 1943

Major Bilger suggested that I go on the boats to Keppel Island for an outing. Two of our boats were going out for training crews. We left with high tide and headed for Great Keppel Island fourteen miles off the coast. Soon the green and tan waters of the coastal sand bars were left behind, and the deep blue of the Pacific began to show, as the powerful boats cut a white swath into it.

Great Keppel loomed up—a dark mass in the blue with a mountain peak in its middle. We got out the chart case and a map of the area and found Great Keppel to be about five miles long by about three wide, roughly oval shaped, with considerable flat space toward the back middle part. It is owned by a woman living in Yeppoon, and rumor has it that she uses it for sheep raising, but I don't know. I didn't see any sheep or cattle there or on the beaches. As it is large and wooded, the island probably would be ideal for cattle or sheep if wells were drilled for fresh water. Certainly there would be no problem of straying cattle and wire fences, and I doubt that there is a predatory animal of any kind on it.

We rounded the north point and landed on a rainbow beach perhaps a mile long—the most beautiful beach I have ever seen or hope to see. Just clean, hard-packed sand along that sweep, sloping into crystal. No debris littered this beach—not a stick of drift, no seaweed, no shells, not a speck of anything for a mile—just smooth sand without even a track on it, almost too beautiful to trample on. We dropped the front ramps of the boats and waded ashore on that magic stretch, and I felt much like the first man who ever set foot on Great Keppel.

We ate sandwiches for lunch, and the boats made ready to go out for practice. I put on swim trunks, stowed the rest of my clothes on one of the boats, and carried only a cloth bag and a knife. I waved the boats goodbye, as I was to meet them later on the other side of the island. They were gone and soon lost in the Pacific, and I was the only living man on Great Keppel.

I was Robinson Crusoe on a deserted island. It was wonderful, just walking down the beach alone—no noise, no people. The incredible blue of the Pacific spread before me, an iridescent changing blue, born of tropic skies. One lone gull flew low and eyed me curiously as he soared on the breeze with motionless wings—no other life stirred.

The tide was ebbing, uncovering more of that remarkable beach at each lap of the surf, and as I reached the far end and rounded the tip, that curved dome resembled a cream-colored china bowl turned upside down as it ran smoothly around the island point and was off again to form another beach almost as wonderful as the first. However, the second one contained a number of interesting, old drift logs worn smooth and gray by the tide, and a wealth of shells at the water's edge.

I had a holiday hunting among them and putting my finds in the bag. Farther along the north end of the island, huge rocks jutted out into the sea, and as the tide was almost fully out by now, many beds of oyster-like shellfish were exposed on the rocks and in the pools left by the receding tide. Securely fastened to the rocks, the shells were deep purple in color, with rough stone-like tops that fitted tightly over the oyster. The pools up among the huge boulders contained many varieties of small shells and small crabs of many colors. One kind of cat's eye shell was there in numbers—a tiny shell the size of a thimble looking very much like a gray, ugly, little stone sticking to the wet rock. But when the animal dies, and the shell is washed on the beach, in the constant grind of the tide the limestone covering is gradually worn away. Underneath is a beautiful spiral of yellow, cream, and red separated by a fine line of white. Odd, that these beautiful shells are not permitted to reveal their inner beauty until long dead and polished by the sands.

The other side of Great Keppel was nearly as nice, except that the long beaches were broken here and there by rocks coming down into the water. The high-tide mark on the sand was littered with hundreds of pieces of cuttle bone (enough to feed every canary in America for years). Apparently the casualities in the Cuttle Family are terrific. The bone is light and floats ashore when the cuttle fish dies or is killed. There was also one large nautilus shell, partly broken, so I took it and explored the wonders of the famous chambered nautilus. It lives in the front "apartment" of the large shell, closing off the others as it grows. Each compartment is lined with pure pearl and is really wonderful to see. Mr. Nautilus may flood any or all of these discarded sections with water and sink or rise to any desired level in the sea, as a tiny hole is left connecting the various spaces he has outgrown.

The boats were there doing practice landings. Later everyone came ashore, and we went for a swim. When the tide began to come in, we hauled anchor and headed back toward the mainland. The sun sank in an almost cloudless sky, but over Great Keppel hung a tattered strip of bright salmon cloud, shredded by the wind. The sky darkened and a very thin moon and Venus came out to lead the night's procession, even while the sky at the horizon in the west remained a brilliant green. When darkness came completely, I noticed that the Big Dipper was visible, lying on its side right on the horizon, which settled any arguments we had had about whether or not it could be seen from this far south. I have no doubt that at some seasons it cannot be seen at all.

May 7, 1943

One year ago today I left Brownwood for the induction center, a start on the many wanderings we have since had. Brownwood to Abilene to Mineral Wells, and after five days in the induction camp, off to Little Rock, Arkansas, for basic training. No one could have had a harsher introduction into the mysteries of army life. The stupidity of that staff still hangs like stinking smoke in my mind, and forever kills any compromise I might have made with myself about army life. It was a "do or die" proposition, and if you died, there were plenty to take your place. Luckily I didn't even become sick during the whole time.

In July we were sent off to Cape Cod, Massachusetts, to a camp that was being hacked out of the bushes; then to Florida, then to California to the first good and decent camp we had been in. Then we sailed.

During all this time I have kept on the sane side by trying to enjoy the things I am interested in. I have had a good job and must have done it well, or else I would not still be in it after nearly a year. For the army officers simply keep people in any place for what they can get out of them, not from friendship. Such a thing does not exist here. A few of them I have found to be fine fellows, the majority, braggarts on the climb for more money and position.

The Gypsy in me comes forward and thrills to new places to see, new countries to explore, new people to meet, new sights, sounds, and smells, new birds in new trees, new insects, new waters, new fish, new winds to blow, new grasses by the road, a new kind of toad, (a strange new moth flew in last night), new flowers on climbing vines, new seasons, new sunsets bright. These are things I would not have had without my army life, but has the price been worth it? Probably I won't ever know, and for now am utterly without an answer. Will it change my way of life? I doubt it, but maybe in the changed world we will find afterward, my experiences will better fit me to carry on in my own way again.

May 9, 1943

Mothers' Day, and I just hope my flowers reached home, along with my cable. We had a special service here, and the Catholics went into town for some sort of special service.

May 16, 1943

Sunday again. The past week has been dull, with rain most of the time. We still have it, but there are signs of clearing. At least the birds are noisy in the trees, which would be a good sign at home. Major Bilger had invited me to go on a real fishing trip today, and I had my shark line all rigged (two hundred feet of small rope with a long double piano wire leader and a huge hook). But the sea is heavy, and it is still raining, so the trip was called off. Damnit!

May 20, 1943

Late yesterday the rain gave up, and this morning the world emerged bright with sun. The tops of the eucalyptuses shine like yellow gold as the early rays hit high and creep down as the day grows older. The parrots scream in appreciation and seek the sunny spots in which to peck their breakfast of eucalyptus buds, and everyone feels better. Blankets can be hung in the sun to dry. Tents can be rolled. Rain in camp is no fun, but I am sure there will be lots of it farther north.

I'm writing this with a gas mask on during a practice drill. Someone beats on a section of bent pipe, which is the gas alarm, and all get their masks at once. No matter what you are doing, you wear it, which gives the camp a "man from Mars" appearance with grotesque-faced soldiers going about their tasks in the usual way. The drill rarely lasts more than thirty minutes.

Another shake-up is due, which drops the outfit back into the old confusion again. Just when one organizational scheme is beginning to work in a smooth, satisfactory manner, it is blasted, and another one is substituted. We will get another regimental commander, and the whole organization of the 592d will be worked over. Sometimes I wonder just what we Americans are doing anyway, trying to win a war or satisfy a group of egotistical, tin-horn professional army men.

May 21, 1943

Just after noon today I learned that I would be sent to Brisbane, four hundred miles to the south, to be "Papa" to some material and equipment going to a group of our men who are there now to bring up boats or take them from Brisbane to Guinea. It will be a good trip and an opportunity to be alone for a few days on my own. It will be a long ride on the odd English trains, but perhaps there will be some little time in Brisbane that is free. "Free" if I forget to do all the shopping people are planning for me! Someone wants camera film; someone wants a book; someone wants a certain sized folder for his girl's picture . . . an endless assortment of things that most likely are unobtainable anyway, since war came to Australia.

Yesterday when I returned to town, the package from Cliff was here—the axe I had asked him to send. He sent two. That Cliff Pouncey[24] just will not write letters, but when he is really needed, he bobs up and proves he is still alive on the other end of the line and as full of interest as ever. The axes were exactly what I wanted. Cliff knew what I needed better than anyone else. Often some little thing will bring him sharply into my mind, usually some outdoor sound or sight or smell that connects up with something we enjoyed years ago when he introduced me to a thousand priceless treasures of the outdoors. Just what my life would have been without his interest, I often wonder! He is as real to me as my own Dad, for they both have had a part in giving me what many men have not had.

May 23, 1943

First I will go, then I won't go. Lieutenant Callaway told me I definitely wouldn't go to Brisbane, and the order that was coming out from regimental headquarters had been cancelled. I was puzzled over such a statement, and later I asked Major Shaul if I was to go to Brisbane at all. He said I surely would, and that as far as he knew, there had been no change in plans. He at once telephoned headquarters and asked. He was told no one had called anyone concerning the matter and that the order was now on its way to our office. Evidently Callaway had decided I shouldn't go and thought telling me so would end it. He had probably forgotten that the order originally came from regimental and was something he had nothing to do with. Shaul didn't express his feelings at the moment, but, of course, he knew what had happened. I have no idea what fool notion Callaway took, but such things are typical of the organization we have.

7 Off To Brisbane

June 2, 1943

I have just returned from a very good trip, after a quick get-away on the twenty-fourth.

There were twenty-two barracks bags, two trunk lockers, and some cases of navigation instruments to go to Brisbane, and it was my job to see that the stuff arrived safely. I took my travel orders by brigade headquarters and began to unravel the red tape it takes to get travel money, finally getting about nine dollars because my travel time to and from Brisbane was figured as three days. It actually took nearly that long to go one way, but I had some money and didn't worry about that end of it. I was told that if it took longer, I could collect more on the trip, but knowing the situation I would rather make it on my own cash than worry with trying to collect anything afterwards.

The truck driver and I went on to town and to the railroad yards, located the yardmaster, and finally backed up to our car where a crew waited to unload the bags and boxes into the tiny English "goods car," a small box on wheels about half as long as our American flat cars. The car was not full, so a marine motor bound for Sydney was put in, then a canvas tied over the whole car. I learned that my little car would be pulled off toward Brisbane about 5:00 p.m., so I went back to town to have dinner and pick up some food for the trip, as I had no idea where or when we would stop on the way down.

Lunch at the Red Cross was very good. Later I found some canned things to take along, also some fruit. Then I met Maurice Roth, who had a going away present for me—a bag of cooked shrimp! He knew I loved it like nothing else the Australians have. Oh boy! The fish stores boil the shrimp and put great piles of it in their show windows. I even like the lovely color it takes on when boiled. It is sold just as it is cooked. You peel your own.

At 5:00 p.m. I was at the yards, where I changed into a suit of fatigue clothes and boarded the caboose or "guard car" as the Aussies call it. The train was ready to go, with my car up ahead of the caboose. As we pulled out, the nicest Australian sunset I have seen flared violently in the west with fiery, curdled clouds spreading into a gigantic fantail across the western sky.

My car turned out to be very comfortable indeed. The back part of the coach formed a separate compartment about twelve feet long, with wide leather seats running the whole length of each side and across the far end. There was no connecting door to the other compartment which was occupied by the brakeman. It was a surprise to find that Australian train windows really work, so I raised those which were open, as it was getting chilly. (You raise Australian train windows to close them!) I had a door at the rear, and a small platform on the outside, a regular private car!

On each side and at the rear there were signs reading: "This train is under military guard. No admittance!" Later I was to notice that these signs seemed to keep people at a distance. They didn't know exactly what that sign meant, or just what a military guard might do. As we clink-clanked along southward, I ate my shrimp for supper.

I dusted off the seats, put my bag, rifle, and gear up on one side, stowed my food in one of the racks overhead, and got out my single blanket to spread on the seat along with my mackinaw. We stopped at one small town and spent several hours on a side track waiting for other trains to pass before I finally lay down on what turned out to be a very comfortable bed after all—much softer than our cots.

How much later I do not know, I waked to hear someone talking outside, probably the train stopping had awakened me. The conversation was between the brakeman and a farmer. It seemed that the farmer was in the habit of riding the night train once in a while to some place twenty or thirty miles up the line. It was more of a hitchhike for the farmer, for he paid no fare but just got on the caboose at the water stop and off again at the next one or at the place where he wanted to stop.

I don't know why, but the brakeman didn't invite him to ride on his side of the car. He was telling him that he didn't know if the American guard would let him ride, but that he might ask. I got up and met the farmer at the door and asked him in a not too pleasant voice where he was going and how he happened to get on at this time of night. He said he only wanted to ride about thirty miles up the road, but evidently the questioning put him in a nervous state of mind. He put down his gunny sack of something near the door and sat down.

I had no objection to his riding, for I had received no orders to the contrary. But I wasn't much interested in his peace of mind either and wanted to go to sleep myself. He asked where I was from and going, etc. Of course he got no information of any kind. He was just curious, but even if I had been in the mood, I couldn't have put out that information. It simply wasn't any of his business anyway.

Just for fun, I picked up my rifle, drew back the bolt, let it go. The resulting noise had almost the effect of a shot from the rifle, and the farmer almost jumped out of his skin. A few minutes later he went out on the platform, and at the next stop (which must have been miles short of his goal) an arm shot in for the gunny sack. That was the last I ever saw of him. He evidently thought this Yankee soldier was pretty dangerous and might just let go at any minute with that over-sized bullet pusher.

Later I thought it was sort of a mean trick, but I couldn't go to sleep and leave him in the car, and he had no right or business there anyway. Of course, in a combat zone he wouldn't have gotten near the train at all. That was my last passenger of the trip. Maybe the brakeman tipped people off if any wanted to ride. I didn't see him often on the journey. He more or less kept away too.

About eight the next morning we stopped in Brundabert, a not too bad looking town, and pulled right up in front of the station, making it all right to leave my car alone for a while. We were to be there for a couple of hours, so off I went for breakfast. As I was in uniform and wearing my cartridge belt and bayonet, no one could have mistaken me for anything except an American soldier. We are known to have plenty of money (a fact that continually seems to astonish Australians) which makes the following incidents even more puzzling.

The "refreshment room" or station dining room was closed, but I could see several people stirring inside, probably getting ready to serve breakfast for some passenger train that was due. I found a side door open and a twelve or thirteen-year-old boy was standing there. I told him I would like to get some breakfast. He at once went inside and relayed the information to someone who said something I could not hear.

Out he came, saying he could show me who could get me something to eat. He led the way around the corner to the railroad platform, and pointed out a man.

"That's the man," he said. I gasped and looked again. I was being referred to a Salvation Army worker! The kid disappeared before I recovered, so I could not lay hands (or foot) on him, as I would surely have done. I am still not sure exactly what it was all about, but it probably was no gag. Twelve-year-old Australians aren't usually so subtly humorous. I did not request breakfast of the good man in the service of the Salvation Army, but went across the street to a large hotel—a wooden building much on the order of our hotels in small towns years ago. The hall ran straight through to the back, and on either side of the entrance way, doors were labeled. One said "dining room," so I opened the door.

A large room contained several tables, all neatly set. One old man was eating, being served by a waitress of immense proportions. Almost as soon as I was able to take in the above facts, the huge woman glided swiftly to the door, backed me out into the hall, and closed the door behind her. I told her I would like breakfast. She hesitated, said she would see, shuffled to the rear of the hall, and disappeared into what was evidently the kitchen.

Soon she returned and said she would show me where I could get a meal. For a minute I was afraid we were again going for the Salvation Army, but she stopped on the porch and pointed out a small restaurant down the street. As in the case of the boy, I had no idea what she really was up to, but in neither case could I find any real grounds to substantiate my feeling that I was being made a fool of. We simply were thinking along different channels, and neither of us understood just what the other expected.

The restaurant appeared to be very good, but again I was puzzled. I gave my order—a very ordinary one of toast, eggs, and coffee—to the girl in charge, and she went back to the kitchen of the small place. I heard her remark to someone there, "What won't these Yankees think of next!" and there was hearty laughter. But I got my toast, eggs, and coffee, and it was surely the best coffee I had found in Australia.

All day the somewhat monotonous country rolled by. Occasionally there were beautiful groves of small paperbark trees and a few streams, but mostly cut-over growth of gum, and little else. At many points along the way, there were groups of one or two or three tents with a few Australian reserves. This railroad is the only line running up the coast, and is important as a link of supply to the north.

My lunch had to be from my fruit, etc., for we did not stop at even a small place for any length of time. Late in the afternoon, we side-tracked at a small station to wait for a passenger train going north, and I got off to stretch my legs in a walk about the station. A very pleasant little country girl of fifteen or sixteen came along and stopped to talk.

She had spent all of her life right here and hated it. I gathered that it wouldn't be long until her somewhat alcoholic father would have to hunt someone else to do the chores, for she wouldn't be held much longer in that dull, small place.

Once about 4:00 at a stop, three small children came timidly back to the car and stood looking up at me as I stood on the platform. Evidently they had been accustomed to riding home on the train, so I opened the gate of the platform and helped them up. Two of them—the little girl and one of the boys—were beautiful children with soft golden hair and blue, blue eyes. The other boy seemed to be a hard-bitten little thing much unlike the brother and sister pair. They were all timid, but finally told me what grade they were in.

The little girl had a small book in her hand with a picture of the cow jumping over the moon on the cover. So, of course, I gathered she had the old jingle. I thought back and recited it to her and asked if that was what she had been studying. She smiled broadly and said, "yes," but I got little response from them generally. They were evidently bush children, unused to strangers. I put them off at their stop, and they waved "goodbye" quite freely, once they were safe on familiar ground.

Toward Brisbane, the country became more pleasant with more cultivated patches and more people. Finally on the morning of May 25, we pulled into the Roma Street Yards. My train was at once side-tracked, so I got off, went to the station office, and called the lieutenant who was to receive the things I had brought down. He said he would send a truck at once, so I waited at the American Railroad Transportation Office and chatted with the pleasant captain there. He was one of the most friendly officers I have seen, completely unself-conscious and real—a thing so rare that it is almost unbelievable. Among other things, we spoke of the new bombing of a place in Europe, and I remarked that a bomb would sure play the devil with this yard here.

"It wouldn't take a bomb," he said. "All the Australians need to hold up things for three or four days is to have one derailed car, or someone yell 'tea!' I think we ought to give this country to the Japanese as punishment."

The truck came and we finally located my car, took the contents, and went to Camp Doomben (the same camp we were in when we first landed). There I checked the stuff, and with the help of some of our boys who were there, took the equipment to where it belonged. This ended my official duties.

That night I saw Lieutenant Duffy who was in charge of our group there, and he said that since I was there, I might as well have some time, so to stay as long as I thought best, because my travel orders did not specify any date of return other than at the completion of my mission. Our major here had already told me to use my Yankee ingenuity and take a vacation.

There was a very good stage show at Doomben that night, so I didn't leave camp. Afterward I found a cot in a tent with some of our men, made my bed, and put up my mosquito bar, as there were clouds of mosquitoes. The other fellows declared they were not bothered by the mosquitoes at all, but I noticed that everyone of them had covered their heads with a blanket by the next morning. The night was very cool. I was not at all warm with three blankets over me. But the weather did not stop the mosquitoes, and they sang around all night wanting to bite me. Maybe they are a hardy Aussie variety not affected by cold.

Since there were few men at this camp (used as a first stop by American soldiers just coming over from the States), the meals were unusually good. So I ate breakfast in camp, then dressed and caught the tram to town. Brisbane is still a city geared to war, and I found that many stores are closed permanently. Others open only a few hours a day. There were plenty of Yanks on the streets, and also Aussies, but a noticeable scarcity of young civilians. The Aussie women have donned uniforms of several branches of the service and are serving much as any soldier in jobs on the home front.

After lunch in Hadded Hall, a very fine restaurant, I found which tram went by the museum and took it. An odd place for an American soldier to go on a day off; in fact, so odd, that I most likely rank as an oddity in the service, but I wanted to find out some things about Australia's natives and several other things. The first wing of the museum I walked into was the National Gallery, a pleasant surprise, for I had not counted on any kind of art exhibition. The paintings in the huge gallery were by artists unknown to me, with the exception of a huge Turner. Much of the work was English, but two large wind-swept canvases were Australian landscapes with beautiful, old river-gum trees and subtle skies all done with skill and daring. From the look of the place and the pictures on display, I gathered that any very valuable works have been crated and stored in a safer place until the threat of bombing is over.

In other parts of the immense building were the Natural History exhibits, and here I lingered. None of the work of the natives could approach what we all have seen many times in our museums (works of our American Indians). Nevertheless, it evidenced much care and work in collecting so large a showing of Australian aboriginal culture.

The natives here seem to be far below our own Indians in all kinds of culture, but the collection included an abundance of really remarkable string work—fish nets, carrying baskets, bags, and just balls of string, all made from human hair. The string was not twisted but crocheted with needles made from bird quills. There was no beautiful flint work, and the race seemed not to have ever progressed to the point of doing more than using a sliver of flint for a knife by simply covering one rough end of it with a wad of tree gum for a handle.

There were hundreds of specimens of native birds and animals, and I found some of the parrots I had seen in our trees here. All in all, it was a profitable afternoon, and I came away much wiser about Australia.

Most of my second day was spent in hunting assorted things which various people wanted from the city. Phonograph needles were one of the practically non-existent items, also camera film. At lunch time I found a small fish bar, and had some very good fish, along with a conversation with an Australian civilian about America. It seems all Australians are interested in America and like to hear us talk about it.

On Saturday I was determined to find the place I had heard of where koala bears were kept and finally located a bus going in that direction. The place was called Lone Pine and was fifteen miles out of Brisbane. My bus only went to the turn of the road, so I walked the two miles remaining. It was a very pleasant spot overlooking the Brisbane River. I saw a house with a wide porch set with tables—the cafe I supposed. Some people were preparing for a picnic under the trees, and farther on I found a tiny building opening into the yards where the animals were.

I saw that this was the combined office and entrance way of the place. An extremely pleasant woman said that her son would show me around when he came back. He had gone for food for the koala bears.

While waiting I learned that she, her husband, and the son kept the place and had done so for years. A regular excursion boat ran up the river almost every day and brought visitors to Lone Pine.

The son arrived, an intelligent lad of about seventeen with the most pleasant manners and keen speech I had come across in this country. We went to the koala cages and went in. Ian Reid introduced me to Cuddles, a young bear about eighteen months old. Cuddles didn't take long in just stealing my heart as he hung on my shoulder and looked at me with an almost human, naive expression on his little face.

Still carrying him, I was shown the different groups of koalas there. Ten mother koalas had babies snugly tucked away in their front pouches. One little bear was taken out of his mother's pouch for my benefit. He was indeed a small one, but I learned he was plenty large enough to be out anytime he chose. When koala babies are born, they are only a fourth-of-an-inch long and very immature and develop in the pouch. The baby promptly climbed on his mother's back, and she went about her business of eating fresh eucalyptus leaves.

Ian explained many interesting things about the bears. He told me that he and his father had built the colony from a very few koalas, which is a rare thing, for they are most difficult to keep and usually die out in a few years. One old fellow was nine years old and still handsome. I have seen many animals, kept all kinds of pets, and studied enough of the world's nature lore to be fairly well acquainted with its animals. So I feel safe in saying that the koala bear is the world's most loveable animal, a real live version of a toy teddy bear. In fact, the koala was the model for this toy now known all over the world.

It was now noon, so I went up to the dining room overlooking the river and found that I could get sandwiches and tea served by an attractive girl. I wanted to ask her to eat with me, but feared I might offend her. Australians are very funny, and sometimes you can be very insulting to them simply by doing what is done every day in the States and considered proper in every way.

After lunch I went back down the slope to the office and looked over the collection of tropical butterflies which Mr. Reid had there. I talked to the handsome white cockatoos by the door.[25] Young Reid was on his way to feed the kangaroos with a sizeable sack of fresh grass. I was surprised by the number of roos he had—several quite large, and one huge wallaroo as tall as a man.

In several big cages were any number of very beautiful parrots. The most interesting were a pair of rare ones with a young offspring about half grown. The mother was red and blue, about the most unusual shades of color I have ever seen on a bird. She was, I might say, "patriotic" red and blue and looked so odd that she had the appearance of being a painted model of a parrot. The male was a beautiful green with red on his wings and a lovely big orange bill. He was so totally different in appearance from the female that I would never have believed them to be of one species, although they were built alike and had similarly shaped bills.

The baby was the "spitting image" of his pa and cute as the devil. He had been hatched in a nest dug out of the side of the hard clay wall of a big cage built against a small steep bank. The bank had been dug away so that the wall of clay formed the back wall of the cage. Down at floor level the two parrot parents had dug a burrow with a small opening, then enlarged it into a round nest. When the baby was hatched, the Reids had chipped off more of the clay in order to see how he was progressing. It was some weeks before the parrots decided to bring him out, and they persuaded him out with difficulty.

During this time the parents were feeding him by taking their usual parrot food of sunflower seeds, etc., chewing a mouthful thoroughly, then carrying it to the baby. This was one of the very few instances I have ever known of a parrot being hatched and raised in captivity, especially a rare species.

Young Reid took several pictures of me holding the bears, which I was interested in getting to send home.

Several people came out to Lone Pine in the afternoon, among them a blonde blue-eyed kid of twenty who was in the Australian Air Force. He was interested in America, and I told him of things he asked about over a cup of tea. (At a certain hour, everyone rushes off to tea over here, and today they did the same—to the large porch and tables overlooking the river.)

He was interested in Broadway, and he wanted to know what the big Greyhound busses were like, and a hundred other things that I had not thought of simply because they were familiar to me. In common with most Australians, he had not figured out our racial problems and asked, "How are Negroes regarded in the States?" I told him as best I could, but knew that making him really understand how we of the south feel, and why, was an impossibility. Why should he be able to grasp it when I meet Americans every day who have lived their lives in New York, nearly eleven thousand miles from Australia—but not very far from the south—who do not have the slightest idea of what the southern Negro is like or how he is living, or why? Also puzzling is the Australian wonder at segregation of the Negro population in our American cities, while the Australians stoutly justify their national laws that no Negroes can enter Australia, and the country strongly enforces it.

This fellow was the first Australian soldier I had met who seemed interested in carrying on a conversation about things worth discussing. He was an interesting person. Although he hoped to visit the States after the war, he didn't exactly think he would like to stay.

As the late bus took me back to Brisbane, I felt that certainly this had been my most interesting afternoon in Australia so far.

The next day was spent in town, mostly looking for books on the Australian natives. A couple of the large book stores had what I wanted and

I ended up with a couple of pounds worth of various books on Australia. Some were to send home to Quirl and Cliff, and one was for Dotson here in camp, who had presented me with a handful of florins as I left.[26]

At lunch time I had another odd experience. The place was crowded, so few tables were available. I ate at a small table with two pleasant middle-aged women, and we were chatting in a friendly manner within a few minutes. But when I arrived, they had nearly finished their lunch, so they left shortly.

Then two girls came in and sat opposite me. The table was a small narrow one, and not much distance separated us. Naturally in such a situation I would talk to whomever was there, for not to do so seemed rude to me. However, the blonde girl I spoke to first ignored my greeting, which startled me, then made me mad. "Don't you girls speak to American soldiers?" I asked. "I don't know you, and I don't speak to strange men!" was her reply. This startled me even more, hearing this in 1943. "Did a Yankee soldier ever bite you?" was my somewhat sharpish remark. No reply—and those two girls ate their lunch without once speaking or looking across the table to see who was there.

The next day I encountered just the opposite in a girl who plopped down at my table when the place was practically empty, with room everywhere. She chatted in a friendly manner and showed me snapshots of a Yankee who had ditched her for some other Australian filly after going with her for some time. She ended up by waiting for me outside the restaurant.

"Where will we go?" she asked as she fell in beside me when I started down the street. She was just a kid, and I wondered if she had taken on her affectionate ways since the Americans had been thronging the streets of Brisbane, or if she just naturally grew up in an environment in which her actions were accepted as the rule rather than anything astonishing. I chatted with her as we walked down the street a couple of blocks to one of the stores I had located before lunch. She had a surprised look on her face when I said, "So long, kid. You better watch these Yanks. They seem to leave you every time." I didn't see her again, but I'm sure she didn't have any difficulty in attaching herself to a Yank who didn't leave her. She would be fair game to nine out of ten.

The trip back to Rockhampton on a passenger train was much less comfortable and less pleasant than the one down on the guard car. The coaches were crowded with civilians, and I wondered where in the devil all those people were going and why. I managed to get a seat, but woke up all through the night with my head at right angles and a stiff neck. However, the next day there was more room, and I managed to doze some. At each stop the people would dash off like mad into the station, and finally I followed them off the train to see what the attraction was. I should have guessed it! They were going to the tea bar where they all got tea and scones. I fell in too, and the rest of the trip I dashed off at each stop and had tea and scones like a veteran.

On arriving in Rockhampton, I couldn't get a ride out to camp until morning, so I found some of our boys and had supper with them. There seemed to be no hotel willing to take a guest overnight.[27] So I ended up at the Red Cross, where I got a cot. Robert Jones, the Major's Jeep driver, came in for me the next morning and gave me the most hair-raising ride back that I ever had. He is a good driver, but he was flying too low that morning!

8 The Battalion Moves To Cairns

June 9, 1943

For the past week things have been rainy and dull. Then we began to get rumors of a move. Finally orders were received, and we are now packed and ready, but won't leave for a couple of days. Our new destination is Cairns, eight hundred miles up the coast. At one time, only recently, Cairns was in the combat zone. Evidently the New Guinea fighting is progressing nicely. Otherwise the combat zone would not be progressively moved up. Cairns is also nearer the Great Barrier Reef, and much more tropical than here. There should be interesting things to see there, and I have a three-day pass salted down to take whenever I please. (It was won in a declamation contest last week.) I am frankly tired of Rockhampton, so I will be glad to use the pass to get acquainted with the new territory.

Our tents are down, with the exception of our headquarters here. Our office equipment is boxed and stacked. Some of the outfit has gone ahead to work on a camp, and the place is humming with activity. Last night Dotson came by and wanted me to go on a hike down the country to take some books to the old crab fisherman he knew, as it would be his last chance to visit him. We hiked through the bush and swamp, and a couple of times heard the thump, thump, thump of a wallaby bringing his feet and tail against the ground as he hopped. I wondered if Dotson knew where he was going, but he did, and we hit the trail right on the nose.

The old man was reading when we arrived. He was very interesting, being pretty sharp for an old fisherman living in a shack by the creek. He recounted numerous stories to us of animals, etc., in the days fifty years ago when he first came to these parts. He was a good storyteller too. He fought in the Boer War and claims he is still the best rifle shot in the whole country.

His statements about the dingoes didn't jibe with what I had seen in the museum or the living examples I have seen of dingoes. He said a full-blood dingo has no white on him and is very small and, also, that now they are largely mixed with our dogs.

Mr. Reid of Lone Pine holds that the stories of dingo half-breed packs are inaccurate for they will seldom breed with domestic dogs at all. He proved this fact by keeping dingoes with dogs of both sexes for more than a year.

The dingo the Reids have is surely a handsome animal—as beautiful as any dog, a rich ginger coat, white chest, white feet, strong head, and strong white teeth. The female was not so handsome because she was paler and more inclined to be slinking and unfriendly. The male came to the fence of his large pen, rubbed against the wire, and wanted to be petted and rubbed as most dogs do. However, he took a dislike to one man and repeatedly snapped at him. The female was to have pups soon, and the Reids offered me one, an offer I regretted not being able to accept. I would surely like to be able to take a dingo puppy back to the States, but doubt that I could, even if I had one at sailing time.

The old crab fisherman had a very good and understandable philosophy of life. He was free to go catch a crab when he wanted to and eat when he pleased. He had never wanted for anything. He is now old and cannot work anyway, so he enjoys life and reads everything to help him understand the world today. He has a few good friends or "cobbers" and could want nothing more. I found him much more of an intellectual than any "squatters" of his type I had met in the States. In fact, he was well up on what was going on around him, and time after time amazed me by candid statements about this and that. In short, the old geezer had not gone to seed in spite of the fact that he lived in a shanty by the creek and had little money. He did practically nothing at all, and to all appearances, was a "beachcomber."

We safely followed the trail back through the dense bush, and after a hike of forty-five minutes or so, arrived in camp very hungry. We could chisel nothing from the kitchen but an apple, so went up to my tent site, the tent having been taken down in the afternoon. Roth had a carbide lamp burning and was sitting by a small table writing letters. I found a can of minced ham and sliced the contents, but discovered that there were no crackers or bread. Roth promptly rose to the situation by getting out a package of

Jewish holy bread or Passover bread—thin sheets of toasted flour and water—that he had gotten at a Jewish service several days before. Roth did not care for ham, so there Dotson and I sat, eating ham and Jewish holy bread, and I thought this was surely the height of something or other.

Today we sent off part of our equipment—cots, tents, etc. From now on we will sleep on the ground in the open. Our staff will most likely be here in headquarters tent, as we have to be around anyway. About all we have to do here now is answer questions for people regarding shipments, etc. Even the phone is gone. It looks like a pleasant couple of days ahead.

June 10, 1943

The wooden floor of the tent here wasn't like a cot, but I helped it somewhat by putting grass in a mattress-cover bag and slept very well. A company across the road decided to get an early start by getting up hours ahead of time, and from all the yelling and commotion, they must have gotten lost in the dark. If we ever get on the front lines, the enemy will have no trouble locating us.

Things are gradually moving out and the place looks bare. From the way things are being cleaned up, it seems that this area is not to be used. It appeared from the start to be unfit. Choosing it was Colonel Hawkins's last bid to annoy the regiment. He did a good job.

As many times before, today the whole of our "cross section of America" here in the army soured on me in the worst way. It is all difficult to explain, except to say that I usually expect people to be more than human beings, or behave better than human beings usually do. I have never considered myself either smart or clever, and certainly I have had far less formal eduction than most, but I am continually wondering where all these men have been all their lives. Apparently they have lived somewhere where the ordinary things I know of life are not necessary; in their world they evidently do not have to be honest, clean, or upright. They must not find it necessary to have the slightest bit of self-respect, or have any respect for anyone else. They do not find it necessary to have any ideas on anything at all. They simply follow the lead of people around them who are the same. I end up not understanding them at all, but honestly find the show interesting.

Our last mail came through today. We will have to wait now until we get to Cairns for any more of it. There was a letter from Ella and one from Quirl. They surely are faithful in writing.

Things lagged today and we played chess a lot and just did nothing a lot. Seems we are moving out slowly, but I'm sure the Australian railroad just can't handle a big move in a hurry. The last of the outfit will leave Saturday. The movie tonight was so awfully bad, I left. One of those Abbot and Castello things. What there is funny about that fat little greasy man with a stupid face, I can't see.

June 11, 1943

Rain last night. Was I glad I was in the battalion headquarters tent! It was the only big tent left standing. The others were pup tents, and rivers were running under all the beds. When the rain was at its worst, I thought of the tent ropes, so I put on a raincoat and sloshed out to loosen them to keep the stakes from pulling out and letting the tent down on our heads. A little later Captain Baker stormed in with his blankets. He had been in one of the new jungle hammocks and had made the mistake of letting down the cover, which had directed all the water on top right down his back, making the hammock anything but waterproof—as it is supposed to be—and making him very wet and mad. But today is nice and clear, and the sun will dry out all the wet beds.

June 12, 1943

All ready to shove off this morning. Everything is packed into trucks. Our battalion staff will go ahead of the company as our headquarters company must remain to feed the stragglers until all have pulled out.

June 16, 1943

Five days later we are camped eighteen miles from Cairns, North Queensland, the jumping place to New Guinea and the battle zone. Cairns was once very much in the battle zone. It seems that areas are opened up as soon as possible, for in a combat zone no one is accountable for anything from an airplane to a battleship or a jeep. There is much waste, and opening the areas lessens the supply burden.

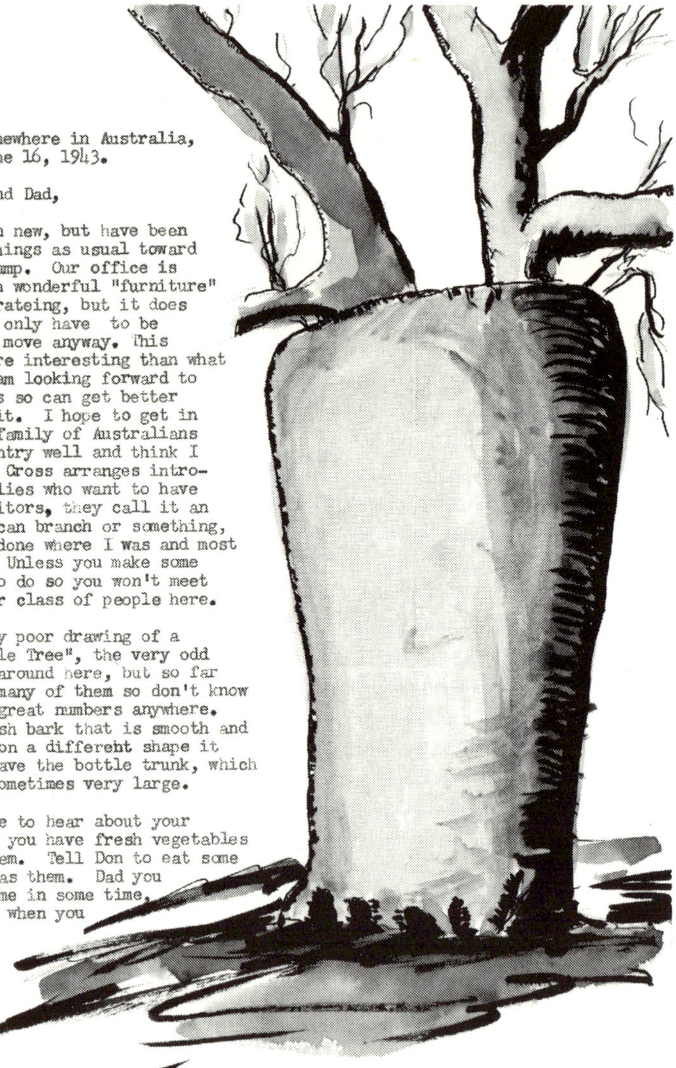

Somewhere in Australia,
June 16, 1943.

Dearest Mother and Dad,

Nothing much new, but have been doing the same things as usual toward building a new camp. Our office is taking shape with wonderful "furniture" of boxwood and crateing, but it does the job and will only have to be left on the next move anyway. This country seems more interesting than what we left, and I am looking forward to my three day pass so can get better acquainted with it. I hope to get in touch with some family of Australians who know the country well and think I can, for the Red Cross arranges introductions to families who want to have Americans as visitors, they call it an Australian American branch or something, at least it was done where I was and most likely is here. Unless you make some special effort to do so you won't meet any of the better class of people here.

This a very poor drawing of a Boabab, or "Bottle Tree", the very odd tree that grows around here, but so far I have not seen many of them so don't know if they grow in great numbers anywhere. They have greenish bark that is smooth and each tree takes on a different shape it seems, but all have the bottle trunk, which is hollow, and sometimes very large.

Sounds nice to hear about your garden, at least you have fresh vegetables when you want them. Tell Don to eat some for me when he has them. Dad you haven't written me in some time, so just get busy when you have a day off.

Write when you can, all of you.

Lots of love,

Gaitha

Saw several big wild Kangaroos the other day -

"This is a very poor drawing of a Boabab, or 'Bottle Tree' . . . so far I have not seen many of them. . . . They have greenish bark that is smooth and each tree takes on a different shape . . . but all have the bottle trunk, which is hollow, and sometimes very large."

The trip up was literally a pain in the neck. The English train coaches were stuffed—twelve men to a compartment! We had four seats about six feet long—three men to a seat which left no room to rest at all. The first night I slept sitting, or tried to sleep. The second night I got into a canvas mattress-cover bag and got under a seat, pulled the bag over my head, used a mackinaw for a pillow, and hoped I would not be jarred out into the aisle and get stepped on. It was much more comfortable than sitting bolt upright.

Australian coaches are a joke, and we wondered if a good pull wouldn't disjoint the thing and leave us scattered on the track. Every plank, door, window, and beam kept up a constant movement to and fro, each piece moving in a different direction until you wondered just what was holding the thing together. There are no doors from compartment to compartment, so each dozen men was really in a private car. This prevented the officers from indulging in their favorite pastime of walking up and down the train worrying people. We got there just as well, too.

Along the way in some flat grassy land, we spotted a group of kangaroos feeding. Hundreds of brolga[28] were wading in the shallow pools, and there were flocks of ibis.[29] In fact, the amount of wildlife seen from the train surprised me.

Much of the country was bare of interest, and we tried to sleep simply because there was nothing else to do. We stopped three times a day, irregularly, at some of the many small railroad stations for eats, and invariably got mutton stew, bread, butter, and tea. We had some foresight, however, and had brought some cans of food along—also a can opener. Feeding three hundred men was quite a task for a small place. Evidently arrangements had been made for the Australian Home Guard to help with the cooking and serving, for rather elderly men in uniform were there, dishing out the goulash and seeing that everyone got fed.

The country was definitely tropical. On the morning we arrived, we passed tangled, green jungle and hills shrouded in fog and covered with a green matting of vines and trees. Coconut trees were common, and several times we saw trees flowering in huge, fiery red blossoms, which I found out later were tulip trees. Here was a country growing something—thousands of acres of sugar cane in nearby fields. In fact, cane seemed to be the only crop, but a good one. Many flat cars loaded with it were along the sidings, and many fields waited to be cut, while still others were just showing green sprouts above the well tilled soil. I wondered if the cane was a continuous crop, running the year round.[30]

Cairns is an interesting-looking town and a good seaport. After the war, it promises to be one of Australia's leading seaports, as the army is building it up by leaps and bounds with good wharves, etc. It could profit by the war if the Japanese don't decide to make a long-range bomber flight in its direction.

Eighteen miles from Cairns by truck, we have a good location on a gentle slope wooded with nice trees and some wonderful, old river-redgums. Their smooth, creamy-barked trunks stand out against the dark green of the mountain that rises abruptly behind our camp. The grass is tall and mixed with a vicious saw grass, but machetes are mowing it down around the tents and on paths.

June 17, 1943

All of our men have finally arrived, and the job of building camp is in full bedlam. Mack, Charlie, and I have about gotten our headquarters fixed up again for the ninth time to date. We have arranged battalion headquarters over fifteen thousand miles in nine camps in the last year. From rough crating we have desks, tables, and chairs—complete with splinters. But at least, we all have a place to do our work. No floor so far, but we don't worry about that as we could move out any time—and may—from rumors floating around.

A friendly group of Australian hornets has a large nest by the tent here. They are tiny insects no bigger than a fly, but with the spirit of a true hornet, as some of our men found out. Also, there is a nest hanging down on a branch by our tent in the company area. I hope to leave it there, as our tent is pitched some distance from the center of the camp, and there is no occasion for anyone to go there.[31]

The anthills are quite large here—some over six feet high. We have a nice one right outside, so I decided to convert it into a pueblo oven, which it looks so much like. I took an ax and chopped a round hole in the base, then shovelled out the inside. This consists of thousands of chips with rounded edges which are arranged in irregular shapes and form passages for the small, white, grub-like termites. Composed of wood pulp, the chips look and burn like compressed punk and smell like honey. The outside of cement-like clay is four or five inches thick, and on an old mound may be twice that. So when the hill was cleaned out, the mound was hollow and about three feet in diameter on the inside. A round hole was cut in the side up high to act as a smoke hole, and the whole thing looked almost exactly like the pueblo ovens of the Southwest U.S. Indians. A fire kindled in it burned well—an excellent place to burn my papers that must be properly disposed of each day.

June 18, 1943

Hustle and bustle all day! More work than I've seen in a long time, and my day off was definitely "off," for all things went very wrong for me. One of the minor tragedies was that I worked late and missed lunch. Oh well, it was Friday and canned fish day, so not much was lost.

Last night I was on duty. Everyone else went to bed early, and I was left alone in our headquarters tent which is separated somewhat from the camp. I didn't mind, for it is seldom that anyone is alone in the army. The moon was full and made the world beautiful. My thoughts went back to the States, and it made me resentful at being penned down in this ill-organized outfit. I thought of Jimmy[32] and wondered what he was doing, and if he had left the States as a pilot as he had hoped he would. He used to say, "Oh I have slipped the surly bonds of earth and trod the sky on laughter silvered wings." Surely no one ever desired to fly more than he, nor deserved more to attain his desires.

June 19, 1943

Busy again today, but I slipped in time to sketch a koala bear on a letter to Mother, because my letters have contained far too few sketches lately. People used to enjoy them so much.

Our cigarette ration came in today, and I got mine. I'm still saving them for the future. I must really dislike the weeds, or I surely would smoke them here, with cartons of them in my bags, and a new cigarette lighter in my pocket. Quirl sent it when I told him matches were scarce.

I received a letter from Ruth Casebold[33] just now. She is a faithful correspondent, and I appreciate her letters. She mentions Cliff Pouncey getting my letter saying I had received the hatchets. I had written the letter on May 22. He got it about June 6 or 7—pretty good time. Ruth's letter had crossed in ten days.

Instead of going to the show, I decided to sort out my laundry, which is growing too large for comfort. I must do something about getting it off or do it myself. Each new station we get to takes us farther from laundry service, so I will probably have to come to doing it. However, it is really not so much trouble to boil things clean, and most of the time they turn out cleaner than when sent to the too-busy laundry.

In our tent I found Roth and Charlie. Roth was very blue, as he had recently lost his corporal's rating for some trivial thing and, of course, resented it. Dotson is now in our tent, but was off to town. Estadt came in later. We assembled our tent group of five when we first got here—the old bunch that has been together since Camp Edwards, except for Dotson who joined us at Fort Ord. We got him into our tent group, for we all enjoy his ready speech and ideas.

June 20, 1943

Sunday, and I had the afternoon off, but did very little. Estadt, Dotson, and I brought our cots out into the sun and laid around all afternoon taking a sun bath and talking. Then we went over to the bucket showers and took a cold shower—very cold, sure enough.

As usual Dotson brought forth some interesting points on human behavior. One of the most interesting was: "I am convinced we die many times during a lifetime, shed our skins—so to speak—becoming a new person, but retaining some part of the essential characteristics we had before." I realized he was right, just by looking over my own life, one of the most vivid periods being the dozen or so summers spent in camps teaching Indian lore. I was enthusiastic, eager, and felt that I did an exceptional job of it. But now, as I look back, I see that that part of me is no longer so much alive, and I really doubt that I could do the same again with like effect. Cliff and I, along with a group, put on a program for the U.S.O. just before

I entered the army. That time I realized I was out of practice and out of tune with the whole thing, even though I still loved it very much. The old fire was gone and the ashes were still and colorless.

We attended a showing of the movie *Random Harvest*, a tender love story and one of the best movies of the year, according to reports from the States. However, I disliked the fact that most of it was filmed in the dark—or equally drab—English, pea-soup fog.

June 21, 1943

Our third regimental commander, a colonel, is doing exactly as his two predecessors—changing everything. As usual, he decided that those of us who fill what he calls "overhead" jobs must rush out each day and do several hours of training in what we don't do in our daily work. But it is all an old story by now, and we have lived through two changes, so I will most likely survive this one. During each change the morale of the group slumps, and no one gives a damn what happens.

June 22, 1943

Our Staff Sergeant has his O.K. for officer's training and will leave in a week or so. I have been taking up his work here, which is probably pretty foolish, for I won't get thanks for it in this hellish set-up we have where things are cut and dried before the people deserving the breaks ever know of them. I stick with it because it is the lesser of evils, and I do work more pleasantly than the boys in the company who dig ditches, cut wood, and are at the beck and call of every small-fry corporal and sergeant in the outfit. And too, I have been of some use, for you just don't last long if you aren't.

Australian civilians have been here doing concrete work and have laid two shower floors and a kitchen floor of pretty sorry looking cement, but they will probably last as long as we are here. Two huge holes are being dug as drainage pits and several dynamite charges have been fired today. Two of them showered hard clay and quartz rocks from ten feet in the ground all over the immediate area. Battalion headquarters got its share, like a dirty hailstorm. One big rock flew clear to the kitchen and smashed an axe handle, much to the delight of the man who had been using it. Down ten feet and more, the ground is dry and hard, as little water soaks in when it rains, which is odd when down the road you see the dense section of jungle which must take a lot of moisture.

Just as the fancy training program starts (overhead training) we find that almost the whole regiment is now to be put on boats to train with the Australian infantry down the road. Our boats and coxswains will run the landing barges and train the diggers in landing, etc. Just how all this will turn out, I don't know. Maybe we will end up attached to a large Australian task force, and my guess is that the Aussies would do a fine job of it, for they have learned the happy fact that soldiers must train for war and not to look like a West Point parade.

A pair of rainbow birds have been in a dead tree by the tent most of the afternoon. I had identified them but had not gotten a good look at them before. Beautifully colored, with odd pointed wings and two extra feathers in the tail—twice as long as the rest—that look like two black wires sticking in the bird. They flew back and forth, banked and turned in the most amazing manner.

I finally got out of the amateur standing in our chess games by beating Mack, who considers himself pretty good, and making a couple of lieutenants sweat in close calls.

9 IN THE NAVY NOW!

June 25, 1943

We're in the navy now! The navy took over control of the Amphibian forces last night. Although not directly under naval officers, the navy will dictate policy and keep us worked into the navy's scheme of Pacific war. We have just taken on another boss, who I hope will be smarter. There seems to be little doubt that Amphibian forces must be handled by the navy to be used effectively, for—to date—the navy has supervised every landing.

Our old battalion set-up is gone, and according to the new organization, the battalion and company will be one, with Callaway—our present adjutant of the battalion—as company commander and adjutant both. Callaway has told me that I will be given the job of intelligence which I have wanted, but had given up hopes of getting. If he is telling the truth, I will be able to really accomplish something in the camouflage and mapping end of the work.

Two people brought me huge tropical butterflies today, the first since coming to Cairns. I made sketches, but they surely look flat beside these shining jewels of the topics. One is a rather common type for this climate—black bordered wings with metallic blue—just the two colors, but they are wonderful. (This is the butterfly used so much in trays, etc., because of the heavenly blue that, under glass, takes on a jewel-like quality rarely seen.) The other sports flashy lower wings of snow white, red moons, blue dust spots, and bright yellow dots with a rather dull, brownish-black upper wing. The late sun on my desk made the metallic blue take on a warm, rich violet color, but now the light of the gasoline lantern turns it to a cold silver that gleams like metal. It is fascinating to look at these colors for which there is no paint—done by an Artist who knows how and puts His color where there is no capturing it in anything we can grasp and hold and keep indefinitely.

I received a good letter from Mother. She had some of the booklets I sent on Australia and had enjoyed them so much. She thought she would like Rockhampton and hoped I would stay there indefinitely. Don and Dad have a nice "V" garden and are eating all kinds of vegetables from it. Mother has planted Don a dipper gourd to run over the garage. I know she remembers when she and I planted them and how much fun it was seeing the vine grow. She ended by saying, "We think of you every hour of the day," and I know they do—a swell feeling to have when you need something real to hold onto in a far off country.

June 27, 1943

A very dull Sunday. I was on duty all day and tonight. Most of the officers went into town and by dark were returning much the worse for too much liquor. Later, two came in very amused because our Lieutenant Sanders, who is considered very mild and inoffensive, got very drunk and pounded the bar yelling: "I'm John L. Sanders and can lick any man!" Finally he had to be brought back and poured into bed. Things have been so bad all week that they probably wanted an outlet for their feelings and chose liquor. Our new colonel has mixed things up so that no one knows what to do. Evidently he is not all gold, in spite of the fact he comes from West Point.

June 28, 1943

The red tape increases day by day. I gotta get out of here on a pass to keep sane!

I've been watching the white ants. They don't seem to be at all confused by red tape of any kind. Someone broke a six-inch hole in one of the large hills and drove a section of green pole into it flush with the wall of the hill, but with some room around it. The termites at once started plugging around the wood with mud, and evidently desired to get all of the pole inside the mud wall, for they were starting their repair job with the idea of building a large "blister" to take in the butt of the wood.

During the day only a few were out, but last night thousands were working. The "blister" was covered with their plump white little bodies as each one brought up from somewhere deep in the earth, a grain of mud less than a pinhead in size. Each found the place where he thought his mud was most needed and pounded it in place with quick blows of his body.

Watching them by flashlight, I at first wondered why an ant would suddenly take a spell of Saint Vitus's Dance, but found by close observation that he was simply pounding down his contribution to the work. They were building like architects, erecting mushroom structures and filling them in from underneath to the desired level. This morning the outside of the repair job was apparently finished, but with a small stick I found that the ants had completed the outside shell, sealed it off from the air, and were busy working at backing up their work from the inside to form a four-inch layer of solid mud. Getting the outside completed enabled them to work in the cool and darkness they like. Whether they will eat the green wood, I do not know, but intend to find out before we leave the site here. Some of the hills are built over dead fallen trees and stumps, but I am not sure if a green wood would attract them.

Roth was transferred suddenly from the company. He had friends in the personnel department who got him a place in the battalion headquarters of the new Maintenance Battalion. Evidently they had heard that he was unhappy and had lost his stripes. So they started looking for an opportunity to get him out to some other place. Roth was very happy about going, as things here had gotten pretty sorry for him. We will miss him in our tent group.

July 1, 1943

June is going—an odd June of cool weather and no fresh mesquites or cactus blooming. No Texas sun promising a scorching summer ahead. A small tree out front here is turning orange and red, the first sign that the tropics know autumn, for most of the foliage is green though somewhat shopworn from a long summer. No doubt spring will see the whole jungle burst into bloom and take on the appearance most people associate with it.

A hurricane warning just came through, and our whole staff rushed off to the beach to get the boats to safe anchorage, as they are moored on an open beach with no protection. There probably will be a monsoon season in the spring, which will give us trouble in the South Pacific.

One small group of our men left for Guinea today. No doubt we will trickle out that way instead of going in one group, as the waters up there are still far from being safe in the event of plane attack. Our information is that one or two small boats are fairly safe as they are not considered worth risking a plane for. All our boats are armed with machine guns and would be dangerous for a plane attacking them.

July 2, 1943

Yesterday I fired on the range, which was a change from my regular duties. We fired at small targets set on posts in the gum scrub up the road. When the firing was well along, the saplings began to fall as they were cut through by the 30-calibre bullets. Before the day was over, a number of sizeable trees crashed to the ground, and more were chewed to the point that a few more shots would do the job. The targets were paper, so the trees got the full force of the shots. I am now familiar with my rifle and feel that I could do a pretty good job with it in a pinch.

Charlie, with whom I have worked so long, is fairly frothing at the mouth at the prospect of my getting the new job. He didn't give a damn for the job, but wanted that sergeant rating so badly that he is almost crazy. He had written his wife that he would get it—a foolish thing to do in this uncertain army. He now feels that she will most definitely think him a heel if he fails to come through. Poor Charlie was born and reared in New York City and knows little but what he has managed to pick up in small jobs there. He once astonished me by asking, as a flock of pigeons flew over, "Are those pigeons or sparrows?" My faith isn't so great as his, even when I have been told I will get the job, and I do not intend to tell anyone anything about it.

As a result of the change of organization, fifty men will have to be transferred out of our company. The list of those to go looks good, as most of them are absolutely no good to us at all. Many are troublemakers of the finest grade. Some have real ability, but can't be trusted for one reason or another. Maybe in another company they will see fit to start over, but, at any rate, we will not have the worry of them.

July 4, 1943

The grand old day—or is it? It finds me ten thousand miles from home trying to do my part toward keeping that home in the condition it was in when this day first originated. As it was my Sunday off, I took the opportunity to go down to the beach and sketch, but only did one watercolor of trees by a group of cottages with red and green roofs—very tropical with the very blue sea beyond. It will make a good oil when I get back and have time to work it out.

As I left, I noticed the grove of coconut trees had visitors—three Australian soldiers busily engaged in climbing up and twisting off the big nuts with a stick, which was hard work. They had piled up a dozen or so and were doing well, when up walks the woman who owns the grove! "The coconuts are six pence each," she said. "How many do you want?" The Aussies were surprised, but game, and said they wanted at least eight of them. Seeing that they were not willing to buy the lot, I took two myself, two being all I could carry very well. They are quite large when in the husk. I don't envy any farmer who has anything that can be eaten growing near all these soldiers, both Australian and American.

We had early supper, and at the table Robert Young, our first sergeant, said he wanted to take a bicycle ride. We went down through the toll gate to the big beach and rode about three miles along the edge of the breakers on the hard sand. Every once in a while we would have to scoot higher on the beach as an unusually big wave came in. The beach is a perfect stretch of clean sand several miles long, backed by immense old paperbark trees, some six feet in diameter. Above these rises the green mountain as a dark backdrop for a scene, movie-like in dramatic beauty. Coconut trees waved in the warm breeze, and a tulip tree flaunted its huge red blossoms. I came back with a flower over each ear like a Polynesian, for that lovely oceanside certainly is at least similar to what could be expected in the land of the hula and aloha.

Dotson was here when I got back, but had to go on guard on one of our boats. He didn't look forward with relish to a night on a pitching, moored assault boat. Even in good weather the things heave mightily, especially when anchored where there is a good ground swell.

July 6, 1943

A blue night and I am on duty again and as "down under" as I have been since coming into the army. My assumption of June 22, must be right, and the later promises I was given by Callaway were apparently empty. It seems now that he wants to ignore the new schedule of organization and give the job I wanted to a guy who never heard of the work and who has never even wanted to do it. All of which makes me mad and Callaway a two-faced liar. Although Lieutenant Gutknecht, with whom I work, talked to the major about it, as he wants me to do the work, I don't feel that Bilger will interfere since he has given the command of the company to Callaway. If I don't get the job, I will drop my interest in the work and do what I am doing. I don't intend to do what I have done and the battalion headquarters job too, as I have been on the camouflage work since long ago.

Feeling so down about this was something I didn't expect, but found that I had slipped into the usual human way of ambition and greed for something in the way of position and more money. Why I should do this, I do not know, as many times in my life I have found unhappiness in ambition. Old Dan Beard summed it up neatly when he said, after ninety years of active life, "I have toyed with the opal bowl of ambition, but its dregs are bitter."

For a long while tonight I lay on the bench out front and looked up into the stars and saw farther than human conceit and petty injustice. I realized how small a thing it was I was letting worry me. I could reach out my hand and touch the cool smooth trunk of a giant eucalyptus tree by my side. It reached high and beautiful into the starry night and would still be there, unruffled, when the war is won or lost by mortals who are, after all, only here for a little while. Only the foolish and callous find joy in the pursuit of the things I was disappointed in not getting.

Sometimes I am frightened like a small child at the thought of what I would actually be if I became what the army strives to make a man and what civilians call "a good soldier" without knowing what they are actually referring to. I am sure things would not bloom for me, and the surf would not sing, but would become merely salty ocean on a colorless beach. It all brings back the old lost feeling that has dogged me always with an indescribable gnawing—sometimes glorious, sometimes tragic—but always most tragic when I try to follow the herd. I am no better or no worse than a million others, yet often feel that I have no place among them, no snug niche.

Once Mary Pouncey found and read to me something from a book she had. I can see her now with the book in her slim hands, across the table in her bright kitchen, reading the story that told me for the first time that she understood that I must many times feel lonely and deserted if I dedicated my life to a search for beauty in all things. Perhaps she alone understood; or perhaps others understood, but could not express so subtle a thing as thirst for beauty in this all too often ugly and unhappy world. Mary Pouncey is a staunch friend. My failure in material things would not shake her.

10 A Three-day Pass

July 11, 1943

I arrived back late yesterday after my three-day pass. Wednesday I could not stand the place any longer, so asked for and got the pass, packed a clean suit of khakis in a musette bag, and took one of the trucks to Cairns. At the Red Cross I found several of our boys eating and had supper with them. Later I looked up the town's only bus station and found that the only bus to Mossman, up the coast, left at 8:00 the next morning. I had heard of Mossman and decided to leave crowded Cairns for a quiet spot.

After spending the night at the Red Cross, I met the bus and found it to be much in the condition of the train coaches—loose in all joints, old and battered, with a two-wheeled trailer attached to house the charcoal burner. Gasoline is so scarce that many cars have been converted to use charcoal, with clumsy contraptions belching smoke and flame as they leap along.

Our Leaping Lena took the road up the coast in full swing, but after all this time of more or less risking life and limb, I am used to it and enjoyed the gorgeous scenery as we careened around cliffs and thundered down hills. Somehow the trailer hung on and supplied our means of locomotion.

Few coast roads could be more beautiful than this North Australia, and the road hugged the lower edge of the green, green mountains above it, now and then dipping down almost to the breakers, then dashing up to overlook the turquoise and opal ocean from a sheer cliff. The ride was definitely worth the risk.

About noon we arrived in the quiet village of Mossman, a delightful sleepy place, and stopped at the town "newsstand" (which carried little news of any sort). When I got off and stood looking around the place, an old man shuffled up and asked, "Lookin' for a place to stay?" I said I was. "Most of the Yanks stay over at the Queen's," he said, pointing across the open square to a large, wooden building with a porch across the second story front. "Queen's Hotel" was in huge letters.

A fat lady was arranging flowers in a small hallway. She finally found the register in the bar after looking everywhere for the dog-eared book. I signed it with my time of arrival, and was then shown up the stairs, or rather the fat lady yelled up to someone named Pat, who turned out to be a handsome kid of seventeen or eighteen, most likely of Italian extraction, but with fair skin against her black hair. She showed me to Room Six, a tiny room with a small single bed, a small dresser, and a relic of the past—a water pitcher and wash bowl.

Six other American soldiers were there, all of them on furlough from New Guinea. The seven of us were the entire American population of Mossman. After we got acquainted, they told me the hours for meals and how the routine of the place went in general. They were somewhat put out that Pat would not even go to the movie with any of them, and they could only content themselves with catching her on the stairs and snatching a kiss (which I found she really didn't mind at all). Apparently she had married an Australian just before he went to Guinea and was having nothing to do with the Yanks who came to Mossman, even though she was the most attractive girl I saw in that town.

We sat on the porch in comfortable chairs and looked out over the town. In front of the Queen's was the town square, an empty irregular piece of ground less than a block in length into which all the streets ran, leaving room in the middle for a neglected, irregular, grassy spot. Through the center of this ground ran the tiny, cane-hauling railroad track to the sugar mill at the other end of town. Every few hours the toy-like engine wheezed through pulling thirty or forty cars full of sugar cane to the mill. After each train had passed, several old cows came out from somewhere and wandered leisurely up and down the track picking up any small pieces of cane that might have fallen off and chewing it with a very pleased look on their bovine faces as the sweet juice drooled down. Once in a while a horse would wander out for a stroll.

Each of the three hotels had a bar. The most popular one was directly across the square from our hotel, and it was the only one which opened early. About 11:00 the boys would watch for its doors to swing open and then make a dash for it. At 12:15 our lunch bell would ring, and if I happened to be on the porch, I would yell for the boys in a voice which rang over the whole town and brought them back in a hurry.

I had been told the mill was interesting, so on my second day in Mossman I went to see it. When I arrived, the white-headed manager (Mr. Crees) was in the yard. After talking with him a while, I found him to be clever and interesting. He had managed the mill, which he and his brothers owned, for twenty-five years. He said he was very short of help and couldn't spare anyone to show me the mill but ended up by doing it himself.

The place contained an amazing amount of machinery that took the raw cane, cut and crushed it, boiled it, evaporated the juice, and finally turned out pure sugar into one hundred pound bags. Mr. Crees had taken an interest in the mill from the start and had planned and purchased most of the machinery. Being in an isolated part of the world, he had established a machine shop in the mill and was able to turn out any parts needed, from small bolts to huge castings. The chief engineer, also named Crees, showed me the tanks and mechanism of the evaporation tanks, then we went by the manager's office, where I was introduced to his office force. We all chatted, and they asked questions about America.

Later in town, I met a niece of the old fellow. She made the surprising announcement, "My uncle told me about you, and I have been hoping I would find you before you left." All of the people were like that—as friendly and wonderful as small town people are in most places. They apparently liked the Yanks sincerely, for as yet they had been visited only by small numbers of soldiers and had not had the soul-crushing experience of thousands of soldiers stomping the place into the ground and making life unbearable for all. The girls got together and planned a dance for the seven Yanks. But something came up, and it had to be put off a day, so I missed it.

The city engineer made a trip every day up the gorge into the mountains to see to the dynamos which supplied Mossman with electricity. On one trip I rode up with him in his Dodge pickup. From town the mountains rise cool and green. Usually the tips are shrouded in clouds and mist, but this morning it lifted, revealing sharp peaks. The largest peak behind the town held the "Good Shepherd" more than half way up its green side. A granite formation, the only rock visible in that green blanket, the gigantic granite is the most perfect natural formation I have ever seen—a robed figure looking down at an object at his feet. As you look at it, you need not use your imagination one bit. It is all there, as if it had been erected high above the city by an industrious Australian Borgulum.[34] Far from being as smooth as it looks, the country we went into was rugged and mighty, with granite boulders the size of the hotel scattered about. A road had been cut to the light plant built beside a swift, jungle stream, for it had to be erected where water would furnish the power.

On the road we passed an old man who was cutting away the encroaching jungle with a bush hook to keep the road clear. He was an old-timer who lived at the plant along with his dog as a sort of watchman. He had a garden, pineapple patch, and papaya bushes and apparently enjoyed his life. It was rather a surprise to go into the cement-floored room and see the well-kept dynamos in the neat, clean place. They somehow looked out of place as they thundered modernity in a pagan place. A path cut through the thick jungle to the creek, and a crystal clear pool was surrounded by immense, round granite boulders. I remarked about the stillness of the place, and the engineer said he had been impressed by the same thing many times. He said you could not find much wildlife anywhere in the jungle—few birds, few animals. A few wild pigs and duck-billed platypuses, and an occasional cockatoo, but no birds nested there, and few visited the place regularly. Evidently the heavy, damp growth offered little in the way of food, and less in comfortable surroundings to nest in. All of which explodes a popular theory that the jungle is teeming with life of all kinds.

Coming from the inland plains and dry country where there are literally millions of birds and animals, the engineer himself had been amazed. The tall trees were festooned with vines, and tree ferns with ten-foot leaves grew thick. Every rock had its cover of soft green moss. The old man had to continually cut the trail in order to keep it open.

Back at the clearing, I saw a number of the beautiful metallic blue butterflies on lantana bushes, and was told that many rare and lovely species were seen there from season to season.

On the way back, we stopped at a turn to look for a diamond python or carpet snake that always managed to be in sight. He had become a sort of cobber[35] of the engineer. We found him snoozing in the sun by the trail, and he hardly gave us a second glance. Ten or twelve feet long, he was a beauty and seemed to know he was safe. Two of them had lived in the area at one time, but some soldiers had killed the other one.

Yesterday afternoon I put my things in the Galloping Goose which was parked in front of the village newsstand of Mossman and spent a couple of hours chatting with various people before we started back. I promised to see them all again, for I had every intention of spending any leave I had there. However, when I arrived back, I learned that the lovable little town had been put "off limits" to soldiers of our regiment—an insult to the friendly people of Mossman who thoroughly enjoyed the Yanks. The only reason given was that there were no MPs at Mossman. Evidently there must be two MPs to watch each soldier, and sending a squad up to Mossman to watch half a dozen perfectly sane soldiers would look rather silly. There was little opportunity for anyone to get out of hand there. By their very attitude the townspeople prevented this, and they were too fine to disappoint. But the real truth of the situation was—as usual—overlooked by a West Point mind.

An order had come through making me a corporal, but I was far from delighted. Evidently Callaway had fixed things up good and based his decisions on someone else's advice. I will continue my work here and, possibly, most of the company work too, but am through with any of the work I did not get responsibility for. Anyone who does that will have to figure out on their own the problems that I have already worked out, for I will simply be too busy to touch it—and I don't mean maybe. At least, if I am not busy, I will say I am.

Callaway has said he will ask for a transfer, and I don't blame him. He was eligible for a captain's rating long ago, but never seems to get it. Evidently his work isn't popular in the regiment, for others have passed him by and gotten their captain's bars.

11 A Year Older

July 15, 1943

Past noon, and suddenly I remembered that the fifteenth had some special meaning for me. It happens to be my thirty-first birthday. In past years it has been in pleasant places that I awoke to find myself a year older. Last year it was in bleak, dirty Camp Edwards on Cape Cod. Since that day we have traveled thousands of miles across earth and ocean. Thirty-one isn't old, but it dern sure ain't no spring chicken age, and I feel older than ever before in my life! I'm as tired as I'm likely to be at sixty-two—if by any chance I am around that long.

I remember the time when a man of thirty seemed so old that my youth could not comprehend just what someone that age could see in life. Mother was about my present age when I was born, and little older when I romped the pine woods of Mississippi wondering at the wistful, pine tree song of the wind. Now I understand it better, for I, too, have wandered far and still find no special satisfaction in one place, but keep looking. There is no particular joy in being thirty-one. Your youthful ambitions have some what cooled, burned low. Things of interest come more slowly. You realize more keenly what you have missed through fortune or by your own bungling. You see others—younger—outstripping you in your old fields of conquest, and you prepare for the shock of middle age. You wonder what it is, just as you wondered about thirty when you were fifteen. You begin to get baggy under the eyes and thicker in the middle and realize that if you ever had a day of good looks (God knows I didn't) or youthful zest, it is a goner sure enough. But to compensate, you usually are blessed with more sense, and people find it harder to pull the proverbial wool over your now not-so-naive eyes. Time still pursues on light feet and clips his coupons year by year.

July 16, 1943

Lieutenant Trundle brought in a fine piece of live coral, tan with tips of beautiful lavender, covered with little buds of growing coral. He had gotten it while in a rowboat off the Great Barrier Reef. The only drawback to this fragile and beautiful wonder of the great reef was its odor! It had an overpowering, repugnant smell that filled the whole place—something like the odor of crushed raw fish and crushed garlic all at once. And not just one fish or one button of garlic! I put it up the hill in the sun hoping it would dry out and lose whatever gave it such a potent aroma. (It did so, but also lost its lovely color in the deal.)

July 19, 1943

As yesterday was Sunday, I had most of the day off. After lunch Dotson, Charlie, and I climbed the mountain behind camp as we had wanted to do so long. It proved to be steeper than we had anticipated, at least forty-five degrees and sometimes steeper. It was quite a climb! Much to my surprise the trees, etc., were no different than below, mostly ironbarks and a number of golden wattles blooming with their tiny balls of golden yellow fuzz. Long grass grew on the ground, much like the sage grass of the South (in the States). It must have been fine fodder, for several horses had climbed the mountain to feed on it.

After an hour or more, we found we were on top of a ridge, but not on top of the range, which loomed farther away and higher still. However, we were satisfied and sat for a long while surveying the scene below. The whole coastline was spread below like a relief map with the sea stretching out in a smooth sheet of water so nearly the color of the slightly overcast sky that it took keen looking to find the horizon.

The houses which I had sketched and the coconut grove at Palm Beach looked like a tiny arrangement on a sand table. Our camp was not visible at all in the timber below. The trees do not seem thick when you are in camp, but evidently, cover and hide our tents perfectly. Coming down was easier, but we had to fall flat frequently to keep from rolling to the bottom. The only birds we saw at all were a lone cockatoo flying into the jungle below and a tiny, scarlet honeyeater with black wings and scarlet back and breast.

I was surprised and disappointed at finding no life to speak of anywhere on the mountain.

After my description of the pleasant town of Mossman, all eight of our men who went out on three-day passes in the first group to leave, went there knowing it was off limits. They all had a good time, but four of them were caught by the MPs twelve hours before they were to start back. The other four did not fall into the clutches of the army law and finished their stay, arriving back yesterday.

Only our particular regiment is off limits there, which is puzzling even to those responsible for enforcing the order. There was really nothing the four men could be charged with, but everyone concerned tried to make it as embarrassing as possible for them, from the MPs to Callaway, who called them up and acted generally nasty about it. I am sure he figured my having been to Mossman (I was the only man out of the regiment who had been there before) had a great deal to do with the others going. But there was nothing he could do or say to me about it, as my trip there was perfectly legal. Evidently the place is being watched closely for 592d men.

July 22, 1943

I received a letter from Mother after a couple of weeks of silence. Evidently she is feeling well, and things generally are fairly satisfactory. She mentions the fact that things are getting more scarce all the time in the States, but apparently most people are very game about it. She expects to get a very good price for my car, as automobiles too, are getting scarce. Neither she nor Dad drives, so they really have no use for it. She hopes in every letter that the war will end, but, of course, couldn't hope so half as much as we who are here.

A couple of nights ago we had a visitor in camp—a curlew with an awful voice. He called long and loud, and everyone awoke with a start in the middle of the night. It sounded even louder in the quiet of that hour. He would manage to keep quiet for a few minutes or until everyone had dozed off again. Then he "gave out" his raucous call. A sergeant finally got up and decided to scare the bird away, but the clever curlew simply out-stalked the sergeant and kept hanging around until he decided his joke had gone far enough. Last night he returned, but with a partner, doubling the noise of the previous night as they called to each other. I suppose tonight he will return with the whole curlew family. Maybe we are being punished for some offense to birddom.

July 23, 1943

All day I've had the urge to paint, and I'm sure that no matter how long I stay in the army, I will just keep on wanting to pick up a brush. There is little time, but I manage to find a minute now and then. Someday in the somewhat hazy future, I look forward to painting again in my land of mesas—Arizona and New Mexico—where the very air is full of color, and the sun is warm, and the land is quiet. That country is my land of heart's desire. Maybe it is the place I will be content to settle in when the war is done.

July 25, 1943

After finishing work on the details and records of the day, I took the 1:00 truck to town, just for a break in the daily go-round here. Cairns had its Sunday soldier crowd, but little was going on. No milk bars or restaurants were open, but the Red Cross Canteen was crowded. Some Australians, as well as Americans, were walking along the low sea wall overlooking the busy harbor. Here and over the town I noticed a number of marines from Guadalcanal,[36] distinguished by their triangular arm patches; also more sailors than before, more airmen. Sea planes came and went, swooping into the coast behind the mass of new docks and warehouses on the waterfront. Ships big and little plied the bay, and some giant warships stood far off near the horizon, apparently too large to enter the channel, or else not desiring to anchor close in.

As I sat on a bench taking in the busy scene of the harbor, two small, gray doves—with blue around eye and bill and barred breasts—calmly walked up under my feet and began picking among a pile of peanut hulls to find any bits of food. The beautiful little birds were completely trusting and hardly looked at me—a serene contrast to the booming waterfront of a city at war. Evidently the birds live in the thick trees along the strip between the street and the low sea wall, much as our pigeons in small towns live in the courthouse steeple, for I heard others of them cooing softly.

The Red Cross Canteen had hamburgers, so I got one and a cup of coffee. It wasn't like hamburger you would find anywhere in America, but as good an imitation as the coffee. The Red Cross tries hard to make American food for the Yanks, but they are, after all, limited by the Australian cooks and Australian kitchen help who know their own way of cooking. The result is that most of what emerges from their kitchen is neither American nor Australian.

The Sunday night program at the Red Cross was a mixture of American swing and Australian song and tap dance. Some of our Amphibian engineers were there with a dance band as good as any professional one—the best music I have heard in a long time and a kid who could really sing! An Australian lady sang, but it sounded rather flat after the sparkling talent from home had performed. In fact, there is some musical something Australians just do not have. They cannot turn a tune into a vibrating, living thing. They simply sing and play the notes, and the result is usually pretty unsatisfactory.

Caught the early truck back about 9:00. It was only ten when I arrived, but everything was quiet. All lights were out. I had not realized how early we go to bed—not because we have to, for we could stay up all night if we just wanted to, and no one would say a word. There is simply nothing to do. No wonder we gain weight with all of this sleep and a life out-of-doors! The food isn't wonderful, but we eat it; you have to when there is nothing else around. All of which shows me that people must be the most adjustable of animals, getting used to anything in a hurry.

July 26, 1943

About all I was able to do today was to take the bicycle and ride down beyond the toll gate on the hill, just to see the sea and the green mountains stretching up the coast. Beauty never fails to make any day seem somehow worthwhile. It was almost dark when I stopped at the place where the road takes a sudden dive down the steep hill to the sea. In sleek swells the water rolled in and finally pounded itself white on the long stretch of sandy beach below. The sky above the mountain tops displayed a dramatic light-splash below the deep blue clouds.

Coming back I noticed the smell of burned-over woods and saw that the fire I saw when returning from my pass had finally burned itself out—but not before reaching the road and scorching acres of eucalyptus and paperbark trees. The Australians evidently burn off the pasture land each winter, a custom we in America have about discarded, for it is destructive and really does more harm than good. Usually, as here, the young trees are killed, and some of the old ones finally die of injury. You can hardly find a woods in this country that has not been burned time after time and the trees blackened many feet up their trunks.

I was glad to see the fire had not gotten as far as my favorite, big, old paperbark. No doubt this tree—its bark white and ragged from the ground up, standing above the smaller trees like a stern old grandfather in tattered trousers—has weathered many brush fires.

July 29, 1943

My friend Dotson did K.P. yesterday for the first time in six or eight months. He was much put out about it but couldn't find a single way out. Until a week or so ago four or five men had been doing the mean jobs—kitchen work, cleaning latrines, etc. Those doing this work were what are known as "basic privates," usually men who are not assigned to any special job, or who are not capable of holding a skilled position. I didn't see any reason why five men out of eighty-five should continue this when we have thirty-seven other privates who could get off the irregular jobs once in every ten days for company duty.

Our first sergeant went on a three-day pass. While he was gone, the acting sergeant and I worked out the new list, got it approved by the company commander and executive officer, and posted it. A terrible scream went up when the men gathered at the bulletin board—they were being cheated, etc., etc. Some tried to find legal excuses to keep off duty, but none did. Finally all agreed it was only fair, after all, to share the work.

As Lieutenant Callaway is now both company commander and battalion adjutant, I do work for both places. I decided I might as well try to do the boys some good, as long as I am working with the company and the men. When the first sergeant came back, he raved and ranted, but the system was in and working well, so he couldn't do one thing but leave it so. Someone said (and justly I think), "He ain't got guts enough to back up anything!"

As we were preparing to go to bed last night, someone began singing somewhere up the way in one of our tents. I knew at once that it couldn't be any of our group—either officers or men—for it has indeed been a long time since I have heard such a voice: powerful, sure, and beautiful. Finally I looked up the tent and found a group listening to an Australian soldier. He had come over for a visit with some of the men he had met and was entertaining them with the finest singing this outfit has probably ever heard. Scores from Italian opera, classical favorites, some of the better popular songs—all sung with personality and skill. This Australian could sing! The fellow was once a professional and did many stage appearances but decided that the war was more important. Now he only sings for his friends once in a while.

I received about the second letter in a whole year from my Dad today. He sure gave all the news. Mother writes regularly and tells what is going on and how she and Dad are, but I was tickled to get a letter he wrote himself. He had six days off for a vacation and rest. Wish I could have been there to take him places during that time.

The news sure looks good now! Musso is a goner, and Italy seems to be a push-over. Hurry, hurry, hurry! So we can close up shop and GO HOME!

NOTES FOR PART I

[1] Ella is the daughter of Gaitha's mother's brother.—*Ed.*
[2] Roy is Ella's husband.—*Ed.*
[3] Maude and Dot are the unmarried sisters of Gaitha's mother.—*Ed.*
[4] The troops were not told where they were going until they reached their destination, which proved to be Austrailia.—*Ed.*
[5] The sooty albatross was commonly called a gooney bird by the sailors.—*Ed.*
[6] Nickname for Don Giddens, son of Gaitha's sister Elizabeth, and her husband.—*Ed.*
[7] Dotson was an army tentmate. His first name is not available.—*Ed.*
[8] G. N. Quirl, an area Boy Scout Executive from Brownwood. Both he and his wife, Elizabeth Quirl, wrote to Gaitha during his years in the South Pacific.—*Ed.*
[9] Brown was a popular American comedian of the '30s and '40s caricatured by a wide-mouthed smile.—*Ed.*
[10] Brownnel and Martin, Army tentmates. First names not available.—*Ed.*
[11] Later, six more machine guns were added at that location.—*G.B.*
[12] I've never identified the bird since, although I suspect it could have been the small, but beautiful, little parrot known as the "elegant parrot," which whistles wonderfully, yet does not talk in captivity.—*G.B.*
[13] Robert T. Smith, a Boy Scout contemporary of Gaitha's with whom he kept in touch while they were both in the service.—*Ed.*
[14] Trucks couldn't go into town over this bridge, so we had to walk in.—*G.B.*
[15] Mack McCleary, a friend of Gaitha's since Camp Edwards at Cape Cod.—*Ed.*
[16] Suzy, a pre-war girlfriend with whom Gaitha corresponded after entering the Army.—*Ed.*
[17] Army Post Office.—*Ed.*
[18] Officers' Candidate School.—*Ed.*
[19] James Ridgley and his wife Marie were friends from New Mexico who wrote to Gaitha often during his years in the service.—*Ed.*
[20] Mrs. Pearl Stallings was a friend with whom Gaitha had worked in the Brownwood Art Association before entering the service.—*Ed.*
[21] He eventually got two months of hard labor in the stockade for this latest trip over the hill, then was sent on to New Guinea with an advanced party.—*G.B.*
[22] On May 12, 1943, the last organized army force in Africa surrendered. The Allies had killed, wounded, or capured about three hundred fifty thousand Axis soldiers and had suffered about seventy thousand casualties in the North African campaign.—*Ed.*
[23] Maurice Roth, one of the original group who became tentmates at Camp Edwards on Cape cod, along with Gaitha, Clarence Estadt, Charles "Charlie" Wilson and Mack McCleary. Dotson joined the group later at Fort Ord.—*Ed.*
[24] Pouncey was an area boy Scout Executive from Brownwood whose wife Mary wrote to Gaitha regularly. Gaitha looked upon Pouncey as a second father and spent much time in his formative years with the couple.—*Ed.*
[25] Later I learned that one of the cockatoos was sixty years old.—*G.B.*
[26] Anytime anyone handed you a lot of silver there, you could pretty well guess that he had been lucky in a poker game.—*G.B.*
[27] The crowded conditions did not necessarily cause this, but I found that most Australian

hotels expected to book a guest for several days. Evidently our harried business man with an overnight stay was a rarity there at that time.—*G.B.*

[28] A huge crane-like bird at least four to five feet tall, gray with a brilliant red head.—*Ed.*

[29] Like the sacred white ibis known in Egypt.—*G.B.*

[30] Upon later investigation, I found that there is a growing season for sugar cane and a slack season when sugar mills are repaired to get ready for the new crop.—*G.B.*

[31] It did stay there for some time, but stupidity will out in some people, so someone decided to remove it one day when I was absent.—*G.B.*

[32] Jimmy was a boyhood friend and fellow Boy Scout of Gaitha's who entered the Air Force when Gaitha joined the Army.—*Ed.*

[33] Ruth Casebold was a member of the Brownwood Art Association who wrote to Gaitha about the group's activities during his absence.—*Ed.*

[34] Gaitha is referring to Gutzon Borglum, who designed the Mount Rushmore National memorial in South Dakota and supervised most of its work.—*Ed.*

[35] Australian word for comrade.—*Ed.*

[36] The Guadalcanal campaign which had begun on August 7, 1942, continued until February 8, 1943.—*Ed.*

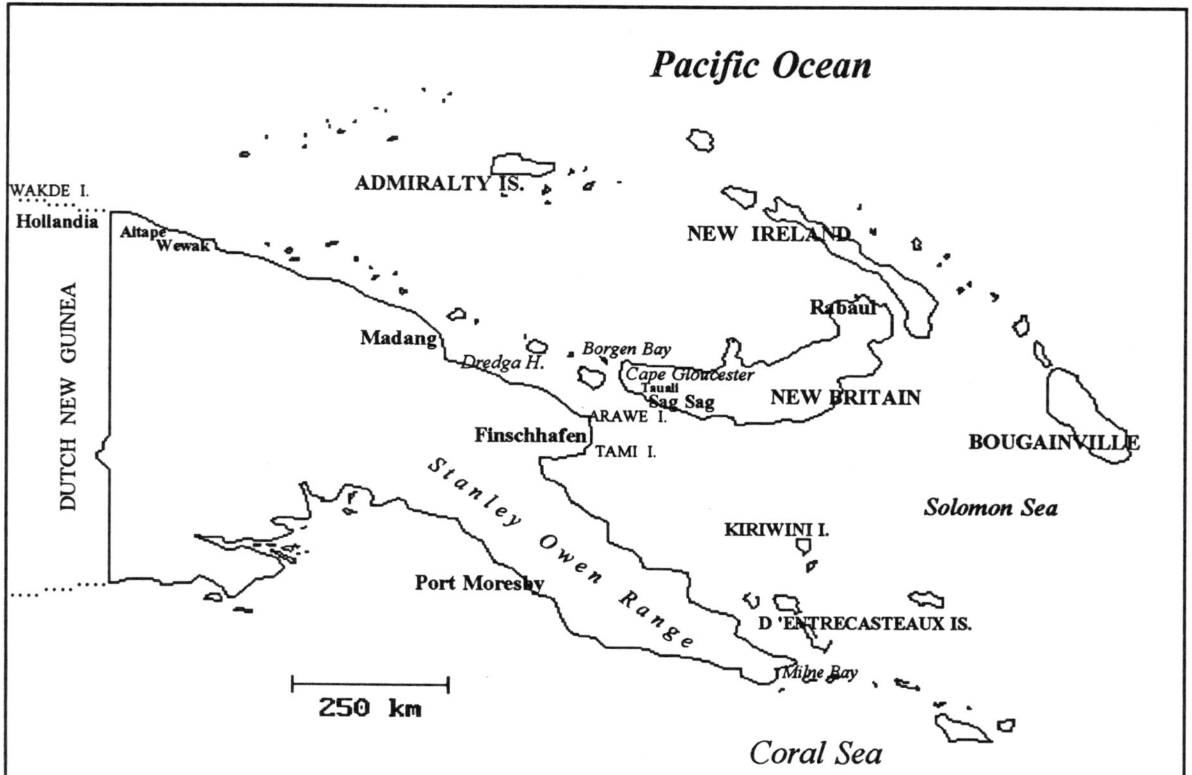

PAPUA NEW GUINEA

PART II

October 20, 1943 to October 26, 1944

12 BEGINNING AGAIN

October 20, 1943[1]

This is "beginning again" for the journal. The first part is now with the Commonwealth Bank of Australia at Cairns, Queensland. Silly isn't it, but someday I want to look back and see just what impressions of Australia I had.

Tents came down late yesterday afternoon. Needless to say, they had not been down thirty minutes until very dark clouds threatened a cloudburst. Usually our tents and the rain come down together. But it cleared later, and a million stars came out. We put up our jungle hammocks and retired therein, feeling safe.

The rain was only fooling. It had gone over the mountain just long enough to lull us into a sense of dry security, then it returned in the middle of the night. The rattle of it waked me as it pounded the rubberized roof of my hammock. I jumped up and began to gather things to take to the one tent that was still up. After that, I crawled back into the hammock and just let it rain. I found that those things are really practical after all. Not a drop of water got in, even though I did not let the sides down.

Early this morning I was up and packed to go. We put all of my things and all of Lieutenant Callaway's things, plus a small field desk, into a jeep. We had to board the boat early as Callaway is ship's adjutant. I went along because someone who does something has to be there—the work must be done.

The country was lovely in the early morning—the green mountains gray with fog, the light green of the cane fields, the brilliant red of tulip trees. Somehow, when I leave a country or place, the last sight of it seems very sweet, indeed. In spite of knowing that I would never feel exactly at home in Australia, there was a touch of regret in my gaze. There is beauty here! The land has its own special appeal.

The ship proved to be the *Moonera*, and she is a busy ship right now. I am sitting in the main office where arrangements are being completed for our men to come on board. When we first arrived, there was nothing to do, so I got acquainted with the ship as best I could. Built in 1935, she is much nicer than was the *Holbrook*, and is smaller, being only about four hundred feet. There seems to be plenty of room though.

The booms are working continuously, swinging big cargo nets full of our crates into the hold. The men who have been loading for three days say they never knew so much stuff could go into one boat. Also being loaded is the *Westralia,* which is tied up close behind the *Moonera* at the dock. Evidently she will make the trip with us.

The crew of the *Moonera* is Australian, just kids it seems. At least they look awfully young. They are all over the ship at once, doing a thousand jobs. Their boatswain "pipes" regularly, but the "piping of the bosun" famous in song and story sounds very disappointing—much like a cracked tin whistle that wheezes more than whistles. Now the piping is no more than a ceremony, for there are loudspeakers in every part of the ship, making the piping unnecessary.

It is night now, but no rest yet. There seems to be an unusual amount of ceremony on this boat, and the officer is here giving exact instructions as to how everyone should treat everyone else, and what such and such an officer expects. Major Bilger is "yessing" him on all points as he takes in the lecture. I often wonder if we are fighting a war or fighting each other over a volume of Emily Post.

Nowhere is the snobbery and jealousy of rank more apparent than on a boat. Each officer goes to great pains to see that he gets a better cabin than any of those below him in rank. The first three grades of sergeants are given a crowded cabin instead of a bunk with the others, but some are honest enough to admit that it is more comfortable up on our deck than in that hot little matchbox of a cabin. Others stay and endure the heat in order to nurse their egos along. They are getting the same quarters as a SECOND LIEUTENANT! (The difference being that twice as many sergeants as lieutenants are stuffed into a cabin.)

The tropical heat is oppressive tonight on the boat. We are still at the dock in Cairns. Maybe it will be a little cooler when we sail tomorrow. The afternoon was even hotter, and the hills seemed to wilt into grayness.

When the late sun slanted across the harbor, it was a wonderful sight, painting the mangrove swamps at the base of the mountains a bright, golden green that came right down to the edge of the water with the dusky mountains behind. Clouds played over the peaks and trailed into the valleys, and their shadows crept in patterns over the roundness of the hills. White gulls wheeled about the ship while small boats passed and re-passed into the inlet.

We put up hammocks for sleeping, and what a job that was! They were given to us in pieces, and we had to tie all the ropes on each end. They are finally up, but I am doubtful that we will sleep too much with the heat and the hammock together. The ship is blacked out, which means that every opening is closed, so we are continually wet with sweat. Even a shower doesn't help at all. I took one to find out! This bunch will be well-wilted by the time we get up toward the equator.

October 21, 1943

After a night of feeling like a pretzel in that hammock, we have a new morning. We have been pulled off from the dock by a tug and are now sailing down the coast beyond Cairns.

Breakfast consisted of weak tea, kidney stew, a slice of bread, and some butter. I passed up the kidney stew—it was on a par with all of that lousy mutton stew we got on the railroad trip on the way up from Brisbane. Evidently the Australians think it is delightful, because they eat it regularly.

Our ship was at first anchored off the old camp beach, while the landing boats were being swung aboard. They looked pretty large by themselves, but as they were swung out of the water and up to the side of the *Moonera*, with the crews still in them, they looked like pea pods. They were lashed to the *Moonera* and left suspended there.

When the convoy finally got underway, I found that there are five ships in all—ours, the *Westralia*, three liberty ships with the protecting convoy of one U.S. sub-chaser, one U.S. destroyer, one Australian destroyer, and two U.S. coverettes. The protecting vessels scoot here and there, out to our right and left, cut across our path in front and rear, and hover around like small hens with very large chickens. The whole convoy presents an interesting sight, and the blue water and sunny skies seem far removed from war.

However, it isn't hard to realize our mission when you look over the array of guns aboard, all manned twenty-four hours a day. Big and little guns, middle-sized guns, but no indifferent guns. They all mean business! The big six-inchers have their shells arranged in handy rows in a semicircle. The crews of the guns are all stripped to shorts, taking sun baths and hosing the deck to keep it cool enough to lie on. But one man continually keeps watch, using a pair of binoculars now and then to search the water.

October 22, 1943

Another day aboard the "Manura," which is the name we have given it. Even a good ship isn't any fun when crowded with troops. As usual the food causes unfavorable comment, although it is not as bad as what we got on the *Holbrook*. To eat we have to go two decks down, climb a steep ladder—or rather, very narrow steel steps—and come back up with our mess kits and a cup of tea. This is quite a trick if you want to arrive on B Deck with anything to eat. Always there is tea, insipid tea, and I have never yet known if it is hot cold tea, or cold hot tea. As expected, the fine meals the officers have in the cool dining room on A Deck contrast with ours.

I have forgotten to mention that our little parrots were brought aboard. Afterward an order came down that all dogs, birds, etc., had to be destroyed before the ship sailed. Several dogs were taken by their owners and left on the wharf, where they presented a pitiful sight as they paced the length of the ship looking up, trying to discover a familiar face. Our little black dog was among them. We had raised her from a tiny puppy.

The parrots disappeared, and I suspected that Chuck had hidden them in an effort to get them to Guinea. Sure enough, he had, but the next night they were found by some snooper of the ship's Gestapo. Their little necks were wrung, and they were thrown overboard.[2]

Most of the afternoon I spent on the deck taking in the cool breeze. Estadt is working down below to give me my first time off since boarding the ship. As usual the sea is very blue—the sky bright with puffs of fleecy clouds.

October 23, 1943

We entered the China Straits (Goschen Strait) before noon with the green hills of New Guinea on our left and various large islands to the right. The channel narrowed, and the convoy stretched out in single file. Soon we were in a very narrow channel with the islands so close that we saw they were almost like a movie set. Thousands of palms,[3] houses, and sandy beaches. A canoe of natives passed on the way between islands.

About noon we entered famous Milne Bay, but it is unexciting looking now, just green hills above blue water.[4] We anchored there a couple of hours, but for what reason I did not discover. All of the activity I saw was one destroyer which came alongside us and passed some papers over on a line. During this time the remainder of the convoy got ahead of us, except for the *Westralia*. The hills of the east have now disappeared, but the Guinea coast is still visible. We have been in very dangerous waters all day, because this strait is a good place to catch boats coming up the Guinea coast.

One interesting incident on board concerned the prisoners from the stockade. Three of them serving various sentences were brought along in the ship's brig, which was a dark cell somewhere deep in the ship that everyone said was so hot it was almost unbearable. The prisoners were ordered to work scrubbing floors but they refused to work under guard. The officers didn't know exactly what to do, but wanted to do their stinking worst, so the men were taken back to their cell, given no food for twenty-four hours, and only bread and water thereafter. After twenty-four hours, all but one decided to work. He stuck it out, and the last time I heard was still sticking to his determination to work without a guard or not work at all. I know the men had been kicked around until they just decided nothing much more could happen to them anyway, so they defied the little bigots right to their faces.

It is late afternoon, and we are making our way up the coast of Guinea. Far off to the east is the dim shape of the D'Entrecasteaux Islands. The liberty ships are now far ahead—so far that we are practically sailing alone. The Westralia still trails us. The landing barges on her sides look like big bugs that have attached themselves. We still have one destroyer with us; the rest have gone ahead of the liberty ships. Many of the shipping problems for equipment have been solved by the liberties, but they are indeed ugly vessels with no lines at all, with almost straight sides, and usually rusty. I wonder if they will do more than outlast the war, for they couldn't be continuously used in trans-oceanic shipping for more than a few years.

October 26, 1943

The skip in dates testifies to the fact that things have been happening thick and fast since we left the boat. We walked down the gangplank onto a huge floating raft, then into our boats, bag and baggage. We came directly to this camp several miles north of Oro Bay proper. The beach was not the wide beach of Keppel Island with its golden sand, but was a grayish black color from the volcanic soil.

To add to the unlovely look of the beach, the army camps have built a mile-long string of latrines down the shore, each one a long walk of poles extending out ninety feet into the ocean with a small canvas-covered structure on the end. As the altitude is the terrific height of from one to three feet above sea level, no holes can be dug for the latrines.

The camp is in a huge coconut grove which was perhaps planted twenty years ago—if it was planted at all. Anyway the trees are from thirty to forty feet high. Near the water are a number of beautiful old Putat trees with slick, dark green leaves. The trunks lean, lie flat, and twist like old oaks, and all of them are immense. Some of these trees have been dropping flowers as large as a small feather duster with pink and white bristles. There are numerous fantastically colored butterflies, and some unknown bird has been calling in the trees. Every bug, bird, butterfly, tree, and weed is strange here, and will—no doubt—continue to be so, for there have been few, if any, books published on the wild things of this country where few white men came before the war.

The natives are quite a show with their bleached and hennaed hair that stands up on their heads in a fuzzy wuzzy way. Yesterday two men went up coconut trees here and dropped the nuts down. They can climb like monkeys by putting the loop of a rope around the insteps of both feet, thus holding their feet together against the tree. Natives are used for labor here too, and, in spite of their small size, are unusually strong.

Yesterday they came to replace a work detail I was on, for it was apparent that we could not stand the heat in that place, plus the hard work of stacking and sorting all the crated equipment for the entire regiment. We sat down and watched them. It was quite a show. They seemed to be jolly and worked cheerfully for their $1.60 a month paid to them by the Australian government. We pay more than that for their work, but they are controlled and managed by the Australians who, after all, understand them much better than we do.

Native dress consists of a piece of cloth wrapped around the waist—nothing more. Some only wear a brief loincloth pulled up between their legs over a belt.

When in Cairns last, I bought ten yards of flowered print and can see that it may have been a good buy. The natives can get tobacco and food, but no one thought of the cloth angle. Many natives seem to need new skirts, as most of the cloth looks like old sacking. A few wear printed goods, all faded. Some have black cloth, but the dirty white predominates. So far I have not had time to do anything as to trading, but if we are here long enough, there will be time.

13 Unloading at Oro Bay

October 26, 1943[5]

The whole move has been tremendous and a test of human endurance if there ever was one! The five ships sailed into Oro Bay,[6] and the unloading commenced immediately, as the ships dislike staying around any longer than necessary making targets of themselves for the Japanese.

Unloading was one of the biggest jobs we have undertaken to date. The cranes went into action immediately. As I left the ship, the last thing I saw was a jeep swinging in mid-air on a cable, waiting to be lowered into a barge. All of the cargo was put into our boats, taken ashore where the front ramps of the boats were dropped, and we unloaded the crates and stacked everything on the beach. Trucks continually hauled it away, but even then, the piles grew into mountainous proportions. It was hellish work in that sticky heat, and we worked on into the night.

Never before had I seen so many supplies—every conceivable thing. Canned food, engines, boat parts, crated equipment of a thousand kinds poured ashore. There was very little petty stuff going on here. When you got hungry, you found a box containing fruit juice and went at it. Several of us found a case of grapefruit juice from the States—none of this Australian stuff—and it was surely fine. About midnight we came back to camp and fell into bed.

One week ago there was an air battle over Oro Bay that must have been an exciting show.[7] Fifteen out of the sixteen Japanese planes were shot down, with the loss of only one of our P38s (of which the pilot bailed out and was picked up). Only one enemy pilot was found—quite dead—shot through the mouth. The crash boat that found him didn't want to haul him aboard, so a rope was looped around his neck, and he was towed behind the boat back to Oro, quite an inglorious trip for one of his majesty's servants of the Rising Sun, and quite in contrast to the fact that he was carried eighteen miles to Buna and buried in the Japanese cemetery there.

We have dug foxholes already. The first day we were here there was a lone Japanese plane over the bay—probably just looking or photographing—but it disappeared, and we didn't see it again.[8]

While we were getting off the boat, a huge flight of P38s went over. I counted sixty in one lot. Later in the day they returned, and many did loops and dives over their field as a sign of victory. They had raided Rabaul in one of the biggest daylight raids to date. Hundreds of planes took part.

From time to time I see some of our men who came up here several months ago and often hardly know them. Most are thin, and all are yellow from much Atabrine.[9] Evidently the climate is a strain, and the food not so good where everything has to be either dried, canned, or condensed. Many have had malaria one or more times but keep going somehow. The loss of weight won't worry me, if that is all that happens. But with malaria, brush typhus, and a hundred other things, even a careful person is likely to fall out with something.

October 27, 1943

Charlie is still in Australia, as he didn't come back from his furlough in time to leave with us. I've done his work for so long now that I wouldn't miss him if he never came back. But by the time he does return, the move will be complete and the camp built. I'm just mean enough to hope he gets caught in one of those casual camps and is kept months "awaiting proper transportation," as is often done with the stray men who get away from their units for various reasons.

Last night we had the first air alert. The siren wailed, and the whistles blew, and people yelled, "No lights!" I jumped up, pulled on my coveralls, found my steel helmet, pulled on my jungle boots, and got into my foxhole beside my cot. The ack-ack opened up down the bay for a few shots, and shortly afterward the "all clear" was sounded. It was high time, as the water from the tent was running on my feet (it was raining), and I saw that the foxhole was neither deep enough nor roofed-over far enough. When I got out, I discovered that I had my boots on the wrong feet, but they work both ways very satisfactorily.

Yesterday afternoon we went up the bay and went swimming, undressing on the rusting hulk of a Japanese barge that had been riddled with gunfire. It was half buried on the beach, and in another six months or so, there will be no sign of it. Nature covers the scars of war on her face quickly, but the scars on our civilization will linger longer.

October 28, 1943

End of another New Guinea day, but one less hot than those before. It was cloudy all day, which gave us a little rest from the wilting, muggy heat. Gradually we are getting used to the place, the monotonous food, etc.

Someone killed the first New Guinea snake for our bunch today—a sort of overgrown grass snake about eight feet long. It was beautifully patterned in bright orange and green and most unusual. It looked like a harmless one, but everything is so strange here that it could be just anything.

Another alarm last night lasting about an hour. The ack-ack opened up down the bay, but we never knew what was being shot at. I know that at least one of our tent mates was thoroughly frightened, and I wondered what will happen when we really get under fire. Anyway, the reactions of the men and officers will be interesting. Already we have two officers who have been up to Finschhafen and showed up much less than anyone thought they would. Both are big six-footers who always gave the impression of being very rugged, but both broke down in a disgusting manner. The story has gotten around, and the men look at them sideways when they pass. These two cannot now hope to hold any respect from anyone.

October 29, 1943

Determined to get coconuts, I unpacked the pole climbers from the supply room and went up a couple of trees this morning. The natives have pretty well stripped them, but a few nuts remained.[10] None were very ripe, but the juice was good, and they contain a surprising amount of it, much more than the ripe coconuts we are familiar with in the States. Unless I can find a tree with ripe ones, it won't be worth any more climbs like that. It isn't easy to get up that high and it usually takes a hefty whack with a good machete to release the coconuts.

Letters from Quirl and Mrs. Stallings arrived, both full of news. Mrs. Stallings says she has sent a Christmas package containing some of her melon rind preserves that I always liked so much. She used to have them when the Brownwood Art Association met with her, and I always threw away convention and manners and stuffed those preserves something awful. She remembers it and knows I would like nothing better.

Several of us rode down to the Forty-Second area to the movie, and along the way I had a chance to observe the foothills of the Owen Stanleys in the distance. Their heads shrouded in clouds, they became foreboding, mysterious, and lost in ages past. Few white men have traversed them. Much of the interior is still unexplored, peopled with primitive tribes. I don't know what parts of the country the Australians and Americans came over, but that campaign must have been one of the hardest in history. I know we lost far more men than the newspapers reported. The Australians did likewise, and the Japs lost men by the thousands.[11]

Two nights have passed now with no visit from "Washing Machine Charlie." Maybe he got tired, or maybe the anti-aircraft nicked him. Anyway, we have not been disturbed.

Late yesterday the sea began to be very heavy, and the cold, gray breakers piled up on the very narrow strip of beach. I wondered if we were in for a storm, as the sky threatened something unusual. Evidently there are few damaging storms here, for none of the trees show signs of it, and they are very old.

October 31, 1943

Sunday, and the usual Sunday afternoon swim and sun bath. Tonight we went to a movie, *The Human Comedy*, as fine a show as I have seen in a long, long time. Certainly the best since coming over. It was unusual in that there was none of the Hollywood pretense to make the characters other than ordinary people acting in an ordinary way. Most of it was based on what happens to be my own personal belief—that people don't die, but live on as a part of a better world. We have their contributions with us even after they are not here in person.

November 2, 1943[12]

Today we had a large group of natives cutting kuni grass across the road for some more tent space. It was more than waist high and thick, but they went to it with flashing machetes and did a splendid job of clearing. The grass fell back as the row of cutters advanced, each one using a small stick to hold back the grass in front of him as he swung. The grass was piled up, sprayed with gas, and burned, because of the danger of typhus-carrying ticks. I was more interested in the natives than in the ticks, however.

There were four of them who spoke English of a sort. Two mission boys and two "Number One" or "Boss Boys" who carried small, carved canes as a sign of authority and did absolutely no work—just kept the gang at it.

Before noon I went over with some of the stuff I had brought along, most of which caused no particular interest until the flowered cloth was brought out. It was a sensation, and the work stopped right there as the natives crowded around. Evidently a loud "lamie"—as they call the piece of cloth wrapped around the waist—is the ideal! The rich red piece I had was the height of something or other in the native mind. Seeing that the work was at a standstill, I left, promising to ride up to the village when work was done. But even more than the cloth, the boys wanted—of all things—peroxide! A bleached and red-dyed head of fuzzy hair is the ultimate in native styles.

At 4:00 I got on the truck with another fellow and sixteen of the natives. We were in the back of the truck, as I didn't want to miss any of the country and also wanted to get better acquainted with the natives. I had my bag of goods along. I opened up cigarettes and gave each man a smoke. Each one took one, saluted, grinned a betelnut-stained grin, and said, "Okay!" This seems to be the standard native reply to anything, and probably is all of the English they know.

We drove away from the sea and into the mountains, gradually getting farther and farther from the main military roads until the last of the camps was passed. At a turn in the road was a bridge over a swift, fresh mountain stream, the sight of which the natives couldn't resist. They set up an awful howl to stop. We did, as time was plentiful, and they jumped off the truck and ran screeching to the water, stripping off their lamies as they went.

In they plunged! Some went under so suddenly and stayed so long that I wondered. But they were simply taking a bath under water to get rid of the day's dust. None tarried longer than necessary, and most climbed back into the truck stark naked and dripping wet. Neither fact worried them in the least, and they "dressed" at leisure as we went along. Evidently they have not yet learned the acquired habit of being ashamed of their bodies.

The road got rougher. We climbed and doubled back until you could look down, down, down to the road you had just left. The tall jungle trees rising on either side of the road were matted with vines. The natives kept looking and pointing and talking among themselves, but I never did see one thing along the way to cause their excitement and never learned what was so interesting in the trees. The road got so rough that I stood up and made a face at the pounding I was receiving. This sent the natives into screeching laughter, and I again noticed the effect of the betelnut on their teeth. Evidently they all chew it for its mild narcotic effect, or is it mild?

The village was located on a high, green knob of a hill with a small, irregular patch of coconut palms. The last place you would think of finding plenty of coconuts would be in a native village, but—strangely enough—the trees were loaded and, evidently, had not been picked for a long time. The houses were small, square, palm-thatched, mostly on poles up off the ground. An Australian soldier was in charge of the village, which turned out to be a men's work village and not the home village of the tribe.

"You Yanks don't know how to handle the natives," he said. "If you let them get by with anything or treat them too kind all of the time, they get out of hand. You just aren't used to whaling hell out of people." I can see that the natives could be easily spoiled.

I traded one man a lamie of the flowered cloth for a dozen bracelets of woven fiber that are worn above the elbow and below the knee, probably having some tribal significance. One man wanted to trade a spear, but I surely had no use for an eight-foot spear, even though it was interesting. Made of wood as hard as iron, it had notched teeth in the business end.

We left the village but found a group of natives bathing in a small stream near the entrance road. Most of them were out of the water combing their hair. I called to them and made it known that I wanted a comb. Several were offered, and I chose one and gave the man a lamie in return. It was more than he had ever received in exchange for a bamboo comb he had spent three or four hours making.

The trip had been worthwhile and had netted a dozen bracelets and one comb, but evidently the Yanks have already somewhat spoiled things, because cigarettes are no longer a novelty or a scarcity. The native's alert mind has been quick to take advantage of the generosity of these foolish, new, white people who have appeared in their land.

Twilight, and the ack-ack down the bay is putting on quite a show. It is probably just practicing, as there has been no alert. The shells seem to float out across the bay in a long, slow string of red balls, then the first one will burst in a flash, and each succeeding one will do the same, but not until it has reached the same spot. Sometimes the pattern of fire will be changed, and the shells all explode in a row. Sometimes two guns fire at once, mixing the string of floating red beads in the sky. I have heard that the shells go three miles before they explode, which accounts for the fact they seem to move so slowly. Three miles is quite a distance.

November 3, 1943

I have a piece of pottery which was picked up where the road was cut through, similar to primitive pottery from any spot in the world. I have seen mound builders' work in Arkansas almost exactly like this somewhat thick, brown shard with a design made by fingernails in the wet clay. The simple geometrical design could have been scraped on with a piece of shell or bone. One of the natives was around, and I showed it to him. His comment was only two words: "Woman make." Evidently this was to tell me that the women still make such things.

14 A Mission Village

November 5, 1943

I am just back from one of the most interesting and exciting days of my life! This morning at 9:00 I left by boat with our chaplain, Reverend Newman (the missionary), and several others, heading for the mission station which is run by this Australian of the Anglican faith. Because he has been in the army hospital for an operation, Reverend Newman has not been to his mission for more than a month.

The ride took several hours. We traveled down the bay many miles beyond the farthermost army outpost of Oro Bay. "There is an overland trail," the padre said, "but in the nine years I have been here, I have only been over it once. It is an almost impossible trip by land."

As we began to near the mission, he pointed to a distant shore where we could just make out a row of grass huts. "That's the village!" he said. "The mission is on the hill." We landed on the sandy beach and saw nearly naked natives running to greet us from all directions. They hailed the padre and showed instantly that they trusted and respected him. The ramp of the boat was let down, but the surf was too deep to wade out in our clothes. The natives immediately saw the situation and began coming in pairs to the front of the boat where we stood. We put our arms around their shoulders and were on dry ground in a flash. Apparently they enjoyed being helpful, for they showed broad grins as they worked.

The distance from the boat to the village just off the beach was a thousand years. There was not a stick of anything civilization could claim. Not a nail in a hut, not a tool of any kind to be seen! A few natives had faded pieces of cloth for skirts, but the majority wore tapa[13] cloth they had made themselves. All had small, black earrings of tortoise shell in their ears. Some wore beads of shell and seeds, and many had tattoos on their faces. All of the faces were happy. These people have not taken on the cares of the world as we have.

I walked down between the rows of grass houses fascinated by the first truly unspoiled people I had ever seen. Old women with withered breasts; girls with firm, pointed breasts; sturdy young men; lame old men; toddlers as naked as jaybirds; tiny babies on mothers' backs. Strangely enough we were accepted in the village without reservation. Our coming was a holiday. They saw so few white people, and from their attitude they had contacted only kindly ones.

The padre knew them all. He stopped to inquire about this and that and heard various stories of what had transpired while he was away. "Why aren't all these boys in school?" he asked in the native language. The resulting explanation was a long story about someone being bitten by a crocodile and the children were afraid to cross the stream. The padre understood all too well that the story was pure fabrication. There was a good, safe raft for crossing the stream, and a stretched cable to pull it across with. Even the noncivilized children will play hookey!

We came to a woman making an intricately woven mesh bag of native string. After some conversation with her in her own tongue, the padre remarked to me in an off hand sort of way, "She says she is getting along fine, but could go faster if she had a needle." "I have the needles all right!" I told him. At first none of the group believed me, but I went to the boat and got the trade bag.

The news spread like wildfire. "Needles! The white man has needles!" And the women scurried off to bring their best tapa cloth to trade. I was swamped by offers. Five darning needles for one tapa became the standard of trade. The tapa piled up, and the needles disappeared. Finally they were all gone, but before they were all traded off, my soldier friends begged me to sell THEM needles, because their money was not attractive. Money was of dubious value to the natives, but a needle could be put right to use. I said "No!" and meant it. I had cornered the market and didn't intend to let the opportunity be lost to someone who didn't think of the fact that natives like needles, fishhooks, and plug tobacco. What a fool I had been to trust my judgement only to the extent of a few dozen needles!

The native men traded woven bracelets for fishhooks and plug tobacco, and I soon had thirty of these. I traded some cloth—enough for a lamie—for two tapas and ended up with thirteen pieces of this unusual cloth made here for everyday wear. Trading had been farthermost from their minds when they made it, so the design and workmanship was sincere, a rare find in this upheaved world.

Several of those in the party got tapas for two and three shillings, but money trade was slow. "Ask the native woman what she will do with money," I requested of the padre. He did and was told that someday a trading store might open up. They had heard of such things, but evidently they anticipated no immediate use for the money.

Now I noticed that the needles were getting around. The women seemed unselfish and had divided with others. Their needle case was the last expected place—in the nose! Most of the women had their noses pierced anyway and were not wearing anything in them, so the needles fitted fine and were safe there.

Sitting there surrounded by natives who smelled of coconut oil, I was extremely happy trading and watching their frank faces—faces that had not learned deceit—had not learned to hide emotions—none of the artificial, acquired tricks we have taken up. If a woman felt like jumping up and clapping her hands when a bright-flowered cloth came out of the bag, she did just that. All this was the rare essence of something that so few have the privilege of seeing. I am lucky!

I had wanted several black cowrie shells to put on silver chains as necklaces to send home, since these shells are very beautiful and quite appropriate for that purpose. So, I asked about them. The padre inquired about these shells but found that the natives would neither sell nor trade them. Apparently they mean more than money or trade goods and have a deep religious significance. I have heard that they are the symbol of fertility.

The trading slowed as the more attractive goods gave out, and I closed the bag. We wandered back through the village followed by a band of natives. An old woman—almost toothless—looked out of a hut and smiled. She had been watching all that happened from her mat inside. A man came up with a most unusual head of hair, long ropes hanging down over his shoulders—ropes the size of your little finger and each one beautifully greased to make the hair stick together. Quite a mop! Most of the women had very short hair. Some of them had it cut as a symbol of mourning for relatives who had recently died. This is a common practice among primitive tribes, I knew.

As we stood on the beach talking to the padre, and he in turn talked to the natives, I asked about the betelnut. Reverend Newman asked a woman about it, and from her hut she brought a stem on which grew six or eight light green balls the size and shape of small pullet eggs. She took one, bit off the end, and opened the hull. Inside was a pinkish ball of a bean, veined like a miniature brain in a pod. A user would put a bit of this bean, along with a small ball of lime, under his lip. The lime works on the betelnut, and the result is a violent red juice—the redder the better. The woman suggested that Reverend Newman try some, and he jokingly refused. She saw the joke and offered it to me, laughing long and hard at the face I made. She had not expected us to chew betelnut.

All waved goodbye as we pulled out for the mission which was a short way up the beach. We took the erring school boys along, also a couple of the men. This time our boat anchored in the mouth of the small stream—the one that could not be crossed because of crocodiles—and the boys began carrying all of us to shore again.

We took an army stretcher from the boat to shore for Padre Newman. The hill to the mission was steep, and his recent operation would not permit him to make it on foot. The willing natives lifted him on the stretcher, and we fell in behind and climbed to the green hill where the church and mission school buildings were located. We came up out of the dense growth and onto the mission hill with its grass houses, the large church, hibiscus bushes bright with bloom, an odd tree blooming in pink masses.

The boys carefully put Reverend Newman on the ground as various mission natives came up to greet him and tell how the school had been getting along. A woman called to us from the high window of a house on poles. Two men who had been educated as teachers talked in English. The padre told them to get back to classes, and we would be around to visit.

The first class was writing on slates, simple syllables of their own language, which has been put into written form by the missionaries. At three other buildings various classes were in progress. The largest building had crude benches, a dirt floor, and a grass roof, and was built on a pole frame lashed together with lawyer cane, which seems to be the universal binding for everything. The other buildings had floors made by weaving huge mats of flattened cane and putting them over a frame raised off the ground. The children sat cross-legged on this floor and recited simple lessons in a somewhat singsong way. Later all the students gathered in the larger building.

We stood outside and leaned over the low bamboo side of the open end of the structure. They sang a number of familiar songs. Their voices and rhythm were remarkable and far surpassed their ability at writing and arithmetic. Singing was a natural thing to them.

It was past noon when they were dismissed, and we all suddenly knew we were very hungry. The interest in what we saw had made us forget food. Without being told, the woman who had greeted us from the window put a large container of water on to boil. She knew the padre would make tea for his guests.

While the billy boiled we went up the slight slope to the church, which was the best built building of the lot. Care had been taken here, as was evident from the huge, beautifully woven mat behind the altar; also the mats on either side and above it. Fresh flowers were arranged on the altar, and carved on the front of it by native hands were their words for "Holy, Holy, Holy."

Reverend Newman told us that he tried to make mission life as pleasant as possible for the people here. Once a month a "ladies' guild" is held when the women come to sew, talk, and have tea and cookies. Apparently women with pierced noses like tea parties as well as the Mrs. Vanderbilts, and most likely discuss the same problems over their tea. Undoubtedly the mission had relieved the monotony of their daily lives, and they liked it.

We had brought along a large can of Spam, a gallon can of tomato juice, and various other things. With the tea we had an enjoyable meal. The native woman helped cheerfully. She was having a good time—it wasn't often she entertained visitors here. Evidently she was quite a character, and her keen mind and wit were evident. She was the wife of one of the teachers and spent most of her time here helping with the mission. She liked the tomato juice, and we shared it and the lunch with her and several of the children who were around.

The woman was so helpful that I decided she deserved a new skirt to replace the worn one she had around her waist—her sole garment—so I got a piece of the bright cloth for her. "It's a gift for you," the padre said. Her face was reward enough for anyone, and evidently it had been a long time since she had received such a gift. She offered profuse thanks in English. I know one lady who will be the height of fashion when the sewing circle meets the next time!

By this time the meal was over, and a dozen or so of the children of all ages had gathered again, each with a huge red hibiscus blossom in his hair. We fell into the gay mood, and soon had these blossoms in our helmet straps.

"These children are only a generation removed from their cannibal ancestors," Reverend Newman explained. "Many of their fathers have eaten human flesh. Twenty years ago they were headhunters as wild and savage as any such people on earth."

Time to get back to the boat and begin the trip to camp. The padre was carried down the hill again by our happy group with flowers in their hair, followed by a group with flowers in our helmets. Reverend Newman was to go back to the hospital for further recuperation from his surgery. We bade goodbye to the boys after we were in the boat. As we left the inlet, the group of brown figures stood knee-deep in water, backed by towering palms and jungle greenness, each fuzzy head topped by a flaming hibiscus, waving a reluctant farewell.

We threaded back through the coral reef and were at last out in open water. When I looked back again toward the green shore and towering Owen Stanleys, I saw that a rainstorm was sweeping down out of the mountains. Now it blocked out the shore in a blue mist, and nothing of the mission view remained. The wind tore the hibiscus from my helmet, tossed it high in the air, and dropped it into the foaming wake of the boat. A plane roared low to identify our boat. We were back again in a war for possession of the world.

As the boat sped back, the padre said, "Say, if you have any fishhooks left, I surely would like a couple. I have a line, but hooks are sure scarce."

I had just two, and he was very welcome to them!

15 ARMISTICE AT WAR

November 11, 1943

Only tonight did I have time to realize that this is Armistice Day—celebrated for over twenty-five years as the end of war. What irony! Especially hard to take in the place we are now. We have moved to Hervey Bay, slightly south of Oro proper, and we find the camp site impossible. The mess hall is being built on poles over the water, as there is no room on the forty-five-degree hill behind. We climb the slippery, muddy hill to a slightly flat place where we are pitching our tents.

The whole move, from Australia to the present time, has been poorly managed, poorly planned, and confused. Our incompetent leadership shows up more and more. Not one of our officers had the guts to protest this senseless move to an impossible camp site. The Australian authorities wouldn't even let the natives come over here to work, so we are trying to get things up the hill.

I wonder what is taking place at home now and if they are celebrating this hollow victory of a quarter century ago. What do the thousands of men—now middle-aged—who went through the useless hell of 1918 really think? They probably realize now that their work was hollow mockery. They actually settled nothing, gained no victory. Today we are at it again, but on a scale that makes that war look like a rock fight between street urchins. Why could we today expect that we are fighting for something important? I personally feel that there will come a day when we will be old men looking back on our folly and the waste of our best energies.

At present it seems that we are following the actual front-line troops up the Guinea coast step by step, carrying in supplies and ammunition, bringing back men and officers on various duties. Almost daily we have trips up to the front which is within easy distance for our boats. No doubt we will move in with the push on Rabaul.[15]

We see no end to all this, and most of us think it may even be years before Japan is completely crushed. It has taken almost a year to get up the Guinea coast.

November 13, 1943

Still trying to make a camp out of this hell hole, and there is bitter dissatisfaction among all. The slump in morale is with good reason, but we see no relief from the miserable leadership under which we are forced to work.

This afternoon a group of us took a boat and went out into the bay, turned off the regular channel, and anchored in about eight feet of clear water over a coral and sand bottom. Out there the water is wonderful, and the clean bottom is as interesting as a museum. There were sea slugs, live coral, and a school of little fishes the same brilliant blue as the big butterflies. One man brought up a big sea cucumber, the berchedemere which is much prized by the Chinese as food. Tons of slugs were exported from these waters before the war.

Someone spied the big dorsal fin of a shark, and the cry "shark" emptied the water in such a hurry that the boat seemed to be drawing bodies out like a magnet. Nobody wasted time! That ended the party, but we'd had a good swim and could sit on the boat and look into the interesting water below.

November 15, 1943

On a sudden change of plans Major Bilger was whisked off by the general, possibly never to return to the regiment.[16] One of our companies plus part of Headquarters Unit here is moving out suddenly, presumably to the front. What is left of us will MOVE again across the inlet to the old B Company area. Less than a week here, with heartbreaking work every day! Now it is all useless, and we will pack up to move half a mile. Things look like they are popping, and the regiment may never exist as such again, but will be detachments to here and there.[17]

November 16, 1943

The boat has just pulled out from the wharf taking a dozen or so of our boys to a new destination. They are being transferred to some other outfit and will move off, first to Milne Bay, then probably to the campaign on Bougainville Island.[18] I doubt that we will ever see them again.

Among them was Dotson, and I hated to see him go. We have been friends since Fort Ord, California. He never really got located in this outfit and was pushed from place to place. Also Holdorf helped to give him a push down whenever he could. Maybe Dotson will get a new start now, but I will miss his pleasant conversation when day is done.

November 22, 1943

Since the sixteenth, we have moved again—up a creek through the mangrove swamp and up a steep hill. A winding stairway, cut from the hill and built in with poles, leads from the water to the top of the very high climb. You cannot make the grade without resting on the way up. Once up, the campsite isn't bad. Gushing from the hillside is a large fresh spring which furnishes us with the best water we have had in a long time. There is a good shower below the spring too.

Our Headquarters Company has been split now with some men being transferred on various detachments and some over at Oro Bay proper keeping up our end of things there. Now we have exactly fourteen men here and are camped with Company A, which has barely a hundred men left. Our last full company—Company C—is to go out soon, which will leave the battalion practically nonexistent unless we get in a lot of the men from the States that are arriving by liberty ship. Most of our officers are gone too, and we will probably not get them back. However, anything we get in the trade will be better than what we lost.

Yesterday afternoon Lieutenent Callaway, Major Shaul and I went down to the same village I had previously visited. After finding the place, we landed in a swarm of natives. They were all over the boat at once. I recognized George—the handsome kid who had been most active in helping us on the visit with Padre Newman. I talked with him, as he knows English fairly well. He is one of the brightest of the mission boys and a fine specimen of a native with a bearing much superior to his fellow Fuzzy Wuzzies.

I explained that we had some cans of bully beef and wanted to trade for some fruit. George said that as they had only moved to this site since the war, they had not yet grown any very satisfactory gardens of bananas, pineapples, etc. However, bananas began to appear. We handed out cans of corned beef in return and soon had a pile of bananas.

I went ashore to trade with the women, since I still had several pieces of cloth. They recognized me as the man who had brought needles before. Although they asked for them, I had none. I finally traded for three pieces of tapa cloth—two of them the largest and best I have seen, of a double thickness and beautifully decorated.

The bully beef gone, we boarded our boat. As we left, I threw down some plugs of tobacco for which the natives scrambled in a good-natured, brown mob, then yelled for more.

The boatman set the boat out into deep water, and with the danger of coral reefs past, we relaxed. Major Shaul said, "Hand me a banana," and we all prepared to have our first taste of bananas in some time. But they were not bananas! We had been skinned, and good. I never knew there could be a fruit that looked so much like a banana and tasted like a green gourd. We looked them over carefully and found several kinds of what were apparently wild bananas and only a couple of dozen very small, edible, ordinary bananas.

We had several coconuts, but they turned out to be almost as bad a deal as the bananas. Most were old ones, which had, no doubt, been picked up off the ground. There were several good papayas, one of which I had for breakfast this morning. Of course, the tapa cloth was good, which ended the decent end of the bargain. We felt very much put out at our ignorance of natives and native fruit. Next time we will pinch every banana, and look carefully at every coconut!

We are going into the third day of a New Guinea drouth, and things are suffering terribly. We look for a rain to break it, but now it is clear and hot.

I have been amazed at the number and kinds of parrots seen lately. Yesterday a black palm cockatoo put on quite a performance out here in a tree. His whistle was loud and clear, and he had quite a repertoire. I am sure that with some training he could do just anything—maybe including grand opera.

Finally I completed and mailed about forty Christmas cards to everyone I could think of. Today we got in a lot of official Army "V" letter greetings, but they are so ordinary that I am glad I made my own individual cards.

November 26, 1943

We've spent days getting established in a new camp all over again. Now we are fairly well caught up with the work and are entering a period of comparative quiet. This isolated hill is visited by few of the "big bugs," so we are not bothered by having them rush in with asinine complaints. The general came to the bottom of the hill yesterday, but decided not to make the climb. That hill is worth something after all! He ended up by going to the kitchen, which is built down there on poles over the creek. He gave the cooks hell about everything, as it would have been very "un-general like" to have gone off pleased about anything.

We had an extra fine meal for Thanksgiving—turkey, cranberry jelly, pumpkin pie! All in all, as good a meal as anyone could have gotten in any restaurant in the States, but, of course, not like home. No meals are ever like that. The tables were located on a large flat-topped barge tied up by the kitchen. They were covered with some cloth that came in for target backing—coarse and unbleached, but better than the bare boards. A festive air was given to the tables by polished red apples and small paper cups of colored candies. We still had to eat from our mess kits, which almost ruined the spirit of the dinner, but still it was a meal you wouldn't expect in this place.

No news of what is to become of us, but there is news of big business to come. Apparently the two big companies are to be put into some action on New Britain. General Heavey made them a farewell speech in which he promised that if everything goes right, the whole brigade will be in the Hawaiian Islands by March, then home later. I wonder why a general would make such promises, for few of the men believed what he said. They all know that Heavey has little real control over our movements. If what he said were true, it would be the best news of our lives.

We have all been doing a lot of shooting lately. Cases and cases of ammunition are available. You take what you want and go out and shoot at anything except one another. We had some good shots at white cockatoos, but no one hit any. All of this is in mighty contrast to the time when men were punished for having even one shell in their possession. We look back on that silly training and see that two-thirds of it was a pure waste of time and will never be used in actual operations. I just hope that as more and more instructors are drawn from men who have actually been through this, the training will become more practical and less foolish display.

A box arrived from home—the first in what will be a happy string until, and probably after, Christmas. The most useful items were a pair of khaki bath towels, the first I have seen. Mother always thinks of all the little things I might enjoy.

A combat zone seems to be the most wasteful place on earth, and I have been shocked time after time by the sight. Perhaps it cannot be helped. In fact, at times I know it cannot. We move so fast and so often that each time things are abandoned or thrown away deliberately. Just now, one of our boats came in with a load of new two-by-fours picked up in the bay. Several days ago a barge loaded with lumber sank between the big liberty ship and the shore, and apparently no effort was made to salvage it. Lumber is scarce here, as few of the trees are suitable for milling. Things are dropped while being unloaded from the ships—anything from a gasoline field range to a case of canned goods—and seldom is anything fished up from the bottom. Canned goods that have slightly rusted from salt water are thrown away rather than clean off the rust and use them. Stuff is smashed in unloading on the beach and scattered and wasted in a thousand ways. Most of us are guilty of contributing to this kind of thing—often through necessity—and I blame a lot of it on poor planning.

We came up here with practically all the clothing and equipment we were ever issued, and the barracks bag was so big and heavy that you could barely get up the gangplank with it on your back. Now our bags are getting lighter all the time. Mine is a shadow of its former self, and a lot more will go until I can pick the thing up in one hand and run up the gangplank.

There is little need for the clean khaki uniforms. No one gives a whoop how you look—clean, dirty, ragged—just so you have on a U.S. Army uniform. So when we get out of this Pacific scrap, we will most likely have a pair of G.I. coveralls and a rifle.

November 28, 1943

Another visit to the native village this Sunday. I had made three lamies during the week, trimming blue cloth with a red band across the bottom and up one side to make a snazzy sarong that would make a "belle of the jungle" all smiles. All of this was done with the aid of our ancient—but still good—sewing machine that has been lugged more than sixteen hundred miles, all the way from Cape Cod, Massachusetts. After being pounded around in ships' holds, etc., it always sews again after some working on.

When we landed on the beach, the usual assortment of natives greeted us. To their surprise we did not let the ramp of the boat down, so none of them boarded. I got off the side and went around in front to find what they had to trade. Major Shaul stood in the front of the boat and handed down the things that I traded them. I refused with determined gestures the worthless fruit and bum coconuts by the dozens. Some of the coconuts they brought even had the milk drained out and the eye plugged up again!

The natives soon learned that this time it was going to be an even trade—no cheating on either side. I haggled and argued and had a lot of fun. I ended up with two beautifully decorated bamboo pipes, three fair tapas, one good comb; two excellent, wide, woven bracelets; and a good bottle made from a gourd with a woven grass stopper. An old man happened to have the bottle in his hand as he passed and was pleased to get a fish line and hook for it. One lamie was traded for a woven string bag, the nicest piece of native work I have seen, made of native string in three colors. However, the woman returned and took it back later. Apparently someone else told her she had made a bad trade. I now wish I had offered something additional for it.

I let Major Shaul have his choice of the pipes (he took the one with the best design) and also gave him the three tapas and two bracelets, as he wanted something to send his wife. I netted a pipe, the comb, and the bottle. I don't like to be selfish with the stuff, especially as Shaul makes these trips possible each week, and because the others don't seem to have the knack of getting anything.

We have had a new character transferred into our company because his old company didn't want to take him into action with them. A private named Leonard, who has been court-martialed seven times. I recognized him as the man who—under guard—had scrubbed the floor on the *Moonera* on the way up from Australia. He has had long stockade sentences and has been given every punishment the army can think up, but still remains pretty worthless to everyone including himself. He has been drunk for two days now on "jungle juice" that someone made from coconut juice, canned fruit, raisins, and what not—sometimes with a good dash of canned heat. The man really should be discharged on a mental unfitness clause, for I am sure he is unbalanced.

November 29, 1943

Last night four bottles of the officers' gin disappeared from their tent. They get a regular supply of it, although lately they have drunk little, as this climate knocks a drinker for a loop. They were very mad, but also fairly helpless, for no one could be turned in for any official action for taking liquor that really isn't supposed to be here anyway. I have no sympathy for the officers in their loss, for they should not have liquor any more than the men. For those men who drink, it is a slap in the face to see the stuff brought in right under their noses when they can't have it. I doubt if anyone will be caught, for, most likely, whoever it was will have sense enough to drink only a little at a time and not get drunk. Leonard definitely didn't get it. What he drank was pure (if there is such a thing) jungle juice.

For the first time since leaving Australia, we had an iced drink—very cold orangeade made from ice water brought from the liberty ship in the bay. It was a treat! I don't know why an ice plant has not been erected at Oro Bay, because anything can be built in this army if it is needed or wanted by the right people.

16 Before Christmas

December 4, 1943

Nothing breaks, and we sit here with very little to do. Our last big company is still standing by awaiting the "go" signal for whatever action they are scheduled to take part in. (Rumor is now Madang, New Guinea.) The bay is full of ships of all kinds that seem to be standing by too, and from up the coast comes the news that ships are anchored all along the way. We have never had more than four or five at one time before. Now there are twenty in Oro Bay itself. But still we know nothing.[19]

Each afternoon there is shooting on the hill above camp where a range of sorts has been set up. We shoot across a small valley at practically anything that can be seen. One of the favorite sports is shooting at the parrots that come by late each afternoon. Someone killed one late yesterday—a happy little fellow with orange beak, a black cap on his very red head, green and yellow wings, brilliant red breast shading into rich purple. He was so beautiful that I resolved to shoot at no more parrots. This particular one was not listed in the book on Australian and New Guinea birds and is probably of an unknown and unrecorded species of which there must be thousands in this country.

Have had time to make three new lamies this week, two by using a clean mattress cover that yielded two nice pieces of cloth which I bound around the edges with blue. Then I stenciled large yellow flowers across the bottom with bright yellow boat paint that happened to be here. The other is blue with rose butterflies across the bottom, done with some red waterproof drawing ink we have here. It presents a striking effect even though it is slightly unnatural looking to a native, I imagine. My trade goods of fish lines, needles and fishhooks have practically disappeared, and so, until some arrive from home, I must improvise something that can be traded.

Today I received a box from Quirl and Ruth, full of small, bright packages which I shall not open until Christmas. We now have six men in our tent. (None of the old tent group is left except Currie and me. Estadt is over at Oro Bay with regimental headquarters. Dotson was transferred and went off with B Company.) One of the four fellows now in my tent, Kevin Coonerty of California, received a small Christmas tree in sections. He is keeping it in order that we may have a tree in our tent. We are all keeping most of our packages and will have a party Christmas Eve. Now we just hope we are not moved before then.

December 5, 1943

Time for another weekly visit to the native village. Major Shaul didn't go but told me to take charge of the trip and go wherever I wanted to. He said the boat would be at the wharf at 1:30 p.m. About a dozen fellows went, and four of these had the intention of trading. The others were simply out to see the sights.

I decided to try the village further up the bay, because we had not been there at all. As we neared its shore, we could see that it was considerably larger than the other village, with a church and several large houses, all of typical grass roof and pole construction. As we landed on the beach, we saw several Australian soldiers on the porch of the large house directly in front of us. The natives came up the beach, and three of the Aussies also came out. While we were lowering the ramp of the boat, the Aussies met the natives and issued a few stern commands we could not hear above the noise of the surf and the boat. However, as soon as we stepped off the boat, we knew what they had been told.

The frost was thick enough to cut. We had been "frozen" before we started. The Aussies were friendly enough and told us they were stationed here with an Air Warning group of a few men. Then they went back to their porch and left us with the natives. It was easy to see that they had been told to let us alone, but a few showed willingness to talk with what few words they could make us understand.

I finally got one young woman interested in a bright lamie and traded it to her for the largest and finest tapa cloth I have yet seen. That was the only piece of anything secured there. We wanted some fruit, but got none. One woman said she might trade some limes for some bully beef, which, of course, we didn't have.

Seeing that the case was pretty hopeless, finally I said, "Crank her up!" The boatmen started the engine, and all climbed aboard. We left the natives in the hands of their Australian overseers.

Everyone was so disappointed that I decided to risk being late for supper and go by the village we were acquainted with. We did, and everyone had a good time. I nearly broke up the party by my sharp bargaining with a man who called himself the village "police boy." Whether or not he was actually one of the appointed police boys who are supposed to keep the village more or less in hand, I never knew. Anyway, he wanted one of my stenciled lamies badly and took me to his hut, where he unrolled a big package of tapa cloth. "I'll take two good big ones for it," I told him. So he and his wife finally decided on two pieces which were only fair and not "good big ones" either, but were interesting in design. I refused them, and the ruckus started.

"You say two!" he said."I say two BIG ones," I responded. "You no trade but you say two for trade!" Evidently we were at odds. The native rushed out into the center of the village shouting, "There trouble here! No more trade! No trade, trouble here!" From somewhere in his brief clothing he produced an army whistle and blew it loudly.

"Get on boat and go!" he cried. "No trade! No come back. We not friends."

I could see that the party was being ruined and fast, so I decided it was time to come down a peg and keep peace. "Let's trade and be friends," I told him.

"Good," he said and immediately held out his hand, which I shook vigorously. The trade was made, and all was quiet again on the village front.

The other natives smiled, for they understood, as I did, that this was his way of driving a bargain. I was glad to settle it, but still I had somewhat the feeling of the week before when I bit into what I thought was a banana.

We wandered around the village to see what could be found at the various houses in the way of something for which to trade. That was when I got dog bit! One of the numerous half-wild dogs darted out silently and fixed himself on my leg. He was a small pup, and my clothing was thick and stout, so I ended the skirmish with two small bruises and no broken skin, for which I was thankful. The natives took a stick and whopped the dog good for his ill manners. These dogs look like stunted dingoes and are definitely some sort of native wild dog.

Down the "main street" of the village I came upon several very old men and women who never stirred from their mats, but looked on the proceedings placidly. I gave each one cigarettes and matches, which they seemed to appreciate. I finally secured six tapas, a woven string bag (an old used one, but a good example of this type of work) which is used to carry articles and when not in use is worn on the head like a snood. These native women are probably the inventors of this head gear, for I am sure they were wearing it long centuries before our women came on the horizon.

An old woman was preparing a meal of taro root and wild sweet potatoes. Among the utensils by her side was an old, coconut shell bowl—polished and black as ebony with age. Its rim carried a worn design. I asked her to trade it for the blue lamie with the rose butterflies. She hesitated, but finally took the bowl to a small boy, talked with him, and evidently reached an agreement, for the trade was made. I gathered that the bowl was the boy's eating bowl, and the old lady (probably his grandmother) showed love and thoughtfulness by consulting him about it.

Later a boy traded me a beautifully carved paddle used for putting lime from the gourd bottle into the mouth with betelnut. It is an old paddle of jet black, hard wood, worn smooth from much use. To me these worn things represent real living and evidence of the way of life of these simple people. Not flashy souvenirs, but as real as trees and earth.

Several of the women had half-finished, woven bags and indicated they would have the work finished by next week, for they have now gathered that we come once a week.

We did stay out beyond supper time, but the cooks had remembered we were gone and had saved us some turkey, mince pie, etc. We had all donated money to buy this turkey and fresh American mincemeat from one of the ships in the bay. Those items definitely were not among our issued rations.

While taking a shower I talked with Marvin Woods, mentioned before as the handsome redhead who is so handy with his fists. He is again up for court martial on a charge of which he says he is innocent. Some officer at Buna charges him with failure to move a boat when told to do so. Marvin says, "How could I move the damn thing when the engine wouldn't start?" As usual I feel our officers are too quick to charge men with just anything if they feel a man has the least resentment of them. It is kind of a balm for hurt feelings when a man shows he does not worship little gold bars. Those wearing the little bars feel themselves to be head and shoulders above those without them.

Because Woods has a bad reputation, he is no doubt suffering from just that. Punishing him further would be an officer's special delight. He was pretty discouraged about the whole thing and talked frankly to me about it when he found that I was sincerely interested. He is supposed to be tough, but he is not, and I felt sorry for him as he talked to me with a catch in his throat like a small hurt boy. I knew I could not help him and told him so, but I tried to show him that he had to take things and take and take and take in this crude army set-up. I advised him to keep his eye on the time when he would be out of it.

Somewhere far back in the past he has had something that threw him off the track. He is a clean-cut, handsome kid of about twenty-three, never drinks or smokes, and is far from the usual depraved characters you usually associate with such a reputation in the army. You feel pretty helpless in the face of someone like that whom you can't possibly help. My conclusion is that the army never really tries to understand anyone, for I fully believe that with a little understanding and guidance, Woods would be a splendid member of any group.

December 7, 1943

I don't know what they call this day in the States—Pearl Harbor Day, I guess. It still remains the greatest naval defeat of this war, and perhaps the reason we are now starting on our third year of war. No one mentioned it here today. It seems a faraway thing now.

December 18, 1943

Things have popped in the last week. We have received orders to organize for an assault mission. Practically all of headquarters has been transferred to reinforce C Company. I went too. Major Shaul is in charge of the outfit, and I will go with him and attempt to keep the records of the trip. We had last-minute meetings discussing which part of the tip of New Britain we were to land on. Discussed conditions and probable resistance.

We were to leave at nine this morning, but received orders last night that it was called off until Tuesday, December 21. Now we are uncertain about the whole thing. Our B Company made the initial landing that started the New Britain campaign and the big drive to Rabaul. No doubt we will land soon enough!

December 24, 1943

Christmas Eve finds us at Finschhafen, New Guinea, making preparations for the landing on Cape Gloucester, New Britain. It is now quiet with only the occasional sound of artillery from Statleburg Ridge where the enemy is being steadily driven back. Statleburg rises across the small harbor and overlooks all of the area. It has changed hands twice, but now seems to be definitely ours.

We are camped on a long peninsula on the south "arm" encircling this excellent and beautiful Finschhafen Harbor. There are thousands of coconut palms here, planted in neat rows but evidently unattended—the nuts ungathered since the war began here more than two years ago. The ground is covered with a thick head-high growth of coconut seedlings and millions of nuts, soft and rotting. In places the trees have been shot off, and at some spots whole groves are shredded from gunfire. Only bright shrubs and flowers show where once stood the buildings of Finschhafen Mission.

In the inlet running into the small end of the harbor two sunken Japanese ships can be seen—their masts and stacks sticking out of the water, still covered with the palm leaves which were tied on all parts of the ship in a vain effort at camouflage.

The water is the color of melted turquoise and jade. The palms wave in a gentle breeze, and all seems as beautiful and quiet as though no fierce battle had ever raged over it. Yesterday I went swimming above the living coral beds where there were amazing fishes and plants—a whole fairyland world in crystal water.

From all accounts we will leave tomorrow or the twenty-sixth. I have often wondered just what I would feel like before going into action, but now that the time is at hand, I feel little different than usual. Some of our B Company boys didn't come back. One was buried yesterday out on the point here. We are constantly reminded by such things that someone has to die as each victory is won. I suppose every soldier thinks of such things before going up, but few speak of it.

I might be among the missing, but it is only human to wish to survive. If I do not, I sincerely feel that my going will be no real calamity to humanity. I am just a small part of what goes on in this big world. I have had a share of living and have relished every minute of it. No one should feel unhappy if I do not return, for I will sink back into the friendly earth and become a part of the blue of tropic waters and the breeze in the palms—a part of the white clouds above green mountains. I will be freed into all the beauty of the earth, where now I am limited to being a sordid mortal. That's all I ask, and I will give up the "golden streets" for that.

Tonight I lighted a candle by the shore as I had promised everyone on my Christmas cards. There was little thought of Christmas anywhere today.

17 A New Year

January 1, 1944

The first day of the new year found the skies clearing and the sea calm. A patrol torpedo boat came in and took the four prisoners away to a prison camp, probably in Australia. I went up around the line and found it greatly strengthened after the attack. More guns, more barbed wire, and more mining of the jungle beyond the cleared space. For a hundred feet or more in front of the line, every tree, bush, and blade of grass had been cleared away and carried off, forming a "no man's land." The place where the battle had taken place was cleared. The eighty Japs had been buried in holes blown by dynamite. They had been buried where they fell right in front of the gun emplacement. After three days, they were beginning to push up the ground, and the stench was terrible.

While I was up on the hill a shell whistled overhead, and everyone ducked for cover. It landed out in the ocean beyond the boats. Evidently the Japanese from Sag Sag locality had set up a big gun. No doubt the stragglers of the defeated force had contacted the Sag Sag group by now and spread the news to them. Because of the intervening hills, the gun could not be depressed enough to drop shells into the line of the camp, but the boats could be seen and shelled. Shell after shell burst harmlessly in the water.

Finally the radio jeep was driven onto a barge and taken out into the bay where the bursts from the gun could be seen. They radioed directions and our 75s opened up. That silenced the enemy gun, and as long as we were there, no more shells came our way.

January 2, 1944

The second of January dawned bright and sunshiny. We dried blankets, washed clothes, and enjoyed the sun. During the night another patrol torpedo boat had brought some supplies and a sack of mail. I got letters from Mother, Ruth, Miss Greenwood, and Ridgley. In Mother's letter was a short note from Marie DeVille wanting to know my address. I had tried for months to locate her. Naturally the mail was cheering.

A patrol of the Fifth Marines arrived. They had walked from Borgen Bay down the coast and reported they had found few enemy soldiers. A whole defense line had been abandoned in a hurry; Jap guns, supplies, etc., were still in place. The guns were destroyed and the supply dumps burned. They found new Japanese clothing and equipment—even hundreds of pairs of new socks, but none could be used because they were so small. The raincoats looked like children's and wouldn't reach to the knees of a marine, so all the supplies were useless to us.

January 3, 1944

On the third of January our 75s bombarded Sag Sag, three miles to the south, with high explosives and incendiary shells, as it was suspected that the enemy was still there. Later a patrol went down and found the place completely destroyed by accurate hits.

The prisoners' pen was occupied by a marine under guard, but I did not have time to find out why.

January 4, 1944

The fourth day was bright and clear and uneventful. Three more Japanese soldiers were killed near Sag Sag. They were apparently hungry and were opening coconuts. Rain blew in from the sea later in the day, and again during the night I found myself lying in a puddle of water.

January 5, 1944

On the morning of the fifth, the sea reached a climax of cold fury. It was a roaring, heaving, gray-green monster pounding furiously at the low bank and occasionally breaking over it into the road. In all our roving by the oceans from Cape Cod to here, I have never seen such a mad sea. The huge swells came shoreward and broke into twelve-foot waves that shook the earth when they hit. Boats came down from Borgen Bay, but landing was impossible.

The marine prisoner spent the night without shelter, the ocean spray covering him as it came flying in. He had been put in the stinking, muddy pen and sat on the same dirty burlap used by the Japanese prisoners.[20] Of all the atrocious things I had seen of war, this hit a new low. There were dozens of places the boy could have been kept, and besides, where would he go if he got loose? After all, he was an American soldier. He was nineteen and a volunteer, accused of sleeping on guard. Maybe he did, and maybe he didn't, and maybe his is a heinous crime according to army law. But there is an end to human endurance, and this fellow had been on the front line on constant alert since we arrived—poor and scarce food, mud, rain, and enemy fire.

I lost a lot of faith in men right there and saw how lightly one man regards another when power is extended too far. The colonel of this outfit held that power and used it in the most disgraceful way I have yet seen in this army!

Three enemy soldiers were killed by patrols on this date.

January 6, 1944

The sixth brought a calm sea, but more rain. More mail had come in during the night, and I got several letters. One from Mother contained a clipping about the recent exhibit of the Brownwood Art Association which gave me a very complimentary paragraph on "Dawn by the Ack Ack Shack," the only painting I have ever done with a military subject and the last one done before I sailed.

There was a "red alert" on the night of the sixth, and our group rushed off to help in case of an attack, but we sat in the mud behind the lines until morning and nothing happened. It turned out that the marines were beginning to "see things" and had fired on a group of stumps. We had sat all night waiting for the stumps to attack. We stumbled in and fell into our beds and slept until about 8:00.

January 7, 1944

The seventh saw the marines moving their ammunition dumps and vehicles. Our boats were loading them. The sea was still heavy, and the boats had difficulty in landing, but the day was bright and sunny. It had been thirteen days since I last wrote a letter to anyone. Although I had tried to find out about getting mail out, I had no luck. Apparently no effort was made by anyone to have mail sent out on the patrol torpedo boats that came in.

A marine lieutenant was wounded by a native at Tauali village. Probably in the pay of the enemy, the native had used a Japanese rifle. I did not learn if any natives were killed, but have an idea they must have been. Anyway the village was burned to the ground by the marines after the incident.

January 8, 1944

The eighth was clear again, and most of the equipment was moved out. We are supposed to leave in a day or so, as the airstrips are safely in our hands at Borgen Bay, and no Japanese troops got by us to reinforce the defeated ones.

Today one of the fellows showed me a poem he had with him called "When I Come Home." Evidently written by a soldier to his wife or sweetheart (I wish I knew who wrote it), it was as beautiful as anything I had come across in a long while. I did not think of any one person when I read it, but of all the friends who have written me.

When I come home, I'll bring my precious dreams,
And you and I will take them one by one
And blend them with the beauty of the hills,
The song of birds, the largeness of the sun.
Then I'll forget the horrors I have known
In this foul place where death alone holds sway,
And you will teach my anguished heart to sing
A song of hope, when I come home someday.

Cling to your dreams, for peace will come again
In shining robes across the eastern sky.
The world will watch the reddening of a dawn
When fate reprieves the millions marked to die,
When Satan, wearied of his hymn of hate,
Calls back the bestial sons of Cain.
When justice walks unchallenged on the earth,
God willing, sweetheart, I'll come home again.

On the night of the eighth, two air alerts were sounded as a single Japanese plane sped high over the coastline. Later there was the dull thud of bombs up the coast, and soon the plane raced back down. He had been to Yellow Beach at Borgen and given our friends there a basket of eggs. Later we learned that five men were slightly injured by flying shrapnel.

January 9, 1944

On the ninth three natives were caught in Cimaroo village as they came down from the hills to gather coconuts at this deserted place. They were questioned by the Australian missionary (now a lieutenant of the Australian Army) who came with us. He had been a missionary at Sag Sag for many years, and so proved especially useful on this mission. Two of the natives were kept in the Japanese pen, but the other was released and told that if he did not come back by noon of the next day, his two friends would be shot. There was great wailing at this announcement, but the native set out at once.

January 10, 1944

On the tenth I saw the missionary out talking with the two natives in the pen and went over and chatted with him. He knew the natives, he said, and was getting quite a lot of information from them. Evidently they had suffered since his leaving, as the Japanese had taken their women, their villages, and their gardens. This particular bunch had been driven out and had moved up farther on Mount Tauali. The Japanese followed, and finally the natives were more than halfway up the sixty-five-hundred foot mountain. They were hungry and thin, but apparently only two or three of them had gone over to the Japanese way of thinking and offered to fight the whites.

During our conversation the missionary told me the story of the two islands we could see just off the coast. The nearest one was a green peak four thousand feet high and several miles long; the second and farthermost appeared as only a low shape almost down to sea level. Five years ago they were the same size. Without warning the island erupted one night and sank into the sea. Another island on the north of New Britain had done the same thing.

January 11, 1944

The eleventh brought rain again, and we sloshed around in it to load the last of our things. We prepared to leave for Yellow Beach at Borgen Bay. One of the last two boats turned sideways and broached on the beach. It looked impossible to get off, especially with no other boats to help. Most of the load of supplies was transferred to the one remaining boat, and all got on it. Someone on lookout spotted enemy soldiers on the beach, and since we had no idea of how many of them to expect, the boat was blown up to keep it out of their hands. We left with our machine guns spitting at the Japs. They were welcome to that hell hole!

The ride up was rough, and again I was thankful that I do not get seasick. On the way we got a better view of the mountain that is the sister peak to Mount Tauali. Though not as high, on its side this one has an active volcano which sends up clouds of steam from its crater. As far as I know, it has not erupted in historic times, but is content to boil and steam from its high perch.

Yellow Beach presented a sight of utter destruction. On the twenty-sixth of December at the some hour we landed at Cape Glocester, this beach was hit. Two destroyers, two cruisers, two Australian cruisers, and various other naval craft shelled this beach while planes rained bombs from the skies. For approximately the depth of two city blocks back from the shore, not a leaf remained on a tree in what had once been dense jungle. Most of the tree limbs had been shot off, and every tree trunk was torn from top to bottom by cannon shells and shrapnel. Few of the estimated fifteen hundred Japanese had stayed through that hell of flying steel, but took to the hills instead. Some had to be dug out of pillboxes with a bulldozer, but all had been dealt with in short order.

We were to camp a couple of miles down the beach, right beside the sea in what looked to be a pleasant spot beneath huge trees. The place had the disadvantage of always catching the northwest wind which tore at everything day and night.

January 13, 1944

On the twelfth we began making camp there, and on the thirteenth I accidentally injured myself for the first time in many, many months. Another fellow and I were carrying a large green log to be used in building a kitchen, when I slipped on a muddy spot and fell with the log on my arm and shoulder. I got up and decided nothing was broken, but later in the day it became so painful that I went to the doctor. He hardly looked at it and assured me it would be all right, suggesting I put it in a sling to ease the pain.

That same afternoon I received the news that I was to go back to New Guinea with the group leaving the next day—not because of my shoulder, but because I was to return with a number of people whose work was done for the time. The shoulder was painful all night, and I slept very little, all of which did not keep me from being up early and ready to leave.

January 14, 1944

On the fourteenth we boarded the LST,[21] the largest of the boats that land on a beach. As we boarded, a mail truck drove off. There went our mail! Now it would have to be sent back to Guinea, thus delaying it longer.

There were many wounded on the big boat, as the battle for Hill 660 was in full swing up behind the beach. A ship's doctor mistook me for one of the wounded when he saw the arm in a sling and said I was supposed to be down in the hospital with the rest. The mess sergeant also decided I was one of the casualties being taken back and refused to let me eat with my group. "You eat at 7:30. Then you don't have all these fellows jostling you around." I couldn't persuade him and waited until 7:30. I was glad I did! "Us wounded" had bacon and eggs instead of the much less attractive breakfast eaten by the hearty chaps. That night we slept well on the canvas bunks and were up early. The sea was calm, and sunrise was beautiful. It usually is over the sea, and I never tire of seeing this splendor come up out of the far horizon.

Guinea was now on our right, and we were again passing enemy-held territory, but any strength the Japanese may have had in this area seemed to have been broken. As we stood gazing over the rail, a Japanese soldier floated by right under us—very dead, but still clothed in his wrap leggings. This told us he was not an aviator, but most likely a soldier who had been shot on the mainland and carried here by the current.

We sailed into Dredga Harbor, the same spot from which we had put out. A detachment of our men were at Finschhafen still, so we got a truck and went up the newly made road ten miles or so to Finschhafen. The group was scheduled to go back to Hervey Bay, but Major Bilger was here and asked me to stay, as he had reports of the New Britain action that he wanted me to do. I supposed my arm would be well in a few days, until which time I intended to do exactly nothing. I went back to Dredga Harbor to get the equipment I had left there and spent the night. So this was the spot I happened to be when I began writing this account of the mission.

18 In New Guinea

January 16, 1944

A new year, and this morning I sit in a quiet coconut grove by the sea at Dredga Harbor, New Guinea. Red dawn paints the palms with soft splendor. Now and then there is the soft thud of a huge blossom falling from the giant putat trees. As a sort of reprieve from hell, I am back in New Guinea again after twenty-three days of the New Britain invasion. I have had no breakfast, but that is a small thing after days of no food, no water, no dry clothes, and the things that make up the inconveniences of war.

As I look over the notes I put down each day of that living hell, I wonder that my brain had enough will power to record a fact, and I was determined that it should be *fact*. Nevertheless, for the first time in my life I was getting the opportunity to see for myself just what material our newsmen used in their often too colorful and evasive accounts.

We left Finschhafen on December 25, and came down the coast to Dredga Harbor to load on the large infantry-carrying ships for the invasion landing. Christmas Day was one of no holiday joy, and the Christmas dinner consisted of a can of beans. We were crowded on the ship, and the convoy of thirty-three ships and many small landing barges set off up the Guinea coast. All afternoon we steamed by a green coastline, all of it occupied by the enemy.

I wondered that we could go by all this territory with such an important invasion convoy without opposition of any kind. Apparently the Japanese are short on planes.[22] Night settled over the convoy, and later we turned sharply to the east to cross to Cape Gloucester. The night was calm, and the marines we were carrying were singing on deck. They were the famous First Division that made history on Guadalcanal, and seventy-five percent of them were the original veterans of that campaign. They were big and tough and mad, all of which helps when you have to land on enemy territory. We couldn't have gotten with any group which knows any more from actual experience.

The attack we were making presented itself as an interesting military maneuver. One unit of our Amphibians, along with a large unit of cavalry-infantry, had landed two weeks before on Arawe, sixty miles below Borgen Bay airfield. Now one group of this invasion convoy was to take a beach-head at Borgen Bay, while the group I was in was to land on Green Beach between Borgen Bay and Arawe about fifteen miles south of Borgen. My outfit was to hold the coastal beach head and prevent any Japanese from coming up from Sag Sag to reinforce those at the airfield and also prevent any of those from the airfield from getting away when they were driven back from Borgen Bay. We were taking in fourteen hundred marines in our landing boats to Green Beach.

The dawn of the twenty-sixth found our portion of the convoy off New Britain. The huge gray shape of Mount Tauali rose 6,500 feet into the hazy air directly ahead. Somewhere at its foot we were to land on a small beach, and what we would find there we were not sure at all. As we steamed towards shore, I saw the destroyers making for points marked for fire. Our smaller landing barges came alongside the infantry ship, and we loaded in, packs on our backs, rifles in hand. After leaving the ship, I was determined to see the show, so I climbed up on some equipment in the barge.

The destroyers had turned their sterns to the shore and were shelling the beach. Each salvo burst from the huge guns in a solid sheet of flame. Now one destroyer raced down the shore and again commenced firing; it would be shelling Sag Sag to the south of our beach. Another was shelling Cimaroo to the north, and the rocket ships were sending rockets into the beach, thundering destruction. A flight of planes swooped low, and each unloaded its bombs. That place was fast becoming a hot spot.

Smoke and dust rose from the shore and made it difficult to see clearly. The shelling ended, and our boats headed for the beach in groups of four, each group landing three minutes apart. I was in the second group, but that was small comfort, as any real action wouldn't even get started in three minutes.

Anyway the Japanese have a habit of letting the first boats get safely unloaded before they open up. As we neared the beach, the first wave landed and made off into the jungle. Before we hit, an amber flare went up as a signal that all was well. It was a welcome sight, but no assurance that it would stay well for any length of time.

We hit the beach with a bump, the ramp came down with a bang, and off rushed the marines. I was in the rear of the boat and among the last to leave. On shore the marines began to dig in. Dirt flew in all directions, and any group of seasoned gophers would have been green with envy. I stood looking around and probably looked pretty silly. But, strangely enough, I was not scared in the sense that word is usually taken. Maybe I had not been in the spots the marines had been and was plain dumb. Anyway, my calmness surprised me, and throughout the stay there, I do not remember ever being thoroughly frightened.

As the marines spread out, they discovered no enemy soldiers, which was somewhat of a disappointment to most of them. My group gathered in the jungle near the shore, and all started to dig foxholes.

Most of the day was spent getting ready for the night by completing the foxholes and covering them with logs and dirt. Marine patrols went as far as Tauali to the south and Cimaroo to the north, and at both places they found evidence that Japanese patrols had been occupying the villages.

At Cimaroo nine packs were found, along with hastily abandoned equipment, as if the first shelling of the beach had sent the owners into the hills. Each of the packs contained a Japanese flag, and the marines were pleased with these interesting souvenirs. Evidently each soldier is given a flag before he leaves his homeland, and his friends and relatives autograph it. The flags are of heavy, white silk with the brilliant orange-red circle in the center. The autographs are in black ink in Japanese characters. Usually the flag is tied around the waist of the soldier in combat.

That day we had little to eat, but did manage to get some cans of meat and beans from the beach. The night was clear, so I slept on the ground by my foxhole. Nothing happened all night; in fact, things were unusually quiet.

The morning of the twenty-seventh dawned gray and soon turned to rain. The sea began to heave and lash the shore. All day the rain fell with only short periods between downpours. I managed to get around enough to find just what territory we occupied. The beach on which we landed was of black volcanic sand and only about ten feet wide at low tide. At high tide the water beat against a low bank of reddish, sandy clay perhaps six feet high. Then the jungle stretched for about two hundred feet along a flat shelf in back of which rose an almost perpendicular bluff about seventy-five feet high.

We were camped along this flat shelf by the sea, and a defense line was prepared to run from the extreme end of the beach up in a half-moon and down again to the sea at the other end of the beach, probably half a mile or more in all. This placed the center of the line directly behind our own group and about a hundred yards beyond the top of the bluff. Even so short a distance from the sea as the hill above the bluff, the country was extremely rough, and it was a tremendous task for the marines to carry up guns and ammunition.

About noon a marine private came in with two long samurai swords. He had killed a Japanese captain and a major who had apparently been scouting the region when he spotted them. He shot one dead. The other ran behind a tree, then made the mistake of sticking his head out to see where the shot came from. Each Japanese officer carries one of these samurai swords which is a family affair handed down from generation to generation. Very long, with a two-handed grip, some of these swords are inlaid with gold and jewels, and one marine told me that his buddy had sold one on Guadalcanal for a thousand dollars, but that it was probably worth more from the amount of jewels in the handle. However, the two swords brought in were not so fancy. Marines have been hacked to death by these swords. On this date, one marine failed to return with his patrol and was feared lost.

The twenty-eighth found no relief from the heavy rain and heavy sea, and the place was fast becoming a quagmire of stinking black mud. I built myself a native-style hut large enough to sleep in. It was merely a platform covered with small poles and a roof made by stretching my poncho on a pole frame over it. There was no string or rope to tie the poles together, so I found a tapa cloth tree and skinned the tough bark to use for binding. It is remarkable how strong a frame can be made with this bark alone. The contraption didn't look like much, but it was dry, at least, and kept my equipment off the ground.

The lost marine was found during the day. He had been bayoneted several times, and his equipment and shoes taken. The marines were fighting mad, and I doubted that anyone would escape death if caught by them.

At 3:00 p.m. a general alarm was sounded as the guns to the south began to chatter. An enemy patrol had approached the line, evidently ignorant of its existence, and were fired upon. Several were killed, and the rest fled in wild confusion.

Still it rained on the twenty-ninth, and the mud deepened. A bulldozer had cleared a road between our headquarters and the beach, and it already had ruts eighteen inches deep.

Sometime since arriving here, I had quietly acquired a strange disregard for things—complete apathy, as complete as any such state of mind could be—a difficult thing to describe, but very real. Maybe it accounted for my not being nervous, not minding the rain nor being wet through day and night. We were never dry! The rain blew in on the blankets, but you just crawled in the wet covers and lay there—if, indeed, you got a chance to do that. Being shot at didn't seem to be especially alarming to me, and I could stand guard for hours in the rain without feeling any special discomfort. In fact, I had ceased to feel anything at all. One day just telescoped into another.

On the night of the twenty-ninth I was in my cozy, wet blanket when the wind began to howl and the rain to fall harder. The storm grew in intensity until it approached hurricane strength. The wind screamed in from the sea, and the surf roared against the bank. I wondered what we were in for and if there was such a thing as getting blown right up Mount Tauali or something as bad. After some time the wind calmed, but at the same time, trouble started on the line above us.

Machine guns broke loose in savage chatter; mortars began firing; rifles cracked. The 81-mm mortars began firing from down where we were, dropping shells into the space in front of our lines. Each burst shook the earth.

The enemy had slipped in, cut the few strands of barbed wire, and charged along a small ridge that led directly into the center of our defense line. The battle raged, and soon snipers slipped through and ranged themselves on the bluff above us—four of them. They sniped the rest of the night, their 25-caliber riflės cracking regularly and their bullets whizzing by.

I did not even get up. Somehow it didn't seem important that I make any effort to move. The marine colonel had ordered the Amphibian group to stay off the front line, so there was nothing for us to do but wait. The snipers were lousy shots, and during the whole night of their shooting did not hit a single person, although hundreds of people were there with tons of ammunition and equipment.

It was as dark as wet black velvet, but our boys sent up dozens of brilliant flares to light up the whole countryside. Any sniper should have had time to pick a target in that light, and there is still no explanation for their complete failure to do so. Towards morning the shooting ceased. The remnants of the Japanese force had fled. Wounded marines began to come by on litters, and we learned that six had been killed.

The scene of the battle was astonishing, and a year ago would have been quite a shock to me. The enemy had charged a narrow section of the line, not more than fifty feet wide, which strangely enough was the strongest point with machine guns and sandbagged dugouts. More than eighty Japanese soldiers lay scattered over the slope in poses of death and various degrees of mutilation from bullets, mortar fire, and hand grenades. It was not a pretty sight, and the smell of the dead permeated the air, making it more terrible.

By daylight the marines were out in the battle areas looking over their opponents, and I found that any atrocity the Japanese commit can be matched by Americans. We have learned to be more atrocious in self-defense, and in this case the losses were more than twenty to one. Our marines are Japanese fighters of long experience and long memories. Wounded soldiers simply had their throats slit by the long knives carried by every marine raider. I watched them and knew that I, too, could have done the same without feeling. Two Japanese who had slight wounds (leg injuries and a toe blown off) were brought down for questioning and put under guard in the hospital tents. Three marines went up on the bluff to hunt the four snipers, found one in a tree and riddled him with tommy guns when he fired at them, caught the other three and came dragging them down the hill by their belts. They were not exactly yellow in color, but a sickly, putty color. A marine officer was along with us as interpreter. He spoke and wrote Japanese with ease and began questioning the prisoners.

They told all they knew readily, and it was learned that approximately a hundred thirty-five men had taken part in the night's attack, which left about fifty still at large. This small force had been sent down from Borgen Bay air strip to fortify this very beach against such a landing as we had made four days earlier, but they arrived after we had landed. Instead of attacking us then, they sat for four days and watched the marines dig in. An attack by them that first day or night would have caused us serious losses and maybe more, but again they failed to follow up an advantage in their favor.

The afternoon of the thirtieth came, and the six Americans were to be buried. As they were carried by, I felt sick for the first time. The powerful words of Robert Service came to me:

Don't cheer, damn you! Don't cheer! Silence!
Your bitterest tear is fulsomely sweet today. . . .
Down on your knees and pray.

This is what he spoke of as he admonished the crowds not to cheer as the boys marched away.

Send to the glut of the guns
Bravest and best of your sons.

These were some of the bravest and best who were laughing only yesterday.

What shall the harvest be?
Unborn of unborn will see.

Yes, it will be two generations before we shall know if they died for a vain hope, as their fathers had done twenty-five years before. I saw cold death marching by that day—I hope I do not stand by that procession again.

The bodies were carried out beyond the lines at the north beach and on to prepared graves in a row beneath tall coconut palms. The sun came out briefly and flecked the ground with light and shadow as each one was put away. Each broken body was wrapped in canvas and khaki tent shelters. Even then the blood oozed out as they were put into the narrow graves. There were no ropes to lower them, so they were simply dropped when they could be lowered no further by hand. One grave was a little short for a tall man; someone took his foot and pushed the body down to the bottom. A short service was held, and the dirt thudded in on the still forms.

I thought, "How unimportant where we lie! How futile the careful record of who occupies Number One grave and Number Two." They have finished with their human clay, and it is ready to return again into the scheme of time.

Late on this day, the heavy sea caught an incoming barge and slapped it upon the beach. No amount of towing and work would remove it, and the sea had claimed another ship—sixteen thousand dollars worth of wood and metal for Davey Jones. The marines lost one of their Amphibian tanks today, too, in practically the same way.

The thirty-first, New Year's Eve, found the sea calmer and the sky bright, but not clear. No rain fell, which was a relief. The three prisoners were getting a home at last—a small pen of barbed wire built around three trees. By now, the prisoners all had names. There were: "Duck Soup," so called because he was captured so easily; "Glamour Pants," because of the odd pajama-like pants he had on (apparently he had been wearing them under his uniform and had now discarded his khaki trousers); and "Joe Jerk," who spoke a little broken English and seemed to be overcome with gratitude for his capture. He smiled at everyone and bowed. No one but a jerk could be that dumb!

The pen was right across the trail from our headquarters, so we were able to observe the prisoners for days. The two injured ones in the hospital met an unexpected and sudden death. A marine guarded them the first night after their capture, and sometime in the night there were two shots. The only explanation was, "One sat up in bed and I shot him. The other sat up when the shot was fired, and I shot him." The marine colonel's comment was, "Now you will have to get rid of them." They were laid outside until morning.

A medical private told me, "I looked outside this morning and there were the two dead Japs right outside by my cot. One had two nice gold teeth, so I decided to get them, but when I returned after breakfast, another guy had a trench pick and was picking them out. I didn't get my gold teeth!" The marine who shot the prisoners got one of our boats to haul them out to sea. There they were dumped with rocks on their necks to weight them down. As they sank, the marine emptied his pistol at them.

On the afternoon of the thirty-first a Japanese captain surrendered by walking into our lines with a white flag. It was an unusual occurrence, indeed. Trickery was suspected, but apparently without foundation. The officer turned out to be an intelligent individual, much different from the three we already had. He was rather neat, wore glasses, was a graduate of Tokyo University, and spoke good English. He had been in the army six years and was now twenty-six. He was simply tired of fighting and could see no glorious victory for Japan. He said his small party had been sent out without supplies or support of any kind, and there was but one end to such an expedition. He knew that none of his group could escape death from either bullets or starvation.

19 Days of Resting

January 20, 1944

Days of resting—and there could be no better place and time. The climate at Finschhafen seems to be making up for all the dreary days on New Britain. It has been bright and dry every day. I have done absolutely nothing since returning except type two reports yesterday. This afternoon I went down to the bay to the *Saturn* to visit the crew, all of which I have known since coming into the outfit.

We took a rubber boat from the *Saturn* and paddled out to the sunken Japanese ship I mentioned before. The control bridge is out of the water, as well as the giant smokestack and the fore part of the bow. The water in the inlet is calm and clear, and we could stand on the sloping bridge and see the deck below with the open hatchways leading into the dark interior. It seemed odd to see the bright, little tropical fishes swimming in and out of the doorways.

The ship is bigger than she appears from the surface. A real steamer! On the deck below us we could see shattered blue and white china—perhaps tea bowls. The fish looked curiously at it as they passed. The steel mast is full of bullet holes, as is every part of the ship. No doubt it was bombed and then strafed. Practically everything moveable has been stripped from the exposed parts, and divers have been into the interior to salvage any valuable material there.

January 22, 1944

Today six of us visited a Japanese hospital which was taken by the Australians less than three months ago. After driving about five miles up the coast, we left the truck and took a jungle trail into the hills, walking through bamboo groves, across small brooks. Fantastic butterflies flitted about in the cool, dense foliage.

At a turn in the trail we came upon a small Japanese burial plot containing fewer than a dozen graves. Each grave had been marked by a square post about four-by-four inches on which was written in Japanese characters what was undoubtedly the name, etc., of the soldier, but the graves had been dug up and grave posts knocked down. One partly-opened grave had a skull beside it, and bones protruded from the loose dirt.

The hospital had been captured by the Australians so quickly that the patients were still in their cots. Perhaps some of the officers and staff fled into the hills and escaped, but most of the place was cleaned up with tommy guns and bayonets. The patients were shot where they lay. There were more than a dozen buildings of poles with native, grass-thatched roofs and mud floors, all built in thickly wooded jungle at the base of a steep hill. Now, after nearly three months, the rain had soaked the place, and it was littered with rotting debris. Full cases of medicine were broken open and scattered, along with hundreds of tiny vials of serum, cases of rotting bandages, mosquito nets, hospital records, clothes, and even a number of the tiny, little wooden "benches" that the Japanese use for pillows.

The place presented a scene of thorough destruction. Nothing remained that was not torn up or rotting in the jungle dampness. The hill had been tunnelled into with a tunnel about four feet wide and barely high enough for an American soldier to stand up in. It ran about fifty feet straight into the solid, white coral-limestone rock, then made a turn, ran for another fifty or sixty feet, then another turn and another entrance—roughly a horseshoe-shaped excavation used as an air raid shelter. Another one was half finished, coming to a dead end after the first turn.

I picked up a small, brown Bakelite rice bowl from what appeared to be an officers' table in one of the buildings and found that someone had scratched his name on it in odd characters. Several of the record books were in fair shape, so I took some leaves from them to include in letters to friends. The pages were absolutely worthless, but someone would be interested in them, as the folks at home only hear of such things and seldom see them. We also took back a small two-wheeled cart that was unusually well made with solid rubber tires and welded iron frame, thinking it would be useful around the kitchen.

January 24, 1944

Last night we had a surprise bombing, and I had my closest call so far.

The movie showing was *Five Graves to Cairo*, and I wanted very much to see it. However, after we had all waited an hour, it was discovered that the usual thing had happened—projector broke down. As we left the movie area, the roads leading out were crowded with several hundred men and a lot of trucks and jeeps.

Without warning, there was a terrific, earth-shaking blast accompanied by a blinding flash. A bomb from a high-flying enemy plane had landed not more than fifty yards away. Everyone stopped, frozen for a second, and then dived off the road and flat on the ground. When I fell, I felt something hot under my chest. I had fallen on a hot piece of shrapnel which had landed an instant before.

Two more bombs fell—both farther away. I shook like a leaf and was thoroughly frightened from my toes up! Not even the Japanese on Gloucester had done this to me. We waited on the ground, but no more bombs fell. The plane was so high that you could barely hear it. It had certainly sneaked in and caught us flat-footed, because not a light was out, and the harbor looked like the middle of Broadway at Christmas. I thought the ack-ack would never get into action, but it finally did, and the giant searchlights stabbed the sky in an effort to pin the bomber to the dark night.

Now we were in danger of our own bursting ack-ack shells, for twenty-one pounds of metal shattered into the air must come down with each shot. Several men around me were bleeding at the nose and mouth from the bomb blast. Coconuts continued dropping from the trees.

As the firing moved south, following the plane, and the shells were no longer bursting directly overhead, I got up and started up the inky black road. Nearly everyone was still on the ground, but I couldn't stay there another minute! Twice I lost my way, but I felt better walking. More bombs exploded, far away now toward Dredga Harbor where the bomber was trying to get a liberty ship for his game bag that night. The damage was one liberty ship hit and one man killed in the bomb blast that landed near us, plus several men injured. Several more were killed farther down the coast. The radar warning system had evidently failed, and it was a costly failure.

I'm leaving for Tami Island in the morning.[23] Major Bilger went two days ago and found it to be an interesting place, so he has arranged for me to go this time.

January 26, 1944

A return from paradise—Tami Island! This tiny coral atoll off the Guinea coast was all the fantastic stories of the South Seas come to life. Our mission was to find out if the water supply would support our regiment should we move there, so we picked up a water expert on our way out and headed for a small, gray speck on the horizon. The speck was the group of three islands that make up Tami, about ten miles off the coast.

We arrived outside the lagoon and carefully threaded our way over the coral reefs into a quiet circle of green and turquoise water. The three islands were linked into the circle by the rim of white surf breaking over the coral, and in the center the lagoon was seventy feet deep. Around the edges where the surf broke, it was a couple of feet, thus making the lagoon always quiet even when the sea outside was quite rough.

We landed on the middle island on a beach of white coral sand. Palms swayed gently above, and all was quiet. But we soon discovered that Tami had been scarred by war. First the Japanese occupied it, then our forces bombed it, and now it showed five huge bomb craters and many trunks of torn palms. The native houses were mostly wrecked, but a few still stood practically intact. We put our stuff by the shack that had evidently been used by the Australians when they were there.

I started to explore. All the island showed neglect, but the hibiscus and periwinkles bloomed bravely, and the ground was covered with pink, crocus-like flowers. An old frangipani tree filled the air with delicate perfume, and there was still some of the feeling left from the days when Tami had been happier. The village cemetery was filled with bright shrubs, and the taro patch had grown out-of-bounds since the natives left.

Two bombs had landed smack in the middle of the betelnut grove, shearing off the tops of practically the last trees. Now when the natives come back and go out for a shot of betelnut, they will be disappointed. There were mango trees, wild cherry trees, and two kinds of nut trees, plus breadfruit trees—all of them bearing fruit.

This island was moon-shaped and not more than three-quarters of a mile long, never more than two city blocks wide. The center was flat and contained all the useful space and useful trees. At each end the ground rose into abrupt coral rocks and thick growths of pandamus palms, so was practically impassable and utterly useless. Around the ruined huts was a litter of poles, thatch, and household articles such as broken wooden bowls, clay pots, etc.

I began gathering up all of the carved wood and fragments I could find and put them on the floor of a house that still stood, so that I could later salvage what was of any use. Never before had I been loose in such a collector's paradise. Each house seemed to have been the site of a particular handicraft, but unfortunately, most of it had been damaged badly. In the center of the island was a huge war canoe, carved from a single log, with each end curving up gracefully into carved heads of mythical animals. It was wonderfully made and measured forty-nine feet six inches—a truly remarkable feat of workmanship.

By afternoon Lieutenant Mahony had arrived—he and Patterson, the coxswain of the *Mercury*. Mahony had decided to come over to Tami, and I was glad to see him. He is one of the few swell guys we have for officers. He probably came because he wanted to spend a couple of days away from the mainland and its confusion.

The population of the island consisted of six pigs, a hen, and a rooster. All of the natives had gone either to the mainland or to the larger of the three islands. The old sow we called "Jeraldine," her four shoats were "the children," the small pig was "the baby." The latter was about the cutest thing in pig form I ever saw, while the shoats and Jeraldine were the same sort of razorbacks that roam Arkansas by the hundreds. The little fellow wasn't more than ten inches long and as striped as a chipmunk. The alternating, dark brown and rust-colored stripes started at his tiny head and continued the length of his body to his curly tail, interrupted only by a white band around his middle.

Jeraldine begged for food and seemed to have been a pet. We gave her various things, all of which she ate noisily, except for our hardtack crackers, at which she turned up her piggish nose and slowly walked away.

The hen and rooster scratched around all day. He was a cheerful fellow, red with white neck and bronze tail; she, a quiet brown lady. The peculiar thing about them was their family relationship. One would suppose that one hen and one rooster on a deserted island would be an ideal couple, but apparently not here. Each evening he escorted her up the island

and soon came back alone to the kitchen shack, where he roosted on a high pole. At dawn he crowed lustily, got down, and went off up the island, soon returning followed by the hen. This happened each day, and we soon concluded that all was not as well as appearances indicated.

The second day I took a flashlight and decided to look into the coral rocks where there were bound to be caves—an old habit I formed with Cliff Pouncey long ago on Gibbons Ranch, where we poked into every crack of rock and often found interesting things to repay us for our efforts. Toward the east end of Tami the rocks rose steep and rugged, and soon I found large crevices and small caves formed by "blubbers" in the coral formation. One of these ran into a room of considerable size—completely bare and apparently never disturbed by human feet.

At the rear of it I noticed a hole not more than thirty inches in diameter, and it had a challenging look which I couldn't turn down. I took the flashlight, squeezed through and came upon what may be the most interesting find of my life.

Here was a room about ten feet across, at the back of which was a long shelf supported by poles. On this shelf rested a variety of native equipment. Several large and beautifully carved wooden ceremonial bowls with weird, half-human figures and queer animals in fine carving. A huge shell horn with a lining of the brightest coral red. (Had it been used to call the tribe to ceremonials?) A string of ninety fishnet floats of wood, many of them carved on both sides. (Perhaps the symbols were to lure the fish into the net.) Straw baskets and such work were falling apart, for even though the cave was dry, the low island air is very wet and penetrates everything. Clay cooking pots were in good shape, but something I could never hope to get the far distance from Tami to Texas.

Here was a movie plot come to life, with the things collectors and students of native lore dream of, but so seldom see. It was a once-in-a-lifetime experience! Almost reverently I took up the shell. It had a round hole about the size of a quarter in the side up towards the end of the spiral. Most of them I have seen have the end cut off instead. Never in my life had I been able to blow a conch shell, but I put this one to my lips and blew. A deep, clear sound came out—to my surprise—and I had blown a conch for the first time! Maybe this one was easier, or maybe the gods of Tami had seen my bare feet, my brief khaki shorts, and the flaming hibiscus in my cap and accepted me as a lover of the tradition of the islands and their magic beauty. At any rate I blew.

The larger of the bowls was three feet long. Another was smaller and could be cradled inside the large one. The two bowls, together with a number of other things, made quite a load, but one I carried gladly. The remainder of the things I left in their place.

The fellows at camp thought the things odd, but weren't especially interested, and not one of them even asked where the cave was located. Not that they would have gotten the answer, anyway!

"I guess you get a lot of money for that stuff back in the States," one soldier remarked.

"No," I said, "I collect it because I am interested. I do not expect it to be valuable."

"You sure go to a lot of trouble with that stuff for it not to be worth anything," was his parting remark. I was furious, not at the simple soldier, but at the whole of our money-minded civilization which moulded him.

These things of Tami were made when men had time to be happy. Time—that most precious possession! Tami's people were free to create beauty from a block of wood, a chunk of clay, a bundle of grass fiber. Behind them were generations of free and happy islanders who each gave to successive generations some of their love of Tami and its surroundings.

Now the lagoon was brilliant green with purple patches and streaks of golden sunlight, bounded by the curve of white surf at the reef. Beyond the reef the sea was blue all the way to the hazy mountains of New Guinea. A white puff of cloud was poised above. These are the things of Tami I will remember when I look at the handicraft in years to come.

One day some natives paddled up to the beach (from the larger island, I supposed) in the finest canoe I had seen in use. It was about thirty feet long, carved from a very straight log, with the same curved ends and carved heads as the larger war canoe I had seen. The sides were built up with wide, hand-hewn boards, each board at least twenty inches wide and running the length of the canoe in a single piece. These sides were painted in interesting designs in white and red, and the whole canoe was bound together with plant fiber of some sort and the joints filled with tree gum. The outrigger was bound with the same strong fiber, and there was not a nail or piece of metal in the whole job. Neither did any of the parts show marks I could recognize as having been made by modern tools.

The man of the Tomote family was on the beach, and I tried to be friendly, asking, "Where your house?" with the idea of finding where he came from. This was a grave error, for he once lived right here in what was now destruction. "My house here!" he almost shouted. "Look now. American boom-boom. House go everywhere!"

Of course, he referred to the Americans bombing the island. "Americans no boom-boom you. He boom-boom Japanese," I told him. He had an answer for that too. "When American boom-boom Japanese, he finish." Meaning that the Japanese had already left the island before the bombing took place. "But," I said, "American, he no know Japanese he finish." "All same, my house gone," he replied, which gave him the last word and somewhat of a victory in the conversation. I had no reply to that, for his house was gone, mistake or no mistake, and the result was the same as if our planes had deliberately done the job. It was time to let that subject die. I didn't want a hostile native after me on this small island.

Two of the boys in the group were around, so I tried to interest them in getting me some coconuts from the tall trees. They showed only mild interest and weren't in any humor to climb for me, so I tackled the problem from a different angle. An old woman, who could have been their grandmother, cracked nuts in the shade of a tree. I went to her and showed her a package of needles, pointed to a coconut beside her, and made it known that I wanted a number of them.

The effect was startling! The old woman jumped up, began to jabber in a high-pitched voice, and rounded up the kids. I don't know what she said to them, but they went up the coconut trees like squirrels and dropped down five coconuts. I told them that was enough. I gave the old woman three darning needles, and she was highly pleased with the trade.

The water supply proved insufficient for a large number of men, for when too much was drawn out of the wells, salt water seeped in. The wells had furnished the natives with water for generations, but we great Americans must have things in quantity or nothing.

The last night on the island it rained hard, but I scampered with my blanket into one of the houses with a roof and did not get wet.

The next morning I put my stuff aboard the *Mercury*, as I was going back with Lieutenant Mahony and Pat aboard this cruiser for a more comfortable trip than in the barge. While waiting for the departure, I hulled a last coconut on the beach, and as we pulled away from the shore, I stood barefooted, in my shorts, a hibiscus over each ear, and drank a toast to Tami—as sincere a wish as I have ever expressed—"Tami, someday may all your scars of war be healed!"

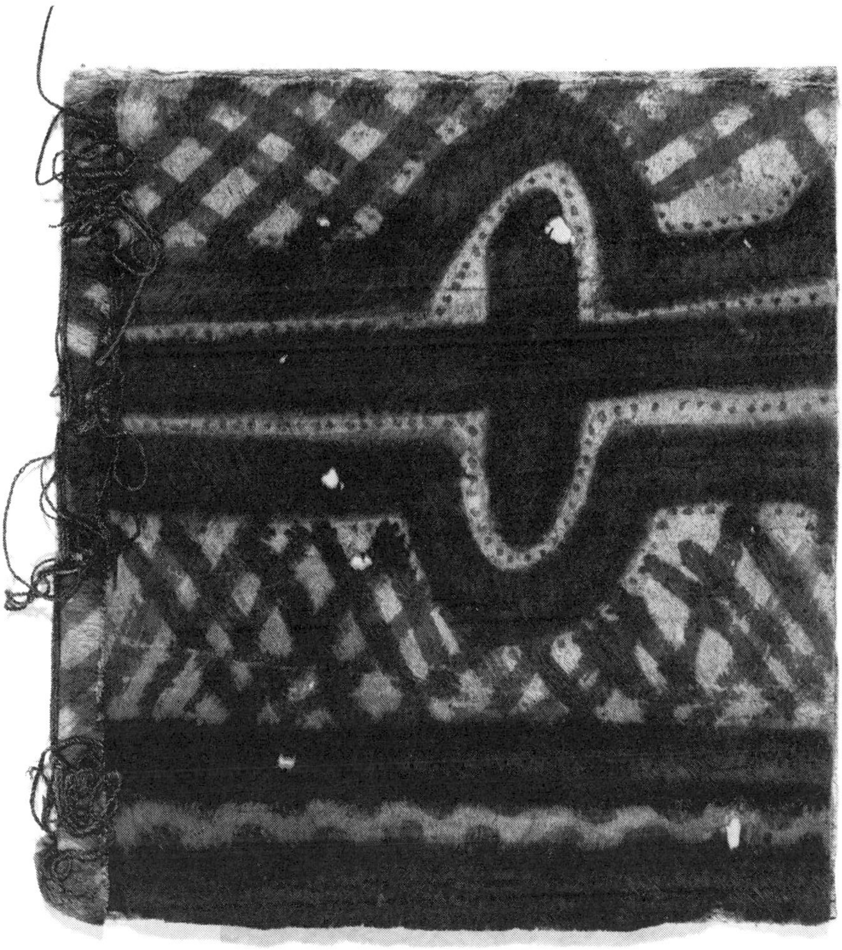

Handmade book with bark cloth cover which Gaitha Browning sent to his mother during the war in 1944.

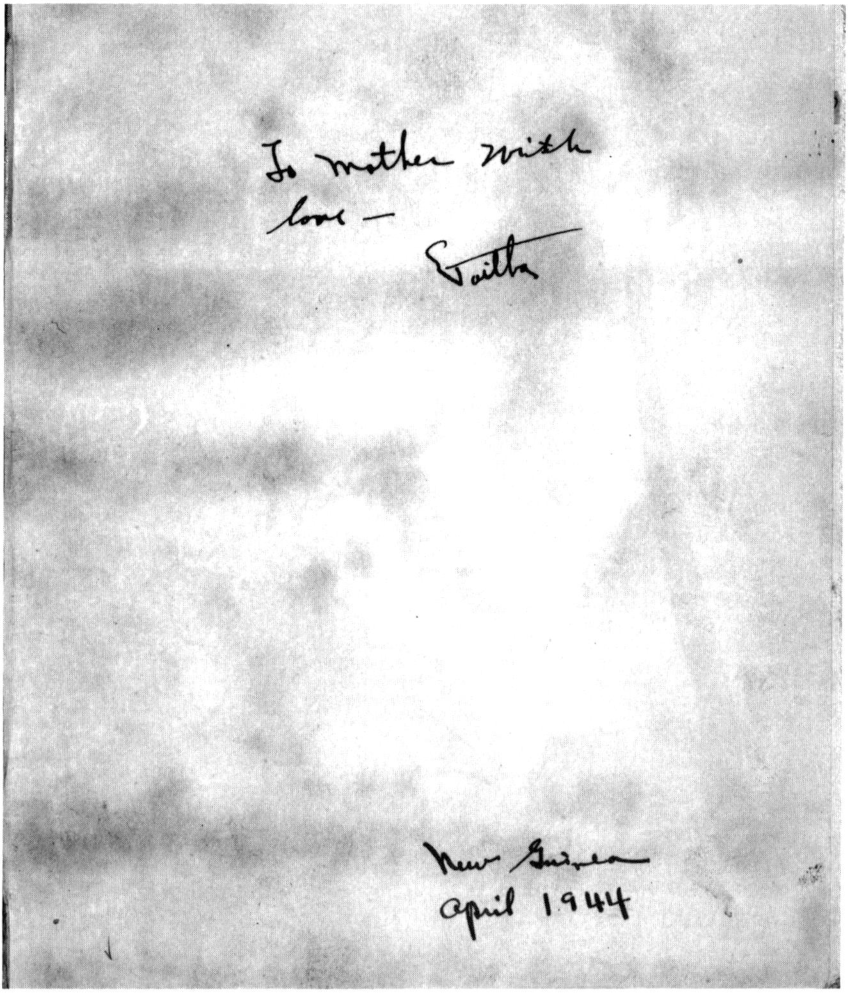
To mother with
love —
Gaitha

New Guinea
April 1944

New Guinea's
People

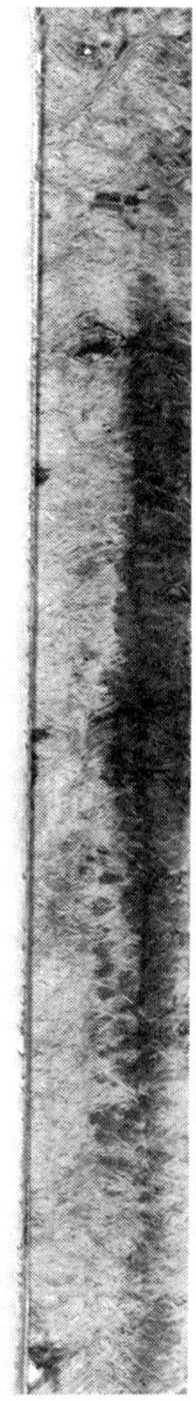

As we in the army travel from country to country, you at home write and ask "What are the people like, what is the country like?" It is sometimes difficult to tell you of these little known lands, such as New Guinea which is most likely the most remote country any army is destined to visit. Before the war there were less than 7,000 white people in this country, mostly owners and managers of the Copra plantations, miners, missionaries and others, now perdominately Australian although at one time the white population of New Guinea was chiefly German.

The natives here are Melanesians, dark people with broad noses and kinky hair, and little of the allure of the long-haired coffee-colored grass-skirted dancers of the movies. We have come in contact only with the coastal natives, who are more or less familiar with white men, but back in the interior are thousands of natives who have never seen a white man and whose lands have never been explored.

The Tapa Cloth in which these sketches are bound is still worn as clothing by most of the natives. It is made from the bark of a tree resembling the American Mulberry.

Like all primitive peoples the Melanesians hold numerous "Sing Sings" or dances, many of them in connection with their religious beliefs but others merely for entertainment. Common among primitive people are the masked dances. (our American Indians have a number of them). Usually connected with evil spirits and religious rites, these dances present a weird sight around the campfire.

This mask was found in a deserted village. The natives had been frightened away by the Japanese and the village was guarded only by the spirit mask.

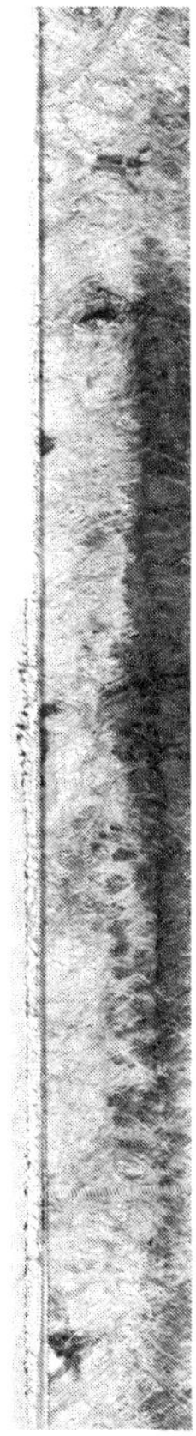

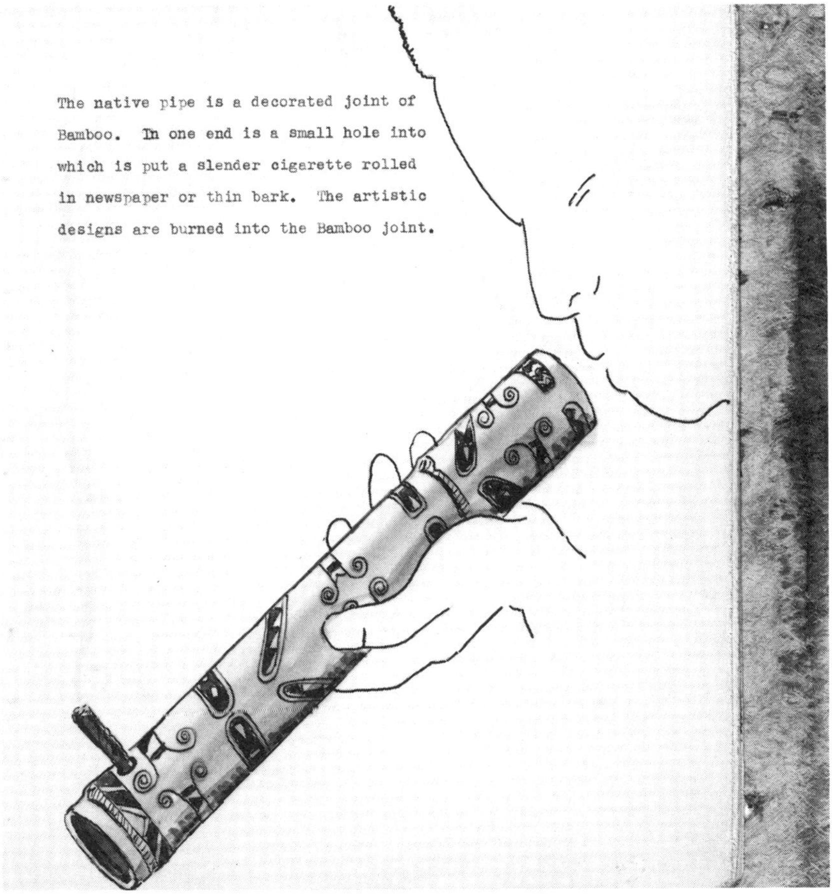

The native pipe is a decorated joint of Bamboo. In one end is a small hole into which is put a slender cigarette rolled in newspaper or thin bark. The artistic designs are burned into the Bamboo joint.

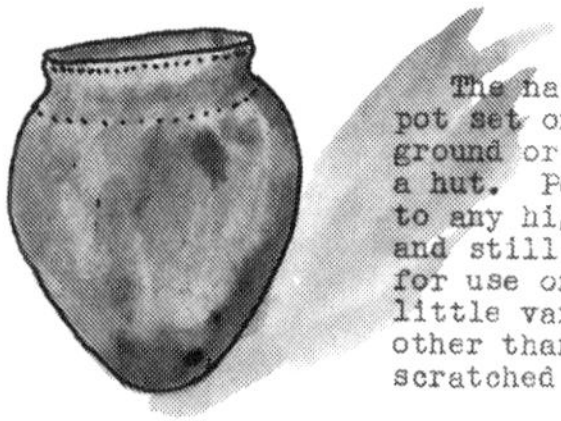

The native cooking utensil is a clay pot set on a small fire, either on the ground or in a box of sand on the porch of a hut. Pottery making has not developed to any high degree among the Melanesians and still remains in the stage of pottery for use only, usually rather heavy, with little variation in shapes and no decoration other than fingernail markings and designs scratched with a sharp stick.

These pots were collected on a tiny coral island off the coast of New Guinea.

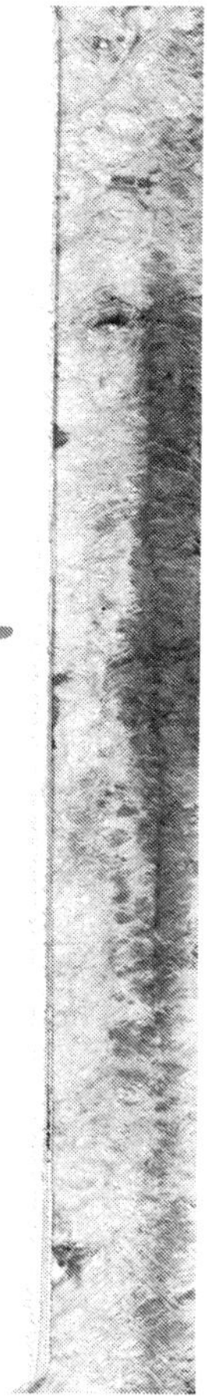

Betel Nut chewing is a common and popular habit in the South Pacific, done much in the same manner as the American smoking of cigarettes. The Betel nut has a mild narcotic effect, grows on a tall slim palm in clusters like dates. It is chewed with lime and produces a rich red juice which gives the impression that the native is wearing a makeup of badly applied lipstick. The lime for this purpose is carried in a small gourd bottle, and is put into the mouth with a wooden stick or paddle, often these lime sticks are beautifully carved.
This native's hair has an orangeish tinge because he has bleached and dyed it, giving him the heighth of fashionable hair-dos. in his hair is a "scratch pin" useful for an itchy scalp.

Lime stick of carved wood and lime
bottle made from small gourd.

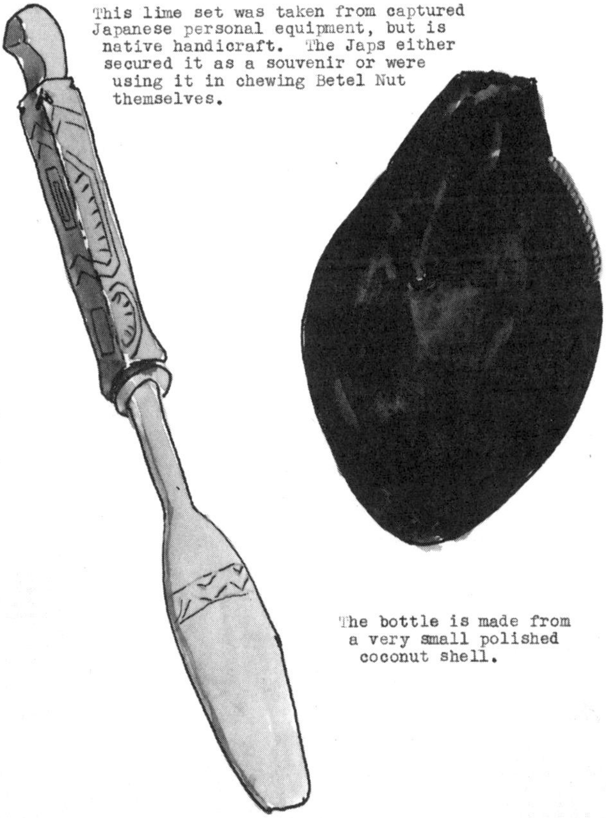

This lime set was taken from captured Japanese personal equipment, but is native handicraft. The Japs either secured it as a souvenir or were using it in chewing Betel Nut themselves.

The bottle is made from a very small polished coconut shell.

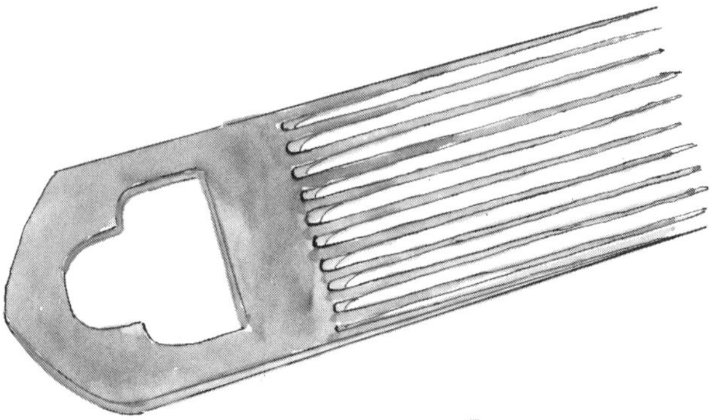

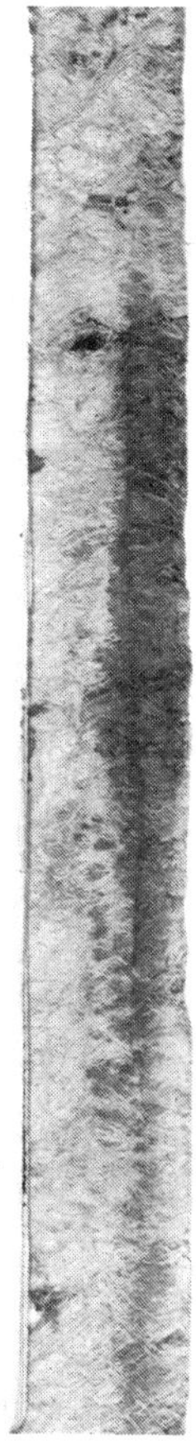

Every native takes pride
in his mop of fuzzy hair,
and carries a comb of wood
or bamboo with which he
continually fluffs it up
to make it stand on end.

Occasionally these combs are made
from polished tortise shell with
inlayed decorations.

THE COCONUT

No mention of the natives of the South Pacific would be complete without the story of the coconut, the two are inseparable. The coconut palms grow by the millions on the flat coral islands and along the coastal regions of the larger mountainous islands. There is no "season" for the coconut, it bears the year round and often one tree will contain ripe nuts, green nuts and blossoms. When a native can find no food there is always the coconut, rich and delicious, of which he may drink the juice of the green ones or eat the meat with a spoon. The meat of the ripe nuts is usually scraped out with a clam shell and eaten.

Most of the smaller food dishes are made from coconut shells, as well as cups and spoons. The shell of a ripe coconut is unusually hard and takes a beautiful polish, often turning ebony black with use.

The leaves of the coconut palm furnish the native with his home, as houses are thatched with this material, also sides of the huts are covered with mats woven from palm leaves.

The Melanesians are expert wood carvers. Here is a fragment of carving from a canoe. The pig is the natives most prized possession and the crocodile is practically the only enemy of the pig in this country, so it is only natural that this wood carver should portray a pig being caught by a crocodile.

No place on earth has the gaudy display of parrots that is found in New Guinea. They are in flocks of hundreds and in all colors of the rainbow. After the nesting season is over the flocks gather, often covering the trees like brilliant blossoms.

This bird was shot and brought in for this sketch, but few of them are killed. Most soldiers remark after killing one - "That is the most beautiful bird I have ever seen, I'll never shoot another one". Mere paint cannot convey the sparkling greens and reds of this splendid bird. Like most birds of this land he is most likely an unidentified and unrecorded species.

Largest of all parrots, the Black Palm Cockatoo is a regular visitor around our camps. His call is an astonishing variety of loud pleasing whistles, which he practices by the hour in the thick green jungle.

The White Cockatoo is the best of all talking parrots when tamed, but in his wild state his only call is an unpleasant raucous scream.

Fantastic things of nature are the rule rather than the exception in New Guinea. The numerous butterflies baffle all description, the flowers are almost all strange indeed. Many of the flowers bloom on the tangle of vines that cover the jungle trees; this one was taken from a tree by our tent.

20 Time for Trading

February 7, 1944

The past week has been quiet (except for nightly air raid alarms and sometimes Japanese planes overhead), and I have done practically nothing. Made two drawings of a machine gun for a fellow who has interested the major in some idea he has for a change of some sort in the firing device. Another one of the thousands of soldiers who hope to revolutionize the design of some army equipment and thus become immortal over night.

Yesterday the boat went down the coast to get thatch from the natives, and I went along. The thatch is made of palm leaves folded over a strip of bamboo and secured with grass fiber, each strip being about six feet long and roughly twenty inches wide. It is put on a roof very much like shingles are and does not leak if properly applied. Our base quartermaster is building some warehouses across Finschhafen harbor and uses this for roofing.

In charge of thatch collecting is an Australian captain who, before the war, was an overseer of the natives in this section. He was an interesting talker, and on the way down I learned a lot about the natives. Also, more about Tami Island. Evidently there were nearly two hundred natives there before the war, but now they are scattered, and most of the men are in the service of the Australian Army as boatmen on the coast. Tami people have long been known as expert sailors and were famous for their big canoes in which they often made remarkable voyages. I found, too, that they were the chief makers of the carved bowls which I had found.

In all, we stopped at five villages, each of which had a pile of thatch on the beach ready for us. Each time we had them load it in the boat. Then the captain paid them for the day's load, as well as what had been picked up on previous trips. Their pay consisted of bags of unpolished rice, cases of corned beef, sugar, salt, and stick tobacco. The goods were paid to the "lulueye" of the village, or head man, who stacked it up on the beach and later supervised the distribution to the families who had worked. Practically every able-bodied man and boy of any size was away with the Australian army, but the old men, women, and even the small children worked at thatch making.

At the second stop it seemed that everyone turned out for our coming, and the women brought baskets of bananas and other fruits to trade. There was little in the way of handicrafts to trade for, as these people had been moved around, chased off by Japs, etc., until they were very poor. One old fellow with white hair and whiskers, and one hand missing, came down carrying a carved, coconut shell bowl. Evidently he had made it for trade purposes today. I went up and looked at it, but he quickly put it behind him and backed away from me. A minute later he did not have the coconut bowl at all, and I wondered what on earth he had done with it.

One of the Australian sergeants who was assisting the captain tried to find out. He spoke in pidgin English and asked, "This fellow coconut belonga this man, where he stop?" The native didn't tell where "fellow coconut stop." The Aussie explained to the native that I wanted to trade for it, but still no response, and we gave up in defeat.

A few minutes later a boy produced the bowl in question from a cloth he was carrying, and the old man was ready to trade. All this business puzzled me, but the trade was made for five needles and a razor blade. Later I spied another of the carved bowls in one of the mesh string bags on the back of one of the women and asked her about it, displaying some of the needles at the same time. As usual, the needles produced enthusiasm at once, and the woman began yelling to a man down the beach. (Evidently the man owned both the woman and the bowl.)

He wasn't interested, but she was persistent and finally got him on the spot. This time the bowl cost me a yard of cloth and five needles. There was little else to be found, so we gave a boy cigarettes to get coconuts. He twisted them off with his feet, then came down and opened one for Glenn Cornett and me. This was Glenn's first such experience, and he was enjoying it. We had the boys load the remainder of the coconuts on the boat.

Most of the other villages were ordinary, and nothing of interest happened. At the last village we noticed a barge pull away as we came up, but paid no attention to the soldiers in it, as it was a common thing to see Yanks visiting the villages on Sunday. Only four or five men were on the beach—no women or children—and the few men seemed in a bad humor. The deal for payment of the thatch went badly, and the natives argued. Finally the captain got the truth from them, because he knew something was wrong there. The barge that had just left contained six American soldiers who had entered the village, hunted up the lulueye and asked him for some women. They might as well have fired a cannon in the village square. Every woman and child, and most of the men, took to the bushes and simply disappeared. The lulueye told the soldiers to leave, but the damage was done, and the village was in an ugly mood.

I wondered if the soldiers were really serious or just trying to see what effect such a request would have on the lulueye. Knowing the level from which thousands of them had sprung, I wouldn't be surprised at anything! Americans are not—as a whole—the noble, big, upstanding, straight-forward, honest, self-respecting men the editors would have you believe. When they get low, they can get lower than any race on earth.

Last night we had Japanese planes overhead again, and bombs were dropped at Dredga Harbor. Our ack-ack put up an impressive barrage, and once we heard the whine of a plane diving, as if it had been shot down. But we never learned if that was the case.

February 10, 1944

My back mail arrived—thirteen letters in all—most written in December, but all very welcome.

For the past week a couple of fellows and I have been taking long swims down below the cliff off the coral rocks. The water is very clear and clean, and you can see bottom at thirty feet. The living coral is wonderful, and so are the fish. Bob McDonald looks and swims like a movie Tarzan and is a joy to watch. We go under water and watch him swim in graceful strokes around the bottom among the fish, and he stays under an alarming length of time. I wonder why more of the men don't take advantage of this fine swimming water. Maybe they don't have time, but I have never done so little since getting into the army as I am doing right now.

February 14, 1944

Yesterday the boat went again to the five villages, and again I left the Sunday dinner (which is usually better than any other, and good food is a premium here) and went along. Last week the Australian captain and I made a deal with the lulueye of Bukauasip village to get me twenty or thirty black cowrie shells, as I am still on the trail of these elusive animals, but after a year I have not been able to find any. The old man consented to get them and assured us they would be ready the next time we came—which is today. Maybe the "quest of the cowries" will have a happy ending—???

The Australian officers this week were a young lieutenant, a captain, and a major—all ANGAU[24] men, or administrators of native affairs for the Australian army. All had been here before the war doing the same work. All showed a somewhat hostile attitude toward the idea of Yankee soldiers trading with the natives. This was the same attitude I have run into once or twice before. We always give the natives too much, the Aussies said, and I soon saw why. The ANGAU men paid them so poorly for their fruit and other products that it wasn't worth a native's trouble to gather the things and bring them to the boat.

The natives wanted to trade with us, but seemed afraid of the Australian officers. One man showed me a fairly good bamboo comb he had carved. He wanted a can of bully beef for it. He quickly hid his can of beef from the eyes of the ANGAU men.

At another village one fellow had some Japanese money he wanted to sell (on the sly), but he wanted only Australian silver money for it, and I had no change. Evidently he had gotten the money either off a dead soldier or been paid for something by the Japanese when they were here. There was evidence of their having been here, because by the beach we found a pile of their mortar shells, still in good condition and dangerous, but ignored by the natives who never gave them a glance. Usually the natives show no interest whatever in such equipment or the wrecked boats that drift ashore. They simply ignore the whole thing.

I offered the man cloth, stick tobacco, etc., but he held out for silver, so it was no trade. But evidently he passed the news on to one of his friends who was interested in what I had. This second man came by, and, without looking directly at me, said quietly, "Trade?" Then, with an eye out for the ANGAU men, he walked away and squatted by an almost burned-out camp fire.

I caught the hint and followed him, squatting beside the fire, too, with my back to the officers. Not that I minded them seeing me trading, but because the natives did mind. This fellow had three pieces of New Guinea silver money, or Territory of New Guinea shillings. This money has been discontinued and is sought as souvenirs by the Americans. The coins are minted with a hole in the center to enable the natives to carry them on a string around their necks. I gave the man a piece of cloth for his coins, and he was pleased. He should have been, as his lamie was in tatters. I was again impressed by the poverty of these people. The war had surely stripped them of everything!

At Bukauasip we were met by the tu tu or Number Two boy, assistant to the lulueye, and my man of the cowrie shell deal was nowhere to be seen. Inquiry revealed that he was in a second village some distance up the way, sick. Neither had his wife shown up that day, which definitely put the finish on another attempt to obtain the shells.

On Tami Island I tried to interest a boy in getting some, as pieces of them were on the beach, and I knew the living bed of them was somewhere near, but he merely smiled. "Where black fellow geri geri he stop?" I asked (or "Where can I find the black cowrie shells?"). "In water on rock," he replied, which was as definite as telling a Texan to look for something "out in the pasture under a mesquite tree," since the whole place was surrounded by rocks and water for miles.

The Bukauasip village was practically in ruins from neglect and Japanese occupation. These natives were living at a village up farther in the hills. The mat mat house stood roofless, but was the most interesting structure in the village. Twice as high as the other buildings, it had a lattice platform high in the top. Here the dead of the village were laid, and there they remained until the bones fell down below. Then the bones were buried and the incident was closed. I do not know the lore behind this queer custom, but it must be fascinating.

Although the day was fairly interesting, I was disgusted at the ANGAU officers' petty jealousy and rudeness toward us. I couldn't resist telling them, "The natives seem afraid to deal with us when you are around, but when we come alone they are quite at ease, and we get along fine with them." The lieutenant just ground his teeth and didn't reply, for he probably realized he was licked already. The Yanks have a way of getting anything they go after, a fact that the Australians both hate and admire at the same time. I could afford to be pretty independent, as they were using our boat, and I wasn't dependent on them for anything. Neither was I under their command from an army standpoint.

Last night we had a full moon, and a full night of enemy planes. No bombs were dropped that I know of, but we were awakened regularly by the thunder of the 90-mm guns. There was also a general alarm on since late afternoon, because somewhere up the coast a large flotilla of Japanese barges had been sighted. Also a prisoner gave information that might have been true, to the effect that there would be an attempt on Finschhafen in the near future.

21 BACK TO HERVEY BAY

February 18, 1944

One year ago today we sailed out of San Francisco and saw the Golden Gate disappear over a choppy sea. Since that time, we have become acquainted with Australia and the often exaggerated island of New Guinea, sailed to New Britain and landed on hostile beaches, seen Japanese soldiers in life and death, and—in short—practically covered the scope of a war-torn South Pacific.

I am continually impressed with the petty things that go on in the army, and in the past 365 days have seen enough to fill a large library. I am convinced that we would be able to win the war more quickly if men would be men and not slump into their more comfortable position of small thinking and egotism.

February 22, 1944

Back in the old camp at Hervey Bay again. We received orders to move back, which sounded good to me. I came down on one of the cabin boats with five others. It was an uneventful trip except for the fact that our navigator, who led the ten boats down, decided his compass was wrong and plotted himself a different course. When daylight came, we were headed for Tufi Harbor, and our own shore was only a thin, blue line on the horizon.

The coxswain of the boat knew we were off, but, of course, only being a sergeant, he couldn't very well tell the lieutenant he was crazy. So we spent a day correcting the error for which an enlisted man would have been court-martialed. We could have well been in Japanese territory by the next morning with an error like that.

Here at battalion headquarters' office I found Lieutenant Callaway off on furlough and Major Hoffinger in charge of the battalion. Hoffinger is generally known as "Muscle Head" and is an overbearing, small-minded person of German-Jewish descent. But Callaway and Bilger both are due

Somewhere in New Guinea,
Feb. 19, 1944.

Dearest Mother and Dad,

Am glad to tell you things are very quiet here, the nasty Jap planes don't seem to come to this place much more, they probably have their hands full elsewhere. Of course I told you we moved back to the camp on the hill and am enjoying the old campsite and the wonderful big spring and its soft water. For the first time in a long time we have really good water to shower with. The old bunch are still in the office, except Lt. Callaway who is on furlough. I might have told you he is from Arkansas, and a typical Southerner, we get along fine. His wife was to send you some of the pictures I took of the natives, did you ever get them?

You were right, that picture Mrs. Stallings showed you did not have me in it at all, as I have never had one taken by a native church as far as I know. When you first mentioned it I thought it might be one of the photos a news man took as we left for combat. I looked around once and found I was looking right into the camera, but this was a movie camera. The news people were all over the place and so was I so could have been in most any of the photos.

Am now looking forward to the rest of my boxes, as they evidently are coming in. Maybe none of them were on the mail ship that was supposed to have been sunk somewhere before Xmas. Was glad to write Mrs. Stallings that hers finally showed up, as she was sure it was lost. It was very nice and enjoyed it a lot.

Love to all of you, and write -- will get your letters now.

Love,

Walter

back soon, so the situation will clear then. Bilger has been in the hospital with dengue fever. Already another combat mission is forming, but it will consist mostly of A Company men and others who have not been on a combat mission. As far as I am able to find out, I will remain here on the hill. Charlie will go, so that will leave Sergeant and me to keep the hill fires burning. It will be a pleasant rest and should be the time for me to finish my book of New Guinea sketches.

I have heard from home regularly since getting back and have even received two Christmas boxes. Mother was overjoyed to hear from me after almost seven weeks of silence.

February 24, 1944

Most of those returning from action have been here on the hill, which made quite a crowded camp, and confusion reigned supreme. The mess hall was overcrowded, and the food pure poison, for there isn't much the cooks can do for that many people. Now a new mess has been set up down the bay, and people have moved out until the place is again calming down to our old tempo.

One of the boys—who has long since gone north to combat—left his two little shell parakeets (or love birds) here—a blue one and a green one. The boys take good care of them, putting their cage in the shelter known as the "barber shop" because haircuts are given there. Each morning the cage is opened, and the birds start their rounds of camp. You often find them a long distance from their home, busily engaged in gathering grass seeds, etc., but each night they return, get in their cage, and someone covers them for the night. They are given such food as we have, but their bird seed is gone, so they are thrifty enough to get their own and seem to do pretty well with it, too.

I received a long letter from Marie DeVille, and it made me want to see her very much. She's a swell, sweet kid, and—to my surprise—she is a riveter in an aircraft factory! Both she and her mother do the same work, and her stepfather is a foreman in the same plant. They all made my year in Gallup ideal, and I'll never forget them for it. We all loved the same things, and enjoyed them together. We all hope to be back in New Mexico after the war. They are making hay while the sun shines and, no doubt, will save enough to build the home they plan in the land they love.

March 3, 1944

The remainder of those who have not yet been in combat are going out in small groups. The orders fly thick and fast and change by the hour. Some of the men have been on boats ready to go three times and are still here waiting for another call. I am not to go this time and will be able to stay here and see how it is to get the news of the other fellows landing. Maybe staying here will give a lot of us an opportunity to gain back some of the weight we lost up there. I had thought everyone had gotten thin since coming to Guinea, but the combat mission took us down to bones. I have to look twice at some people to be sure it is the right man. The food here is fairly good, and lately we have been getting fresh meat regularly.

There are rumors of another move for the camp, most likely up to Finschhafen. If so, all of our regiment will go, as Oro Bay is now way in the rear of the war in this area. There is also talk of us moving to the newly taken Admiralty Islands, three hundred miles north of Finschhafen.[25]

March 6, 1944

Reports from the Admiralties are coming in. We have lost around ten men so far—this time men I knew from long association. It is not easy! Today word was received of three new casualties, among them Loring, the lobster fisherman from the Massachusetts coast. Loring was more than forty and had no business in such activities as the army exacts. He belonged back in Massachusetts with his lobster pots and schooner, where he could have done more good supplying folks with food to supplement their ration points.

I have had many long talks with Loring. He was shy and quiet, but readily recounted his experiences along the New England coast, and they were many and varied. He was familiar with all the wildlife of the coast. He once told me of how the mother seals would push their babies under water when they saw a boat coming, where the lobsters were to be found, what kinds of fish the various seasons brought, and—most of all—he talked of wanting to be back. I don't know where he is tonight, but wherever it is, I hope there are lobsters in every trap.

March 20, 1944

Since March 6, not much has happened. We have simply been on the hill doing very little. Two more missions have gone out, taking every man out of the outfit that could do boat work or anything else of the sort. Those of us who have recently returned are still here, getting used to the absence of Japanese planes and bombs.

Yesterday I spent the day on board the *Dobbin*, a destroyer tender anchored in Oro Bay. David Belvin had sent me a note saying he was here, so I took advantage of Sunday and went out. The last time I saw David he was a somewhat scatter-brained kid whom we called "Commodore" because he always wanted to get into the navy. That was at least three years ago. The intervening time has touched him kindly. He is now a young man with skilled training in machine tool work and a good worker, but he has lost none of the qualities he gathered in his years of Boy Scout training with the old gang we both know so well.

The destroyer tender had four to six destroyers tied up beside her immense bulk, like chicks around their mother. All day long the work went on—repairing machinery, loading torpedoes, overhauling guns, and loading food onto the various destroyers. Evidently an invasion fleet is outfitting from here. I expect to hear before many days that some new point to the north has been blown off the map.[26]

We are to move over to the mainland, back to regimental headquarters area. It will be an improvement over this isolated spot in many ways, for we will have movies, etc., and will be in contact with what goes on in this part of the world, but we will not have the quiet and peace we have known here.

22 On the Mainland

April 4, 1944

A lot of time has gone by, and we have moved from the hill over to the mainland with the result that we now have all the things we have missed for so long—a movie every night, etc. I have taken advantage of the lack of official business and the good light of my corner of the tent to continue working on the New Guinea sketches. So far, I have more than a dozen plates finished, and the thing is at last nearing completion.

From all the rumors I think we will soon move to Finschhafen, not to the Admiralties as per the last rumors. The third and fourth brigade of our type troops are now in New Guinea, and we hope they will take up where we left off and relieve us. (Hope springs eternal in a silly mind!)

A minor disturbance today was Leroy Vangilger getting drunk on jungle juice. He and others found a large can that had been hidden by someone weeks before, and was it ripe! So Van came back completely crocked. He was put under a cold shower, but not before he had a fight, received a black eye, screamed to be taken to the guardhouse, and told the company commander just what he thought of him with no words left out. Van is a good-natured Arkansas kid, but wild when drunk.

More furloughs are being given to Sydney, but I'll just wait and see what comes. It couldn't be much worse here than on the trip down and back. Many say it isn't worth the fifteen days spent there.

April 10, 1944

Yesterday was Easter Sunday—my second overseas. The remembered dates of what happened in Australia a year ago keep rolling around regularly now, reminding me that it has been a long time. The early service was held in a huge, natural bowl at the foot of the mountains, and a large number of soldiers attended. Lanny Ross[27] sang. He is a lieutenant in the outfit over here now. There was a choir of nurses which was fair, but the gals were a pretty hard-looking bunch. Somehow these services carry an air of indifference, as if a concession had been made to war. Little squeaks of half-hearted worship in the monstrous roar of war, I realize more and more that the enjoyment of anything is mostly in being among people you love in a place you love.

After dinner five of us took a jeep and went to the hospital to see several of the boys there. They are in for various things—malaria, yellow jaundice, jungle rot, dengue fever, and bullet wounds. All of them seemed in good spirits. The hospital was a quiet, pleasant place up in the hills with a magnificent view of Oro Bay to the east and a quiet and very green valley to the west. A good place in which to attempt the road back to health and let your wounds heal, so you can go after more.

April 11, 1944

Four letters from home in the past few days. It is good to hear that all are well except for the usual spring colds. Mother writes, "Dad is putting in all the time he can at his work. Help is so scarce now. He realizes this is his last fling at regular work." Suddenly I realized both he and Mother had birthdays in February, and they are sixty-five! A big lump comes to my throat, and my feelings are mixed and confused. The years have gone so quietly, so swiftly, and so surely, and now my Dad and Mother are old people. It is incredible! Only yesterday they were handsome and middle-aged. Only day before yesterday they were young.

April 16, 1944

Another letter arrived from Marie. That swell kid is still the same. She will be twenty-one in July and is scared to think of it. I still see her as eighteen and wonder how she is at twenty-one. She loves Texas in the spring and writes all about the green of the grass and the live oaks, the red birds and pear blossoms, and all the things I have always associated with that smiling land in springtime. She has had her ears pierced and is glad that she can now wear turquoise in them like a Navajo when she returns to New Mexico. What a wonderful soul she is.

Early this morning I was awakened by someone calling softly, "John. John!" I found it was a native—one of those I had photographed the week before. He had a very sorry bamboo comb he wanted to trade, but nothing else. I told him to go away and not come back until he really had something.

Later in the day a man came by carrying a grass skirt and betelnuts wrapped in a large piece of tapa. I stopped him and made a trade for the two, but just what I wanted with the grass skirt I don't know. On Sunday we usually have a number of native men coming by, as they do not have to work then and are free to roam. One demonstrated a song and dance. The whole thing was surprisingly similar to some Apache dances I have seen.

I have just heard the latest report on Marvin Woods, the redheaded problem boy I have mentioned several times. After his last courtmartial, he was put in the stockade for six months hard labor. Later he broke out, took a boat, and headed out into the bay. Another boat overtook him and brought him back. There was more trouble, and now he has received a sentence of three years hard labor. He will be kept here in New Guinea, and if the war ends, he will most likely be returned to a prison in the States to finish his term. I won't see him again, but I won't forget that somewhere down the line of his years, someone slipped up and gave him an outlook that no one else ever tried to understand or correct.

April 23, 1944

Sunday again, and—as usual—somewhat of a rest day. This afternoon five of us took a truck and drove over to the ANGAU headquarters beyond Dobodura. The whole place is set in groves of the tallest coconut palms I have ever seen. There are many grass-roofed houses, all of them beautifully built with woven matting for sides. The native workers there were off duty today and were lounging around on the grass, primping, fluffing up their mops of fuzzy hair and putting flowers in it. All were dressed in their newest and brightest lap laps and looked healthy and happy—altogether the best looking bunch of natives I have seen.

I took some photos of the houses, the ball game, and the "poker game." A large crowd was gathered around a circle of seated men who were playing cards on a piece of old canvas. I never decided just what sort of game they played. One card at a time was dealt face up, and stakes were thrown in each time. They gambled for stick tobacco, matches, and nicknacks. The whole thing looked complicated and was, most likely, something known only to themselves.

May 4, 1944

More than a week ago we picked up bag and baggage and loaded on a liberty ship. Now we are camped below Finschhafen by the sea in a coconut grove. There has been constant rain since we arrived, which has hampered the building of camp.

Out in front of our area is a stretch of coral reef which is uncovered at low tide. On that reef I have found the elusive black cowries. End of the "Quest for the Cowries!" At first it was a matter of finding how to find them. I knew they were there and was determined to find them if it took all night. (It is easier to see them with a flashlight at night.)

As usual, I found that Mother Nature had the last laugh. The cowries have a protection for their attractive beauty. They simply cover themselves with a very thin film to which particles of moss, etc., cling, making them as inconspicuous as a bump on a rock. When they are touched, the film disappears revealing their polished and colorful shells.

Once you learn this trick, you are able to find them easily. After I "broke" the mysterious case, I found thirty in one night and continued to collect them each night. The black ones like to stay out where the surf pounds on the reef. The tiger-eye cowries are farther back in still water. There is quite a trade in souvenir bracelets made from these, and I may jump into the business and collect some cash on the side.

May 6, 1944

I have been pondering over the fact that I have written so little and so poorly lately. Things have lost much of the appeal I found in them eighteen months ago, and I feel stale and tired. Perhaps it started after the combat mission. Perhaps it is a natural state. Perhaps I should get out of the dumps and decide the whole thing is worthwhile—even against my inclination to do so.

May 7, 1944

Sunday again, and this afternoon I had time to go up the road to photograph some natives. Tomote—tul tul of Busika village and surrounding territory—was there with some of his people. They came to take away the big canoe, which is the last piece of their property left on what was once their village site. The canoe must have taken many long months to carve from that straight log, but it was still unfinished, without outrigger or paint. It was rolled down to the lagoon on sticks and tied to a smaller canoe in order to hold it upright.

While the work progressed (done mostly by the women and a couple of young men), I talked with Tomote in my growing vocabulary of pidgin English. Tomote answered my queries about the moo-rook or cassowary bird, which I had heard was to be found here, as well as in Australia.

"Big fella pigeon moo-rook where he stop?" I asked. "He over in big bush," Tomote replied, pointing toward the hills. Then he went on the explain that he himself did not know much about hunting moo-rook, but he had traded for some of the meat from the inland natives a number of times. He said since the natives from the inland spoke a different language, he was not able to find out much concerning the cassowaries.

The cassowary is a giant bird of the ostrich family, completely flightless, but capable of outrunning most animals. Also capable of breaking a man's leg with a kick of its large and powerful foot. The eggs of the cassowary are very thick-shelled and are of a pale green color. The unusual eggs first gave me the idea of asking about the bird, because the eggs make interesting souvenirs.

Late this afternoon one of the small native boys I had contacted last week showed up with a good-sized can of shells and a small, carved coconut bowl. He drove a harder bargain than the older natives, and it wasn't easy reaching an agreement on payment with him. He refused fishhooks, but wanted a new lap lap which I wouldn't give. Finally we settled for half-a-pound ($1.60). He had gotten a good price for his cowries, but seemed dissatisfied with the bargain. On my part it was a good buy, as the can contained about forty-five of the rare yellow shells that can be made up into perhaps fifty dollars worth of souvenir bracelets and necklaces.

May 12, 1944

In the mail today was a long letter from Mae McCay— the most heartwarming letter I have received in a very long time, full of her sensitive appreciation of New Mexico and all things worthwhile. She is truly—as Robert Henri says—"one of my people." I was green with envy of the plans which she and Roy have for a trading post and studio. Roy sent a note along too. He is a swell egg and is showing Mae all the happiness she has missed for so long.

May 13, 1944

Yesterday Tomote came by and tried to tell Callaway something about which he could not make heads or tails, and so, called me from the dining hall to interpret the stream of pidgin English. Tomote was quite relieved to see me, as he now has learned that my small knowledge of pidgin, and natives, is sincere. He wanted to take "some fella boy" (a group of natives) over to Tami Island.

Now, there is no place I would rather go. So I suggested that if we could get a boat, perhaps Tomote would get enough fish while at Tami to feed our company, because our chow has been especially awful lately. Of course, Callaway consented, since anything for his stomach causes him a sensation of delight. The thought of fresh fish to stuff his over long, big intestine would make him do anything.

Tomote was vague as to the number of natives to be taken over to Tami, but finally decided there might be nine or more. So plans were made for him to come here early in the morning when we will go to Busika beach and pick up the rest.

23 GOING FISHING

May 14, 1944

Cunning Tomote! He had a reason for being vague, for when we reached the beach, there was a positive mob of brown humanity scattered over the sand. Some of the Tami people were going home at last, along with their possessions. They began to load on, and soon the boat was practically hidden under piles of palm leaves, baskets of sweet potatoes and taro, cooking pots, baskets of coconut "canteens" for water, straw mats, men, women, children, babies, hens, pigs, and other noisy belongings.

It was a relief to know that only twenty-two of the people were going. The others had merely come down to see their friends off. Norman, the coxswain of the *Mercury*, had to have them move some of the stuff so he could see to steer the boat.

Inside the lagoon at Tami we unloaded the people and frazzle-tail litter of belongings on the beach of the larger of three islands, near the Australian radar camp. Soon the natives and their gear disappeared into the jungle toward the village on the opposite side, and we were left with the Australians. Tomote and several friends stood on the small pier that jutted fifty feet or so out into the lagoon, scanning the blue water. Soon he got out a small, square can of TNT; applied a fuse, crimped it with his teeth, calmly lighted it from his cigarette, held it a moment, and then tossed it into the spot he had selected.

Immediately after the explosion some small boys jumped into the water and began to bring up fish—beautiful silver ones about fifteen inches long, sometimes coming up with one in each hand and one in the mouth. Soon we had a boxful. Then Tomote and another native and a couple of small boys paddled off after more fish.

We chatted with the Aussies. There were about thirty of them manning a radar air warning station, and in nine months there, some men had not been to the mainland. Nothing is on the mainland anyway, and Tami is a place where you could live forever.

Most of the Aussies strolled around in shorts only, some of them quite naked, but all very brown and healthy looking. There is little use for clothes here on Tami, and in their off-duty hours the fellows took advantage of that fact. One, Brad Langley, was interested in showing me the camp, and before we left I had made an Aussie friend.

He was one of those who had been on Tami for many months and now planned his first trip over to our mainland camp. He wanted to remain overnight, so I promised him what hospitality our camp could offer, if he did so. The Aussie tents were set up by the beach in various nooks between huge coral rocks. Behind some were small "patios" surrounded by high rocks in which they had built seats and planted flowers and fixed places to build small fires for heating tea. Everyone seemed quite comfortable, and I envied them all of this.

One fellow offered to row me across the lagoon so I could hunt some cowries, but once over, he discovered he had forgotten his shoes (they seemed to rarely wear them anyway) so he could not wade out on the sharp coral. I found the reef almost untouched by shell gatherers, with plenty of cowries to be found under the loose coral rocks, and spent a pleasant hour or so after them.

Langley offered to make me a cup of hot chocolate when we returned. We drank it sitting in his "front yard" by the shore, as we looked vainly for Tomote, and the sun slid westward. My friends of the *Mercury* expressed no interest in either the island or the Aussies and spent their time sleeping on the bunks of the boat or sitting dejectedly on the wharf—a fact I couldn't be worried about.

A canoe slid across the lagoon bringing Tomote and his fish, and what fish! Every conceivable shape and color and size. Beautiful angel fish, parrot fish, bright blue ones, yellow ones, pink and green ones, purple ones, stripped ones, some with fantastic fins and enormous eyes, spotted ones—the canoe like a kaleidoscope full of tropical creatures. And me with not one bit of color film for my camera! A priceless opportunity lost.

Tomote sorted the fish, giving us the colorful names of them, telling which were edible and which were poisonous—facts he had learned from infancy up. The sea was a book he could read.

We were ready to sail for the mainland now, with only three natives returning—Tomote, his son, and a small boy. Tomote had told me he had a twenty-year-old son, but this was my first sight of him. He had been away in the service of the ANGAU. He was a handsome, sturdy native—probably an outstanding example of a Melanesian male. The boy and Tomote cleaned the fish on the rear of the boat as we crossed.

Before we left Tomote at Busika Beach he had promised to bring me some large crabs. I had learned the native word for the crabs and asked him about them. He always grins broadly in appreciation when he finds I know a new native word. Our conversation sounded something like this:

Me: "Tomote, you savvy Koo-Ka?"

T: "Yes, masta. Me savvy (with a big smile)."

Me: "Where stop big fella Koo-Ka belong Ki Ki?"

T: "He stop long water belong run. No stop soda wata long negiche."

Me: "Plenty fella Koo-Ka, big fella?"

T: "Yes."

Me: "Him plenty good Ki Ki?"

T: "Yes, plenty good."

Me: "One time you come long Malasiga, you bringum me Koo-Ka?"

T: "I bring three day, four day, mebbe."

What I learned, in plain unpidgin English, was that the crabs were found up the small streams that run into the lagoon, not along the ocean. There were plenty of them, and they were good to eat. Also that Tomote would come Wednesday or Thursday and bring some of them to our camp by Malasiga Lagoon. Anytime in the next week or two would be a good guess at when he would show up, for these people have the happy faculty of not allowing themselves to be pinned down to a matter of hour. Anyway, why hurry through a day? It's so wonderful—much too wonderful to split into mechanical fragments of minutes.

May 29, 1944

Since the thirteenth, several bright spots have appeared in the routine of camp—several trips to Tami (which netted a fine collection of cowries), more experiences with the natives, etc. In the past two weeks I have collected $225 from my cowries, and the demand is still red hot. I am usually behind in orders. It gives me something to keep my hands busy.

I have found myself thinking of Marie oftener and oftener. She is the only girl I have ever known who sincerely loves and understands New Mexico, not with her head, but with her heart too. She will never leave it, I know, and maybe sometime I will get the courage to ask her if I can share it with her—all the sights and sounds and smells of sage and canyon and aspen; rain, snow, and sunshine. I know I am more deadly serious than I have ever been. But what about Marie? She has an artist mother and an artist father. She understands the strength and weaknesses of people of the brush and palette. I would spend a joyful lifetime making her happy.

The whole army works in peculiar ways. Today for the fiftieth time a list was brought from regimental headquarters wanting the religion of every man. Now, after all the previous times of asking the same question, they should know—besides it being none of their damned business. So I decided to do just what I had forgotten to do when inducted—declare myself a Mohammedan. As I suspected, it created quite a flurry at regimental headquarters. Nobody had ever heard that there was a Mohammedan in the regiment, so that paper was sent back to be verified. I stood my ground and was very indignant that anyone should question my religion and signed the sheet as proof of my determination. For once there was something in the army that I could demand being done for me. Now, as far as all the army records are concerned, I am a Mohammedan. I must find what direction Mecca is from here.

Elizabeth writes that Mother has recovered from her recent illness but looks pale and tired. How I long to see her! Sometimes it is hard to bear, especially as there seems to be no end in sight. We figured out recently just how long it would take to get our brigade home on the so-called "rotation plan." Exactly SIX HUNDRED SIXTY-SEVEN YEARS! Our quota is one man from the brigade each month. What utter stupidity. What insidious propaganda! Folks at home have visions of shiploads of their boys coming home on "rotation," but we here understand it is only an empty gesture to impress them.

Last week my first touch of fever showed up and made me feel pretty rotten for about four days, but with plenty of the little, yellow Atabrine pills, the fever was licked and apparently left as suddenly as it came. Getting sick is a tragedy here, as our hospitals are only tents, and there is a growing lack of enthusiasm among the doctors. The usual diagnosis is, "There just isn't anything I can do for you."

The indifference is found again in the evacuating of those who are really ill. Every record is kept as free from mention of any illness as possible. A doctor who has fewer bad cases on his record is more likely to get a promotion. So human health and life is sacrificed for a few more dollars and a little more rank with which to impress the empty hero-hunters back home.

June 4, 1944

Another letter from Elizabeth, and the worst news since coming overseas. Dad has had serious heart attacks, and Mother is again ill. Elizabeth was quite alarmed, and I have been blue since her letter arrived. The news is so hard to take, and I feel so helpless and far away. There just wouldn't be anything to go back to if Mother and Dad were not there. They have been my guiding light.

I have sent Dot two hundred dollars for incidental expenses—the little things Mother might not get. If the money were sent directly to her, she would simply deposit it to my account. So even if she has plenty, I want this spent on her.

June 14, 1944

Another letter from Marie! A swell, cheery letter so full of the little-girl charm of her. She has not lost her bouncing interest in things, and I doubt that she ever will. Mae never has, and Marie is a lot like her mother.

I came across an earlier letter containing Marie's account of her last summer in New Mexico. It is a rare piece of writing.

"Summer before last we were still in New Mexico. We were living at the mine. I believe that summer was the most enjoyable one I ever had. I worked at the Ranger Station four miles down the mountain at a picturesque little Mexican village called Peñasco, which means 'Rocky.' It is situated in a small valley, and the Indian pueblo of Picuris is only about a mile away. In fact, it runs parallel to Peñasco, for a little ridge is all that separates the two. The little valley is beautiful and surrounded by mountains; and close by is Truchas Peak, which is fourteen hundred feet high.

"Spring is beautiful there. You can smell it and feel it and see it. The Mexicans start their plowing, and lilacs and yellow irises bloom in all the yards. The fruit trees bloom, and the creeks are overflowing with snow water from the mountains. You can look at a group of cottonwoods and see not a leaf—but you know there will soon be, because there is a yellow-green haze about it. The sky is bluer there than any place else in New Mexico, I believe.

"I've seen just about every little valley around there, and the names fascinate me. There's Llano and Llano Largo and Río Pueblo and Rodante and Velarde and Placita and Angostura and Trampos. (There's the most beautiful old mission there!) Then there's Truchas, Chamisol, Chacón, Mora, and Tres Ritos. They're around Peñasco in a radius of ten miles. Gee, I'll be glad when I see that country again!"

And see it you will, Marie, and if you will let me, we will see it together—for a whole lifetime. If you had no other virtue, sweet child, but to be able to feel and smell and understand the Spring as you have written, you would be a rare mortal indeed! "You can look at the cottonwoods and see not a leaf—but you know there soon will be, for there is a yellow-green haze about them." So few are conscious of that haze, Marie.

24 TRADING AT TAMI

June 17, 1944

This morning we were to have a rifle inspection, one of those asinine things where everybody lines up with his supposedly clean rifle (we have been issued carbines now, which are easier to carry and easier to keep clean), and an officer (who most likely doesn't know if a rifle is clean when he looks) comes down the line putting his eye to the barrel. Lots of guns have gone off that way, and I keep hoping.

Just as the thing started, I was called to the phone and found that the captain of intelligence wanted me at once. So I escaped and went up to find out what he wanted. He had a native whom I recognized as a tul tul because of the two red bands on his cap. The captain was unable to understand what the native wanted. I was to interpret pidgin English again.

The ANGAU had given this fellow his rations for the village for a month, but the rations had been deposited on the beach some ten miles from the village. Ten miles of overland trail in New Guinea is no joke, especially when you are carrying hundred-pound bags of rice, cans of sugar, cases of bully beef, etc. The tul tul wanted to know if we would take him in a boat, pick up the rations, and drop them down the coast at his village. Captain Gudgeon wanted to go on a trip with the natives (he had not been before), so he said all right—if I would go along. He and another officer went, but knew so little of the natives that they were useless except as sightseers. However, I enjoyed doing what managing was necessary anyway. This time I had color film and intended to get some good character studies.

While the loading of the supplies progressed, I noticed a woman coming on board with a large can of meal on her shoulder. But it was her legs and feet that caught my attention. She had "elephantitis,"[28] and her legs were swollen into huge posts that made even her ample feet look tiny. I at once went to the tul tul and told him in no uncertain pidgin that "Mary belong big leg. She no can come on boat." He screamed at her in a high-pitched voice, and she bolted like a rabbit.

Soon another woman with the disease was spotted in the loading group, and I banished her myself by bellowing at her like a veteran. It worked equally as well as the blast the tul tul had leveled at the other woman. Then I proceeded to give the tul tul the very devil for letting any of the elephantitis cases come aboard when I had told him not to. The disease is dangerous in the tropics, and this is one country in which you can't be too careful about such things. Even after the repeated warnings, I found one afflicted woman aboard just as we were ready to pull away. She had slipped on and thought she was unnoticed. So, she got off and joined her sisters of the oversized legs for a trip on foot to the village.

We had all the natives in the bottom of the big boat. This was one time they couldn't get away from the camera even if they wanted to. Some are shy, but usually they are flattered to be photographed.

A woman nursed a brown elf-of-a-baby and made quite a picture, but she was in the shade, so I asked her to move into the sunlight. Her husband came up and decided he should be photographed with the baby, so he took it and struck a rigid pose in the sun. Naturally he couldn't nurse the baby, so my original picture idea was ruined right there. But I got a close-up of the cheerful infant.

Another woman had a baby too and looked hopefully at the camera as she bounced the baby on her knee. But the small fry had sores on his head and was definitely not picture material!

During the photographing I noticed a new "billum" folded in the belongings of one of the women. The billum or string bag is the carryall of the Melanesian woman. It is made from native string that she spins from grass and bark. Billums are remarkable pieces of work, so even in quality that I have a hard time making my friends believe the bags are not made from manufactured string. This one was dyed in lovely, soft shades of pink, blue, wine, yellow, green, and brown—all woven in stripes and squares. Quite a riot of color, but their soft hues blended into a work of art! Later I was told that the women dyed them with "something belong bush"—probably berries and bark and the like.

The woman was hesitant about selling the bag, and even though her husband seemed to think it would be all right, she held back. In spite of all you hear to the contrary, these women usually have their way, like the female of the species all over the world. I showed her a bright, flowered lap lap and package of needles. She gave in right there, and the trade was made.

High on the boat's ramp the tul tul stood like an ebony masthead scanning the sea. I had told him to "look long wata, sing out strong long bad wata." He understood the importance of keeping off the coral reefs and promised to "sing out strong" if any were sighted. However, under his direction we weren't apt to get anywhere near a reef, for he had known these waters from childhood.

He guided us into a good beach near his village where all the natives in that section were gathered. These stops are as mysterious as anything I have found among the Melanesians, for no matter when we take a boat or at what time, they are there expecting us. It is a long way from Malasiga to the village, and it had taken the tul tul a long time to make the journey and arrange the trip. The people couldn't have known whether or not he would be able to even get a boat, and certainly did not know when it would arrive. They swarmed out—kids, men, women, girls, and numerous small, wiry little dogs of the kind found in every village.

Down went the ramp, and I told the tul tul to unload "hurry up" and went ashore to photograph. An old woman was the first subject. She was washing six puppies in a pool, then putting each one back into a large billum. She finished, put the billum on her back, and left, as I wondered if it was an act of love or washing meat before eating.

Several of the young girls had pointed breasts that wagged intriguingly under their missionary-inspired "Mary blouses," and we wanted photos of them as they usually dressed—in lap lap only. I approached the tul tul on the subject, and he seemed a bit surprised. He talked with the husbands of the girls about the matter, and the husbands looked even more surprised. Presently the most fetching of the belles simply disappeared into thin air, and our men got a suspicious gleam in their eyes. Although it was not a fatal blunder, it didn't help any.

One woman finally couldn't resist a package of shining needles and peeled off her unbecoming top covering to reveal an even more unbecoming pair of breasts—one hanging down toward her waist and one short and pointing west (giving me an idea that some people wore clothes for a good reason). But I photographed her anyway and dropped the subject right there. It was time.

As we left, a native came to me with a large coconut shell full of cowries as a gift. He was that grateful for not having to carry all that food over miles of trail. A small gift maybe, but enough cowries to bring me forty or fifty dollars when made up.

When we returned, we found Tomote here, in a very bad humor. We had promised to take him and his food supply over to Tami Island, and he thought we had neglected him for this rival tul tul of the other village group. He had not showed up when we left on this last trip, but he somehow knew that we had gone off with other natives, and he didn't like it. His decoration of three long feathers[29] fairly quivered in his fuzzy hair as he spurted pidgin at me in a tone of hurt indignation. I finally smoothed the situation over by telling him I had been ordered to go by the "big boss"—the ANGAU.

It was too late anyway to get him to Tami before dark, so he finally decided it would be better to wait until morning, then take his canoe, his pig, etc., along—as well as the food. He covered the pile of provisions by the wharf with a large canvas, and I assured him that the guard that was posted there at night would "look strong long im kai kai belong boy." Then he went off to the village to round up some men and women to help with the loading in the morning and to arrange for the picking up of the pig and canoe at Busika village.

It was very late the next day when he finally showed up—almost noon. So I had to forego the trip as I was Corporal of the Guard beginning at 5:00 p.m., and I knew we would not get back by then. With Tomote when he came to the office was the old man who had promised to do the wood carving. Evidently the old man wanted to bring the things himself. One was a beautifully carved walking stick for Callaway. The other was the "man belonga house Tambarin"[30] that I had asked for, but perched on the top of a stout cane. It was a peculiar half-human figure in a somewhat crouched position, skillfully carved, but still unfinished. I gave the old man the white silk lap lap he had been promised, but he looked at Tomote and spoke to him in their own language. Evidently the old man was not accustomed to pidgin. Tomote told me the old man wanted one of the flowered lap laps too, because the carving was "work plenty too mus." Of course, I gave in, and the old man took the carving away promising to do a good job on it—"work im work im work im plenty, make im black fella too" (finish it well and carefully and put it in the mangrove swamp to turn it into "island ebony"). Tomote also collected the second of two lap laps I had promised him for a lot of cowries, which I have not gotten as yet.

The supplies were loaded by three men and half-a-dozen women, after which I told Tomote that Dotson would go with him. Dotson is back with the company after a long stay in the Admiralties, where he learned pidgin. It is good to have him back! He has been gone for many months, and I wondered if he would ever be with us again.

They left for the trip, and I left to prepare for the tour of guard. Later violent rain squalls showed out to sea, blotting out Tami from sight, and it was a good guess that the boat of natives and belongings was getting a good soaking.

June 24, 1944

The photo Marie promised arrived, and she is beautiful in a simple white blouse and checked skirt, with a quizzical smile playing over her lovely face. The camp wolves come by and sigh as they see it. Several come by and say "hello" to her everyday, and get in some digs at me as to why she would have to send the photo to me.

Took another load of natives to Tami, again picking them up at Busika beach. They moved the usual load of everything under the sun. Among the litter of belongings were some fine old pieces of carving and the biggest bowl I ever saw. It was every bit of four feet long! Also, there were some beautifully carved bowls for pounding taro root, and an old drum that was a dandy. The old man who had made it wouldn't sell it, because it was an old family possession, but promised to start right away on one for me. Most likely we will move off before it is finished, as the man works slowly.

At Tami I looked up Tomote. He and his people are building a new village on Oneum Island—the center of the Tami group. He was busily engaged in cutting the head from a steel barrel, possibly with water storage in mind. We went back to the temporary hut he had built while the pole-and-thatch house was being erected. I gave his wife the bright, red silk bag

I had made, filled with needles, safety pins, thread, razor blades, and beads. She should have something for herself, as she has been gathering the cowries I am to get. Evidently she works on the shell gathering willingly for the food and clothing they get out of it. (I always carry them cans of bully beef and small things of the sort.) She did not speak pidgin, and I found that none of the women do, as they have simply no dealings with white men, and therefore, have no use for a common language.

Before I left, Tomote went out by the hut and got my shells—the biggest sack of them I have yet seen. He had certainly lived up to his promise to get plenty.

After washing them and sorting them out, I find there are hundreds of the rare yellow ones. To date I have made somewhat over seven hundred dollars on these shells, and here was enough to double that sum. Being a friend to a native pays in lots of ways!

25 To Dutch New Guinea

July 8, 1944

First news of a new move, this time way around the northern Guinea coast to Wakde—a spot west of Hollandia—in the newly captured section of Dutch New Guinea. Our next payday will see us getting Dutch guilders instead of Australian pounds. Maybe we are leaving Australian territory for good—I hope.

It is a disappointment having to leave my native friends here. They have been a pleasure. It is nice to make a new friend of any kind, but hard to leave him for good and all. You can retain pleasant memories—and I have them—such as: Tomote bringing me a fresh coconut as I sat in the village on Tami; his primitive hospitality so strong and more sincere than ours, showing that people are born with pleasant instincts; his quick smile at each new pidgin word I learned; his dull anger when he supposed I had taken his rival chief in tow; all the human things so similar to our own behavior, but in a place so remote.

July 13, 1944

After the usual mix-ups and hurry-ups and demonstrations of poor planning, we left Finsch[31] around noon with about fifty boats. Estadt, Charlie, two more fellows, and I were passengers on an M-377. The crew of four had, of course, arranged their sleeping quarters in a sort of "cabin" rigged upon the rear of the boat just forward of the wheel house, but we were just "passengers," so to hell with us. Our boat crews seem to eternally resent carrying passengers on their boats, even though they do so all the time. Perhaps we do not know anything about running a boat, but I'd like to see any or all of those hams do what any one of us does each day!

Tonight we passed up the north coast of Guinea. Numerous brush fires were burning along the coast looking like lighted amusement parks by the sea. There were no troops in this whole area, and I wondered just how such extensive fires could have gotten started.

July 15, 1944

We traveled all day yesterday and arrived at Bogia Harbor late last evening. Bogia is a moon-shaped harbor with the whole shore one huge coconut plantation—the largest I have yet seen. One cabin boat hit a rock coming in and started sinking last night. It will be left behind for repair. Bogia is only a fueling stop, but the last stop of any kind before reaching Japanese held territory.

Lying out to sea is a beautiful peaked island, evidently an extinct volcano. It no doubt reminded the Japanese sharply of Mount Fujiyama, as it has—in a small way—all the grace and beauty of that Japanese mountain.

A few miles west the Australians have the Japanese hemmed in on this side, and a hundred miles or so farther on, our boys who landed at Hollandia have them held on that side, gripping the Eighteenth Japanese Army of probably fifty thousand men in an iron vise from which there is no possible escape. Sea supply is cut off by constant patrolling of destroyers and PT boats that have taken a terrific toll of Japanese barges and ships and finally cut them out completely. The enemy may try to escape over the mountains, an almost impossible feat for an army, or make a suicidal attempt to break through to the west. Even with a temporary breakthrough (which they are not likely to bring about), they would be up against thousands of American troops and many hundreds of miles of American-occupied territory seized from Aitape to far down the coast beyond Hollandia.

The fifteenth is my birthday, which I happened to think of as we sat on the boat in the twilight. I'm getting too doggone old to be wasting my time running around New Guinea!

July 16, 1966

We skirted the Japanese-held sector last night and yesterday, traveling so far out to sea that no land was visible except a number of small islands. One island was an active volcano about whose peak hung a cloud of sulphurous, yellow smoke. Evidently, there had been no eruption in many years, for the whole island was covered with green growth more than halfway up its steep sides, and there was even a coconut plantation down by the sea where some land lay flat. There were several grass houses there too, but my idea is that living there is a bit risky. Maybe the thing hasn't erupted in a long time, but it might take a notion to spurt fire and brimstone just any moment. I found a peach can label and a grubby stub of a pencil and made a quick sketch of the smoking island.

Aitape is an excellent harbor, shielded on the east by a group of coral islands. Our first glimpse of the place was one of these islands, ripped by gunfire until hardly a leaf remained on any tree. Aitape is the western extreme of the Japanese pocket, and even as we entered the harbor, we heard the 155s on shore giving the Japanese a hot assurance that they faced disaster. We narrowly escaped being fired upon by our own destroyers and shore guns, because we arrived at the precise time a group of Japanese barges was expected to try running in supplies for the belabored enemy troops. To make matters worse, the ship and our convoy signalman were at odds about challenge signals and spent some time blinking to each other. Finally the destroyer turned broadside to us and signaled the shore batteries to stand by for action. At the critical moment, someone on the destroyer decided we were flying American flags and finally let us go by.

We anchored by one of the islands several miles offshore. It was a fueling stop and repair shop for boats. Later in the day I went ashore to see what had taken place there and found that it had once been used for exactly the same purpose by the Japanese. There was an immense fuel dump that had contained hundreds of drums of gasoline, now a blackened heap of exploded barrels where our planes had destroyed it. The shore was lined with wrecks of Japanese barges, made sieve-like by all kinds of gunfire. As the place had so recently been taken, there were no labor-saving devices, so we pumped the fuel for our boats by hand, each group of us fueling our own boat.

The swimming is good, and we take advantage of as many swims as we please during the day. The smooth white sand bottom is dotted with huge starfish and other ocean creatures that can be easily seen from the surface.

Today there hove in sight an amazing array of native canoes, all with sails spread, and we said, "Here comes the Fuzzy Wuzzy Navy!" It was a beautiful sight as they came nearer and nearer. Each man had rigged his canoe to suit himself, with the delightful result of no two sails being the same size or shape. Some were white canvas. Some woven grass matting. All were picturesque.

July 20, 1944

We arrived in Hollandia Harbor early and found another large harbor filled with every kind of ship, from small native canoes to one huge aircraft carrier. This was the spot where the initial landing was made on Dutch New Guinea, pinning the Japanese Eighteenth Army in.[32] Now the beaches swarmed with men and machinery; roads were being built; camps erected. Probably more work had been done in a few short weeks than the Japanese did in their more than two years of occupation of this port.

Our stop here was brief, and before nightfall we were off again for our final destination. The western sky was a sheet of brass tarnished by purple clouds. The sea picked up the color on its waves. The steep, green mountains rose abruptly from the sea on our left, and each boat trailed a sky-blue wake behind it like a fluffy tail. Night gradually lowered itself over the whole of it, and we settled down for an all-night run.

July 23, 1944

We're in Dutch New Guinea building a new camp again, but this time—instead of coconut trees—we have a forest of immense giants of jungle trees hung with vines and filled with bird calls, all very much like the movie scenes of Kipling's *Jungle Book.* The breeze from the nearby beach comes through, and the shade is cool, the only disadvantage being the rather swampy ground. This area is also very new, and there is still a defense line up back of us, manned by infantry. The woods there are full of booby traps for defense against enemy troops, who—even though defeated and scattered—have a nasty habit of slipping back to do as much damage as possible. Naturally I have taken no hikes over the country and anticipate none.

Evidently the threat of any Japanese action of any large nature is entirely removed, because the harbor here is full of all kinds of ships unloading tons of material. There has not been any Japanese air action since the first day when a very few planes made vain attempts to bomb. However, there is the almost constant sound of artillery down the coast to the west where the action is going on. Each night the 155s up behind here blast targets in the hills—probably places selected by patrols during the day—and never a night passes that a number of the land mines and booby traps do not explode, bringing all of us upright in our cots.

At last we have as a company commander the only officer I have ever known who was a gentleman before being made so by an act of congress. Callaway has gone to another company. Already the change is apparent in the good things taking shape. All the men are very fond of Sanders and always have been. They are overjoyed to have him here. Work is smoothing out. We have our jobs clear-cut and know what to do, and everything is run on the fairest basis I have seen thus far in the army.

July 30, 1944

Sunday, but no change, and no place to go this time. I miss the usual Sunday trips. No late mail has reached us as yet. Things are at a standstill in most ways. The change of company commanders did more to lift morale than anything in ages, and it was about time, too, as everyone was getting plenty low.

The Japanese soldiers are apparently still prowling around in the vicinity, for yesterday one of the guards at the fuel dump was found shot. The place is rather isolated, and only one man was posted there. The sniper probably just slipped within shooting distance and picked the man off and then disappeared again into the jungle. It was a bad thing and made the whole area jittery to some extent. The Japs hide like rats and are killed weeks, and even months, after the area is taken over. Eventually they get so starved and desperate that they give up sniping and try to just exist, but either our men get them or the jungle does.

Bill Flint knows trees. He has lived in the Kentucky mountains and has cut and taken to the mill countless forest giants. Yesterday I asked him to estimate one of the immense jungle hardwoods here. We finally got figures as accurate as possible on a standing tree—seventy feet to the first limb, more than five feet through with practically no taper from base to the end of the seventy feet, containing more than ten thousand board feet of lumber. Multiplied by millions, this is quite a lumber supply tucked away here in the wilds of New Guinea. Someday it will be tapped, for we will be forced to look for just such supplies when we have depleted our American forests—and we will.

August 4, 1944

Our "temporary" campsite seems to be developing into a permanent one, and we are fixing tent frames, flooring the headquarters office tent, etc. During the past few days there has been far less shelling from the nearby big guns, but occasional bombing by our planes. To add to the humor (if any can be found in such an incident) one fellow "saw" a Japanese soldier under his cot and two more outside the tent. Just what such a soldier would be doing under his cot is a mystery, but the fellow was so scared he jumped up and alarmed the whole place. The infantry that has the defense line across the road sent a patrol out, and the place was thoroughly gone over, but nothing found. Now the guy is the butt of all kinds of jokes about people seeing things in the night.

Today the infantry guards said they expected the Japanese between here and Hollandia to try for a breakthrough here. However, the guards were not alarmed. From captured and killed soldiers, it is learned that they are in bad physical condition from lack of food, etc.

Our news summary contains some details of the Japanese pocket between Wewak and Aitape.[33] From it I learn that on the sixteenth when we were in Aitape, the attack by Japanese General Hatazo Adachi's Eighteenth Army had just been definitely broken, and our forces were still destroying the forward part of the Jap drive which had been cut off completely by the Allies. Thus the constant shelling and bombing is accounted for. The news gives Adachi's predicament—having Australians on the east, Americans on the west, the impassable mountains on the south, and the sea (full of our destroyers) on the north—and says he has only "the choices of the damned." Apparently the choice was to try for a break through the American lines, but he gained only more Japanese dead for his trouble.

The task force that left here recently struck at a point east of Sorong and encountered no resistance. MacArthur says this is the last large-scale landing to be made on New Guinea. Whence do we goeth, Mac? Are you determined to take the Philippines so you can ride in triumph through the streets of Manila? Will the few who tell you what to do feel that the sacrifice is worth it? I hope not, you old bastard, built by Hollywood-like publicity in American newspapers, proud of your swagger, quick to catch the publicity angle of any news and use it to the hilt—but hated by those who work near you plus every man in the southwest Pacific. You were nearly *too* clever in the presidential nomination incident and were willing to kill it when you knew that you might get one vote from some silly soldier—no more. Even that brought you further into the limelight, scum of West Point!

The good change of having Sanders as company commander was short-lived. Callaway is back, and—again—the men feel that they have been let down by higher-up authorities. Sanders's good work is even more apparent now that it is at a standstill.

August 11, 1944

This has been a damnable week, relieved only by five letters from home and two from Marie. At home things are running smoothly, if being comfortable could mean anything, but Dad is still in a doubtful condition and has heart attacks if he is up much. Marie is working the night shift, and her last letter was written at 2:00 a.m.

Little firing has been heard around the immediate area, and even the fighting down the coast seems to have moved away from us until only occasionally do we hear the shelling. A jittery soldier on the line occasionally tosses a grenade into the darkness where he sees stumps moving or hears something fall from a jungle tree, but apparently this has become practically "non-combat" territory. Morale is low—the lowest I have yet seen—and my personal morale is exactly zero, making me wonder if it is worth going through day after day after day for another year (which may be spent right in this same climate, among the same people, under the same conditions). Sometimes I envy those who fell early in the game. At least they have rest and freedom. We have neither, and little hope of it in sight.

The sunsets over the harbor are beautiful, and it is restful to sit by the shore and watch the day die so gloriously, giving its warm splendor to each wave, painting the wet sand in rose and pink, filling the air with soft magnificence. Softly, so softly, the night obliterates the harshness of war. The ships fade into the grayness of the harbor as the light dies. The tents and machinery become shapes that are part of the night. Only the moving lights of the harbor indicate the teeming activity of war.

August 13, 1944

For the first time, today I rode down the coast five or six miles to approximately the end of our occupied territory. Beyond there is nothing in the way of camp or road, just scattered Japanese patrols and starving remnants of their beaten forces. The jeep whizzed along the hard-packed, black sand of the beach, past the hundreds of soldiers out for a Sunday swim and sun bath. The sea was very blue, stretching to Wakde Island,[34] but Wakde was an alien piece of earth—no part of this green land. Here on shore there were few signs of fighting, but Wakde presents destruction more fierce than any I have seen. Every tree is shattered, every blade of green. The very earth is shredded, and Wakde stands—a strip of yellow desert—misplaced in a blue tropic sea. Tons upon tons of screaming metal must have gone into this five miles of island to strip it so completely.

Finally the narrowing beach forced us onto the road that parallels the shore—a road that bumped, rolled, and staggered its way through coconut groves and across ditches until it came to an end near the American cemetery. Here we stopped near the entrance marked "Toem Cemetery," so named for the muddy little Toem River nearby. Rows and rows of white crosses in two neat, bare squares—in all, probably five hundred graves. All killed in this whole area are buried here, including those of the battle on Wakde Island.

The ground was raked bare and clean, but behind each row of crosses was a beaten path where the living came to read the small metal tags tacked there. Maybe the searchers had a buddy killed here, or maybe someone had written that Joe Doe from the hometown was killed in a forward New Guinea area, or maybe they were just curious, but anyway they came and searched each tag for a familiar name.

Near the entrance was a tent, headquarters of the detachment that supervised and cared for the cemetery. And there the registration book of those buried here was kept, but I did not read it. By the entrance an American flag flew on a tall pole and cast a long, flickering shadow over the crosses of those who had died for it. This spot was far removed from the noise and bustle of the unloading of ships up the coast, but there was no silence here. Each cross spoke like thunder through the coconut grove, across the pale tropic sky, loud sounds of broken bodies and broken hopes and leaving behind of those who cared. "What shall the harvest be?...Unborn of unborn shall see..." What are we to believe—we who are left to look upon the rows of crosses?

All along the road there were numerous natives, but quite a different lot from the Sunday groups we saw around Finschhafen. Our natives there were proud, dignified, and careful of dress. On Sunday they wore their best lap laps and combed their fuzzy hair up and put flowers in it. Seldom, if ever, did they don castoff army clothing. They seemed to realize that it robbed them of any look of dignity or neatness. These natives were all clothed in very dirty, old army undershirts and shorts, old shoes, all kinds of old hats; and their hair was cropped close, making altogether the most miserable and motley-looking group of Melanesians I have ever seen.

August 21, 1944

Another Sunday has come and gone—another week marked off. Aside from five letters from Marie and Mae and some from home, there has been little on the bright side. Still the dullness of an army camp in a mudhole, of which there is none worse.

For six weeks now the Japanese who are cut off at the point across the harbor, have been bombed, shelled, and strafed without mercy. Every day we can see the planes diving on them and hear the thud of bombs and the rattle of machine guns and cannons. Every night the 155s behind our tent area shell them from here. They must live in a literal hell, but they still live—at least enough of them to be dangerous. Sooner or later, they will be forced to die or come out. And die they will, rather than surrender, if they are at all like those before them.

A lieutenant of the infantry that is holding the front there came by one afternoon and gave us the best firsthand account of the fighting we have had. He was not a personality to spin yarns, and I believed his accounts of the fighting there. We lose men every day. The Japanese are still cunning.

Those captured show little signs of needing food and are tricky and stubborn. Evidently they are better supplied than the enemy forces to our east.

The best catch of this whole campaign was a group of three prisoners taken lately who gave more information than anyone had been able to get before. A lieutenant, a warrant officer, and a sergeant were surrounded and captured alive and uninjured. The two officers offered to talk, but the sergeant, who evidently spoke English, was stubborn and smart. One of the infantrymen simply took his sharp machete and severed his head with one blow. Surprising? Not at all. It is done often, as I saw with my own eyes, so I have no reason to doubt a word of the story.

The irony of the whole thing was that just the same day I had read a memorandum on our bulletin board that gave a hair-raising account of an American soldier having his head cut off with a samurai sword. It had been taken from the diary of a Japanese sergeant killed near Hollandia and said in part: "Today was the greatest day of my life. I was allowed to sever the head of a captured enemy with a samurai sword. My only humiliation was that I had to take two strokes."

My, my! You should have practiced with a machete, Mr. Moto, for you see, our men need to take only one stroke with that! War is war, and the Geneva Red Cross Convention (quoted often in articles about "humane treatment of enemy prisoners") is a long, long way from the front line. There is but one law here, KILL, KILL, KILL!

August 26, 1944

Apparently nothing is due to relieve the monotony and petty dealing of our inadequately run regiment. Our men—not one, but all—are worn out, tired, and sick. Morale is zero. No one feels that the men are any longer of any importance or that anyone cares what we think, so long as we can be driven on and on like good mules.

While doing a four-hour guard watch the other night, I had—for the first time here—a chance to observe the coming of a jungle dawn. At 2:00 I took up a lonely post—lonely not because it was far removed from camp, but because at that hour the world is wrapped in its deepest and quietest sleep.

Nearby was the second of the only two "firefly trees" I have ever seen. Once on New Britain I had seen this strange phenomenon in the jungle—a tree twenty or thirty feet high covered with literally thousands of tropical fireflies. An odd pulsating glow hung around the tree—a light that seemed unreal and uncertain—as if at any minute it might dissolve into the night. Apparently the fireflies were attracted to a certain kind of bushy tree, for they were nowhere else, which accented the whole strange sight. It brought back memories of snow and Christmas trees on lawns back home, but no tree was ever decorated with such splendor.

After some time (I judged it to be between 4:00 and 5:00) a hornbill high in a tree above me suddenly began his rattling call—the first herald of dawn. I had noticed no change in the night, but the hornbill from his perch had caught the subtle change in the earth and sky. Soon after that another smaller bird called, then another, and another. The sky began to pale. Fewer fireflies winked on the firefly tree. The green color of the jungle that had been black in the night emerged. Camp kitchens added their clanking of pans to the bird calls of a waking jungle, and gradually there was day in New Guinea.

26 Exploring New Area

September 1, 1944

Today I made my first trip to what is generally called the native village. In reality it is a newly built compound of sorts where all the natives of this section who have come in from the hills are kept. Very large, thatched-roof houses have been built, and each family occupies a small square along the outer side. There is an aisle down the middle. Apparently race or tribe was not taken into consideration, and everyone classed as "native" was put there. The whole thing seemed to be under the management of young men who were apparently Javanese or one of the similar races.

They wore neat khaki shirts and shorts and carried pistols on their belts. Each man wore a shoulder patch bearing the words "Netherlands Indies" which showed he was a part of the Netherlands Indies Native Army. No Dutch were present, nor have I seen any since coming here. So apparently the whole administration is up to the native soldiers, who looked neat and intelligent and entirely capable of the job. On seeing them I suddenly realized that I had seen no Australians since coming here. We are out of British territory, and, of course, even in the present emergencies, the Dutch would not welcome British as administrators of their subjects.

An astonishing mixture of races is found here—so different from the pure Melanesian stock of New Guinea's eastern shore. To be sure, there are Melanesians here also; but along with them, unmistakable evidence that we are approaching the "melting line" of the Indies border where world fuses with world in painless stages, generation after generation.

One little woman was really beautiful, with an oval brown face; almost-straight, black hair done up in an odd knot on the top of her head; a deep wine blouse, and a very Oriental rust-colored, figured skirt or sorong that came almost to her tiny, bare, brown feet. The right side of her face bore a curved design in tiny, blue dots of tattoo, probably of tribal significance. She was carrying a delightful brown baby, and the whole made such a rare picture that I felt the world had lost something valuable because no portrait painter was present to immortalize on canvas this Melanesian-Javanese mother and child.

Another girl boiled a pot of rice over a small fire. She was outstanding for her beautiful, golden-ocher skin and her snow-white sorong. The sorong was simply a piece of white cloth wound about her shapely body as only these people can wind a sorong. It started just above her firm breasts and ended below her knees, all being accomplished without fastenings of any kind. The girl's hair was somewhat fuzzy, but had been bleached and dyed a reddish color that almost matched her startling skin. Her teeth were white and even.

In the village were several Chinese, pure Javanese, and many who could have been either or both, with a dozen strains thrown in. Two small children, perhaps little more than a year old, looked suspiciously like their pappys might have been G.I. Joes of the Japanese army.

A large warehouse shed was crammed with Japanese supplies consisting mostly of rice in woven straw bags. I suppose these supplies were given to the natives, as our forces wouldn't use the things, and we would have to feed the residents anyway. Much Japanese material was captured in this area—most of it useless to us.

In an open space in the center of the village, all the men were gathered for some sort of drill and roll call. I noticed that they were all very nondescript looking and showed surprisingly few of the color differences noticeable in the women. They were seemingly a group of shabby, dark men clad in various wild costumes like untidy tramps. I finished my roll of color film by taking several photos of the two women, along with some shots of the village houses, etc. Then we departed. There was nothing to trade for here. The people were homeless and poor.

September 6, 1944

Today one of the fellows shot the first cuscus I had ever seen close up. It was first seen high in the treetops swinging from limb to limb with a nonchalance that simply shouldn't go hand-in-hand with swinging by your tail that far from the earth on bending branches. Finally a shot registered, and the cuscus tumbled down. About twice the size of a large opossum with a large round head, large round eyes, a soft coat of white and bright rust brown in a bold irregular pattern; feet with a thumb and five fingers, and a stout tail for clinging, he looked almost as cuddly and innocent as a koala bear. Just why Mother Nature chose to fit him with his thick coat of somewhat wooly fur is a mystery known only to her, for he would seem not to need it in this climate. He would, no doubt, be an interesting fellow, and I am sorry we do not have him alive.

September 10, 1944

I have spent some time in the past few days doing a large layout for some tropical sketches; finally getting the composition in fairly well, and the whole thing washed in with watercolors and a big brush. At least the ideas will be on paper to work up someday when time is mine and not the government's. Nobody's time should have been utterly wasted for the past two-and-a-half years as mine has been.

September 16, 1944

The past six days have been one disgusting twenty-four hours after another with only a few letters to break the stretch. Dad seems to be on the way back now and is again up around the house a little. This news helps a lot. Marie writes and is still her own sweet self.

As to the army, we have been treated to its worst in a hundred different ways. A new area commander took over—a general whose name I do not know and care less about. He probably wants another star, for he immediately went completely nuts. Orders came fast and stupid—the first being that everyone would carry a rifle wherever he went. Now that is all right in its place, and I doubt that anyone would have to be told to do so if the need were present, but it happens that this particular general is plain green with no practical experience overseas. (He was probably made a general hurriedly from a colonel when the need arose.) Now he orders everyone to wear khaki uniform and leggings, supposedly so that if you are killed, you will die neatly (with shined shoes).

All the old garrison tricks are popping up now, but those of us who have been here twenty months are poor material for tryouts by a fresh new general too lately from the States. To add to the confusion, our great leader,

Callaway, sits like a giant, pudgy cheese-ball and mulls over the orders, adding suggestions from his pea brain to make things more complicated.

September 23, 1944

The usually monotonous green of the swamp beyond the road suddenly exploded into flaming red, as trees covered with vines burst into blossom with huge clusters of delightful brilliance. This is the first wild display I have seen in all of the tropics where flowers are supposed to grow like the Hollywood movies' version. I wanted to go native and make myself a flaming lei, but most likely all the G.I.s would have thought I was stark crazy. Anyway, the mud is deep and black in the swamp, and there is plenty of it between me and the blossoms. Another example of my eternal craving for real beauty to put my hands on, and my usual inability to reach it. Sometimes I think I will die without ever having put my hand on the flower I insist on reaching for.

September 24, 1944

We are definitely moving now to Hollandia to join up with a task force for a big invasion. No one seems able to guess just what is up, but we think it is the long awaited Philippines campaign. Being uncertain of the future, we will leave most of our office equipment behind, such as tables and chairs and tent floors. We have carried these all up the Guinea coast, but will build again when we get to the new destination.

Tonight is "beer night" when each man is issued three bottles, which he pays for himself. The army finally got around to the beer question and the shipping of it to the SWPA.[35] As I don't drink it, I give my share to Ed Niaber, so he has six bottles instead of his three—and he is fond of it. I threaten to hold out on him quite often, as each man has to draw his in person, and I have to go after it for him. Some men trade around and secure as many as twelve bottles at a time, but even that doesn't have any effect on anyone. So I gather that, most likely, at the order of the army, the beer manufacturers "water" the beer, so to speak. As we have had a large refrigerator, our beer is cold. Most generally it is given out hot, and ours will be, as soon as the refrigerator is taken by another unit. We never keep a good piece of equipment any longer than it takes some other unit to find out we have it. Our company is known as a "soft touch," and neither Callaway nor Bilger have guts enough to protest the taking of our equipment. This is the third refrigerator we have had so far.

September 25, 1944

A day of work tearing down camp. Over and over again we do it—build up, tear down, move and build up again. The labor seems so futile. Tomorrow we will finish the job, load on boats, and be off to Hollandia.

September 26, 1944

We left Maffin Bay[36] at 3:00 a.m. in a good sea. As usual the boat is short of sleeping space. At least this time, we are on one of our own boats with our own men running it, which makes a more congenial group than the mixing of different companies' men.

September 27, 1944

Arrived at Borgen Bay and went into the inner harbor to anchor. As we came in, we passed alongside a large native village built on poles in the middle of the straits, and I determined to visit it and see how these people live.

September 28, 1944

We came ashore to our new campsite.

27 More Mud, New Territory

October 3, 1944

This campsite proves to be no exception to our long line of very unhappy places, or maybe we just hit it at a bad time. Here we have sticky, black mud-gumbo ankle deep, and it clings to shoes like glue—slippery as grease when wet. The 532d Engineers group has been here since April and claims to have packed the ground down for us. What was it when they came?

The place has been defended by a number of machine gun posts until a couple of days ago. Now they are no longer deemed necessary, as it has been weeks since any Japanese have been killed, and even then, only a couple of starved, half-crazy ones. The thick jungle behind camp is full of evidence—their camps and scattered equipment, odd foods in jars and bottles, wooden kegs of pickled fish heads and soybean sauce (still good, or as good as it ever was), two-toed shoes, their little wooden "pillows," their blasted foxholes, and their skulls.

I picked up one skull and brought it back to camp and left it on Ed's cot. Latcr the fellows took pictures of it and will, most likely, never get the photos back either. The army has gotten the holy jitters about the skull question, and we receive repeated warnings of court martial, death, and any number of absurd threats for possession of Japanese bones, teeth, etc. *Life* published a full page photo of a girl with the skull her friend had sent her from Guinea, and such publicity didn't help any. Even Tokyo Rose used the photo as an example of the "barbarous" Americans' attitude toward a "superior race."

After a couple of days of dry weather, the ground is hard as rock, but thirty minutes of rain can turn it into black goo. Disgusting damned place!

There is a lot of fuss and confusion as preparation is made to leave in a couple of weeks or so. Evidently we will follow up the main landing and unload ships with our boats. Nearest guess is that we will land about fifteen days after "D" Day.

October 6, 1944

Today I visited the native village for the first time—not the one in the channel, but one that is very near the camp here. That is a good way to get out of the war. Just step into the Stone Age. The village is a large one, built on poles in the water, but—unfortunately—it is practically abandoned since the army came here. I couldn't blame the natives for leaving a place full of American soldiers. A few families remain—most likely to see after the village, for I am sure the people will be back as soon as we clear out.

An old man was making a spear in the shade of the palm grove by the shore. A woman came by with water from the stream, but instead of the clay jar she once carried, she now had substituted a castoff army dehydrated potato can. It sat ugly and out of place atop her kinky head. A boy with a six-word English vocabulary came up, and we began finding out what they had to trade.

Our barter was a stack of large signal flags that were to be destroyed. We decided to use them here, as they were good lap lap material, in spite of their bold stripes, squares, and circles. An old man brought out a number of fine old spears with carved, ebony-like wooden shanks and bone points. At two spears to a flag, we got a number of weapons, and the natives got an assortment of clothing that will drive a navy signalman mad if they dress in it and appear on the shore.

Ed took some pictures of the village and of us on the walkways to the houses. Each house has its stick and bamboo "sidewalk" running from the shore out to the house. Then the various houses are connected by a network of such walks.

The whole village must have been wonderfully picturesque when occupied by hundreds of people, but I wondered about the walks. It was a job to go even a few feet on one of them, and I concluded that it was a game in which the family that went the longest without any broken legs won. Every board sagged. Every one was loose. The ends flew up. The pole supports leaned. I stopped and came back—cautiously—past a native woman who walked upright, calm, and collected, with a huge load of vegetables on her head. She didn't even glance at the walk and seemed unaware of the imminent danger she was in.

We are still preparing to move, but things are more clear now. Evidently we—the Second Brigade—are playing a very minor part in the big Philippines show. Rumor has it that General Heavey insisted that we go along in order to claim a part in the Philippines campaign—which is very like him. He or one of his "yes" men dubbed him a "fighting man if there ever was one" which fits him about as well as it would Madame Perkins. He will take his Brigade Headquarters Company in behind the assault troops. The harbor is full of warships, more than I have ever seen before, and this is only one of the gathering points of the invasion forces. How many more there are, we can only guess.

There is some delay, and we may be here awaiting transportation for some time. Nights are dull. There is so little to do that even conversation stales after a while. Although we have had mail from home, there is little to write the folks about. Two of our men left for rotation to the States. Both were over thirty-six. One—the Greek, Philipatos—left roaring drunk, waving a beer bottle as he rode off down the road. I remembered that he had come into the outfit two-and-a-half years ago in the same condition and reflected that he most likely will end his life happily drunk.

The picking of men for rotation and furlough to the States is pretty much up to Callaway, and it was no surprise to find that he is planning to send our baker, who is only twenty-five, has never been anywhere near combat since coming overseas, has had a furlough in Australia, and has never been sick a day. The way to Callaway's heart is through his tremendous gut. In all fairness, I will have to say that no matter who goes home, the rest of us will be mad, for we all want to go so badly.

A few natives have been around, but these are not nearly as interesting as those of the east Guinea coast. A small boy came by with a very large papaya, and I bought it from him for a few cents Dutch. He seemed flabbergasted that I would discuss the price of the fruit in his own language. He didn't realize that my Malay is limited to counting money and precious little else.

My new "dog tags" came today, stamped with the "M" for Mohammedan. It would make little difference as to religion once you were a casualty in battle, and I doubt if any chaplain we have had would know what the "M" was for.

October 12, 1944

A tropical drizzle has been falling all day, and this afternoon a blue-black cloud came up from the south, promising a real rain. However, it fizzled out into more drizzle, giving us a damp day, but not enough rain to goo up our mud puddle.

We have closed our kitchen and are eating with B Company across the road. Their chow is too, too terrible—Spam, Spam, Spam! which I like, but not three times every day. If it isn't Spam it is some terrible chili that looks and tastes like dishwater. Ed is sick tonight and blames it on the chow, which is most likely a good guess. It will probably be some time before we have our own kitchen and decent food again, as our whole kitchen group is staying here in the rear echelon.

I've been trying to round up things here—getting rid of extra equipment, mailing home my latest acquisitions from the natives, and sending Quirl the last of the cowries. (I finally cleared more than a thousand dollars on them.) I don't want any loose ends when we pull out, only the smallest amount of equipment possible.

October 15, 1944

Late today I walked down through the banana grove to the palm grove by the village, the most beautiful and graceful I have ever seen—not planted in rows plantation style, but leaning this way and that, backed by the far blue-green of tropical mountains, made more interesting by the village just off the beach. There was a restful quiet here, and nothing disturbed the mood of twilight falling.

The tiny mission school stood on shore, surrounded by the remains of a bamboo fence now flattened here and there. Gay flowers still bloomed in the enclosure. The building was practically intact; the seats, still inside. What had these people learned at this place that had enabled them to live more fully? Too often we press upon them something they could not hope to absorb and something they have no use for in their way of life, and end only in confusing them.

October 18, 1944

Still no news of our forces hitting the Philippines. We had expected it before now. Apparently Nimitz is attempting to knock out the Japanese Air Force before an invasion begins by land.

October 22, 1944

Our troops have landed in the Philippines at last.[37] MacArthur has blown his horn long and loud, and I hope he is satisfied. From the news we get, things are going well, but we heard that "our beach" is under artillery and mortar fire, and we hope that by the time we arrive, the Japanese will have been pushed out of range. The landings seem to have been in even greater force than anyone expected.

Out near the shore here are the remains of an old, native burial ground uncovered when our bulldozers scraped off the ground—ironically enough—to make room for our chapel. After the recent rain, I picked up numerous beads, shell ornaments, etc. This was my first contact with the Melanesians of the past—just how far into the past I could not know, but judged from the trade beads scattered about that the burial ground must have been used after the coming of white traders and could have been started at the insistence of the mission fathers. Burial customs varied in these parts, and I doubt if any such cemetery existed before the late 1880s.

At one spot the scraper had barely uncovered a burial that seemed especially rich in all kinds of things, so I took a knife and scraped the sand off. There were a dozen or more shell armbands, many shell rings of smaller size, thousands of beads, broken pottery, numerous dog teeth drilled for stringing, and several white porcelain "dog teeth." Some enterprising trader of the early days had found that dog teeth were used as money and had brought in these excellent imitations. I have seen none of these glass teeth in all of New Guinea, so they must have disappeared from the market long ago—perhaps most of them going as these had. The trade beads were identical to those found in ancient American Indian burials; both came from the European traders.

One of the boys has been stationed at the island of Kiriwina, where the natives seem to be fond of pigs. The boys said they were able to pick up any number of them in wood. My pig is about six inches long and done in heavy, dark mahogany. His body is carved with odd spirals, two of which continue to his head and end in curls that form his eyes. Altogether it is a clever piece of work! I called the pig "Jeraldine" after the sow on Tami Island, but on closer examination, changed his name to Jerry.

I have sketched the village several times, as my film has not arrived, and I must get enough ideas to do at least one oil of this interesting place. One afternoon I gave a native the pencil and asked him to draw a house. He did, and one that was so original it made my conventional sketch look odd indeed. He drew the inside and outside of the house at one time. The bed-racks seemed to be on the roof, but he explained to me that they were really inside. The roof carried two queer items resembling weather vanes, but where has this native seen such a thing? At least I know now where Picasso gets his ideas. And people call him original!

October 26, 1944

Another trip to the village with pencil and paper. This time some of the old men took an interest and drew for me. I had taken the box of colored pencils along thinking they would provide interest but found that, apparently, color is unimportant to them. I insisted the first old man take his pick of the dozen colors in the box. He chose a sky-blue one which was about the last color I would have guessed would attract him. Each man who drew was offered his choice, and each decided on the blue. Only once did one hesitate; he took the yellow one, but made only one line with it, then exchanged it for the blue again. The drawings were interesting and certainly original—all of various animals and fishes these people knew, a tree frog, a giant lizard, a shark, etc. Here were real, live, primitive men doing the same delightful drawings I had seen in rock paintings in Texas. Those Texas Indians are centuries dead, but the primitive instinct of their time is alive in this far spot.

Today I made a trip to the native garden for papayas. Fruit is so scarce we have almost forgotten what it is like. The garden is a large one, built on the almost forty-five degree angle of the kind that inspired the stories of the Ozark farmers who plant corn with a shotgun. Both banana and papaya trees cover the hill, and the ground is covered with native sweet potato vines. I saw no other vegetables, but there must have been some in other patches somewhere, for the natives have passed by with peppers and other things.

The papayas seemed to have been long ungathered, because many ripe ones hung half-eaten by the birds. I had no trouble finding as many big ones as I could carry, but discovered that going down the hill was even more difficult than coming up. With no arms to check my downward progress, most of the trip was made on the seat of my pants. The native woman who goes to the garden with a sack she can hang on her back is smart. Maybe the steep hill was the only place that could be found which was well drained. Too, it was rich and slightly sandy, but the garden was a good two miles or more from the village—quite a walk for your food.

All equipment is loaded, the office is closed out, and we are simply waiting for the signal to grab a pack and board the boat. All of which leaves me free from duty and taking it easy for the first time since the weeks in Finschhafen immediately after the Gloucester mission.

Today we received word of a terrific naval battle in the Philippines area and are awaiting more news of it. Let's hope they paste 'em good![38]

NOTES FOR PART II

[1] Allied forces had captured Finschhafen, New Britain on October 2, 1943.—*Ed.*

[2] One dog remained hidden until we were almost there, and it was a pity he couldn't have been brought on to Guinea. On the Westralia a prissy little white dog did get smuggled all the way, and today was trotting proudly down the road in his harness. His soldiers were taking good care of him.—*G.B.*

[3] Later I learned that most of the coconut plantations in this section were owned by one of the big American soap manufacturers.—*G.B.*

[4] Located at the southernmost tip of Eastern New Guinea, Milne Bay was the scene of a major Allied victory in 1942 when a large number of Japanese ships and planes were destroyed by Allied bombing.—*Ed.*

[5] As this is dated the same as the previous entry, it appears to have been written that night after landing at Oro Bay, or perhaps early the next morning as Gaitha was setting up the office.—*Ed.*

[6] Oro Bay is located just north of Hervey Bay on Australia's eastern coast.—*Ed.*

[7] This was the last mass raid ever made by the Japanese on Oro Bay.—*Ed.*

[8] Later we heard that it was chased and shot down, which was most likely correct, for the big air field of Dobodura a few miles away was one of the largest in all the South Pacific.—*G.B.*

[9] A yellow, crystalline synthetic compound (quinacrine hydrochloride) used especially during World War II in treating malaria.—*Ed.*

[10] I found out later I was wrong. The trees had been stripped by our own men on orders from some fool officers who thought the nuts would be a "menace" to safety if they fell.—*G.B.*

[11] Late in 1942 Japan launched an overland campaign against the Allied base at Port Moresby, located on the southeastern coast of Papua, New Guinea. Its troops came within thirty-two miles of the town. American, Australian, and Dutch forces then took the offensive.—*Ed.*

[12] By late October 1943 Allied forces had advanced up the Solomons chain to Bougainville Island. U.S. troops landed on Bougainville on November 1, 1943.—*Ed.*

[13] In the South Pacific, an unwoven kind of cloth made by soaking and pounding the soft inner bark of the paper mulberry tree. Tapa was so important to the aboriginal Oceanic people that they domesticated the paper mulberry tree.—*Ed.*

[14] In the South Pacific, an unwoven kind of cloth made by soaking and pounding the soft inner bark of the paper mulberry tree. Tapa was so important to the aboriginal Oceanic people that they domesticated the paper mulberry tree.—*Ed.*

[15] Bad guess!—*G.B.*

[16] Another bad guess!—*G.B.*

[17] This, too, later proved to be untrue.—*G.B.*

[18] The fighting to place Bougainville Island in Allied hands lasted from November 1, to November 24, 1943.—*Ed.*

[19] In December of 1943, Allied troops landed on the nearby island of New Britain. On December 15, the 592d boats participated in the main attack on Cape Merkys and in the support landing on Andwe Island. The actual assault was broken into four operations.—*Ed.*

[20] Although I did not know it then, he was to spend six days there with no shelter and no bed.—*G.B.*

[21] Landing Ship Transport.—*Ed.*

[22] The shortage of Japanese planes was a fact I was to note many times later.—*G.B.*

[23] Tami Island is located fourteen miles off the northern coast of the Territory of New Guinea.—*Ed.*

[24] Australian-New Guinea Administrative Unit.—*Ed.*

[25] After brief enemy resistance, the Admiralty Islands fell to the Allies in March of 1944.—*Ed.*

[26] This was the Hollandia landing.—*Ed.*

[27] A popular American vocalist of the 1940s.—*Ed.*

[28] Elephantiasis, commonly called elephantitis, is a tropical disease in which the blocking of the lymph vessels by a parasite leads to great swelling of the tissues, especially in the lower part of the body.—*Ed.*

[29] The hair ornament was interesting and much like those I have seen various Indians in the States wearing from time to time. These feathers were most likely from the tail of one of the huge guaria pigeons.—*G.B.*

[30] "House Tambarin," I had learned, was a reference to the shelter housing religious realia of the tribe.—*G.B.*

[31] Finschaffen was frequently shortened to Finsch in conversation.—*G.B.*

[32] Land-based planes of the Allied Air Forces softened up the Hollandia area destroying over three hundred Japanese aircraft in early April. Landings were made at two points near Hollandia in the summer of 1944. A major air and staging base was developed in the region, where most of the higher headquarters in the Southwest Pacific established their command posts.—*Ed.*

[33] The Japanese Eighteenth Army based on Wewak carried out an attack on the Aitape area during July and August 1944, employing more than twenty thousand troops there. But U. S. infantry and cavalry forces coordinated by U. S. Headquarters Eleventh Corps broke the forward push of enemy troops and began pushing the Japanese Eighteenth back toward Wewak.—*Ed.*

[34] In the spring of 1944 carrier-based U.S. planes had struck Japanese air installations at Wakde and Sarmi to the northwest of Hollandia.—*Ed.*

[35] South West Pacific Area.—*Ed.*

[36] Maffin Bay was needed for a forward staging area. It was taken after the U.S. Sixth Infantry Division captured a strategic hill in a series of bloody assaults. The area was secured by late June with about four hundred fifteen U.S. Army troops dying in the Wake-Arara-Maffin Bay region. American wounded numbered fifteen hundred. Almost four thousand Japanese were killed and seventy-five taken prisoner.—*Ed.*

[37] Following intensive action by Allied land, air, and sea forces, the first landings on Leyte were made October 17-18, by U. S. Sixth Ranger Infantry Battalion, which took possession of islands in Leyte Gulf. Between October 20-23, the Tenth and Twenty-fourth corps established beachheads on the east coast of Leyte.—*Ed.*

[38] A group of Japanese battleships, cruisers, and destroyers advanced on Leyte Gulf from the south through Surigao Strait and were fiercely attacked and defeated by U. S. Seventh Fleet surface vessels before dawn on October 25, 1944. Further fighting followed when a force of enemy vessels moved into Leyte Gulf through San Bernardino Strait.—*Ed.*

PART III

OCTOBER 30, 1944, TO JUNE 22, 1945

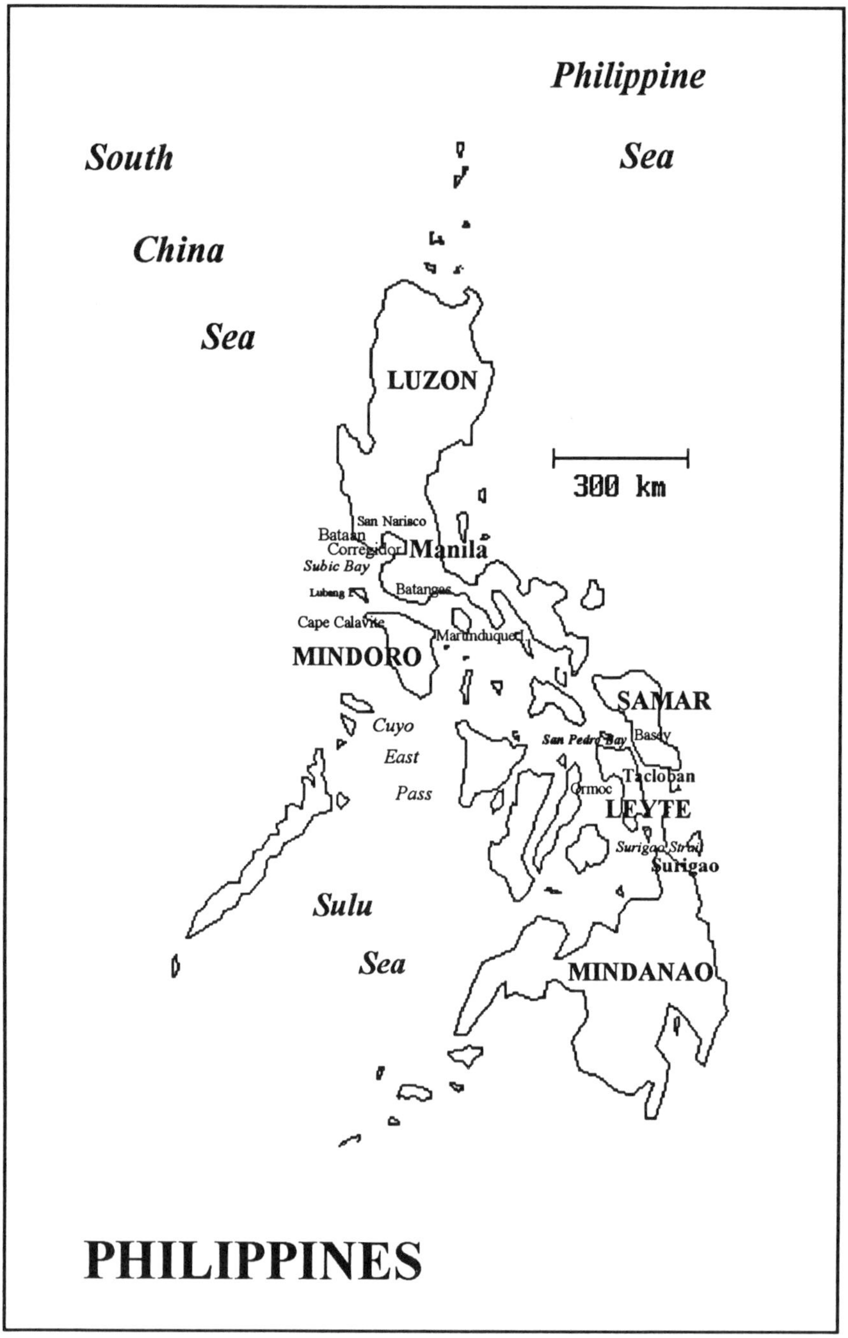
Philippine
Sea
South
China
Sea
LUZON
300 km
San Narisco
Bataan
Corregidor
Manila
Subic Bay
Lubang
Batangas
Cape Calavite
Marinduque
MINDORO
SAMAR
Cuyo
East
Pass
San Pedro Bay
Basey
Tacloban
Ormoc
LEYTE
Surigao Strait
Surigao
Sulu
Sea
MINDANAO
PHILIPPINES

28 A Non-Pleasure Cruise to Tacloban

October 30, 1944

On the high seas again, sailing along the north coast of Guinea. We loaded on the Loading Ship Drydock (LSD) yesterday morning. The LSD is quite a ship, one of only twenty or so in existence, made to carry small ships for long distances. The back end simply lets down; the gigantic well-deck fills with water to a depth of about six or eight feet; the boats come in; the back goes up; the water is pumped out; and away we go—a big ship full of little ships.

Our boat crews just stayed on their boats, as they had living quarters arranged there, and, too, it was cooler than below decks where we were. I got a top bunk down in the compartment. (The top bunk is still the best.) The place was hot as hell, but not unbearable with two fans and a blower-ventilator going all the time.

We are not crowded on the boat, and the food is excellent—though getting it is another question. We line up on deck in one of those endless lines that go all over the boat and finally down a ladder into the dining room. The food is the best we have seen in a long time. Yesterday we had delicious ice cream! Always there is ice-cold water. I thought Callaway would let me alone on this trip, but already he has called me to type some lists of men for the life rafts. Each man is assigned to a certain raft in case of having to abandon ship. The fellows in the ship's office were very friendly, and I found one who was from Texas. Apparently their job is much the same as mine, but done under more pleasant conditions.

The convoy consists of six LSDs and one destroyer escort, but we are to pick up more boats off Biak or somewhere. Tonight is a wonderful tropic display of silver moonlight over a silver sea with men and guns silhouetted against it—too beautiful to be headed into the vortex of war. I started reminiscing.

The past year floated on the silver of the sea. It was a strange year in a strange land, and I reflected that there had been the same old pang of reluctance at leaving a spot I would never see again. Certainly New Guinea is a remote land that, until the war, few white men had trod. I got what I could from it. I caught the island in the passing of an era in its history, for never again will white-sailed trading vessels lazily ply the coast. Never will sleepy ports wait weeks or months for a ship to call, for New Guinea has become a part of our shrinking world. How long until the interior is known? How long until we know its value to the world? Once even America was considered a poor colony and a liability to England!

October 31, 1944

All day we have plowed through heavy rain and heavy seas, and it has been impossible to stay out on deck. Most of the boys have spent the day at cards with American coins which they got from the ship's crew. They found that twenty-two months without handling any such change has made them slow with their own money.

During the day I met Smith (Smitty) of B Company, who told me he had a Kiriwina pig for me—an unexpected, but much appreciated, gift. I knew he had a friendly western way about him but did not discover his past until I went down to his boat to pick up the pig. Smitty is a professional rodeo rider from Montana; has won numerous awards including his silver-mounted saddle; has ridden in all the famous shows—Madison Square Garden, Fort Worth Stock Show, etc.; was once stomped into a pile of broken arms and legs by a wild horse, but longs to get back to his ranch and his riding and training of his show ponies. It seemed odd to meet a broncbuster in the middle of the Pacific. The pig is the nicest one of four I have gotten—a very large and belligerent pig in dark wood.

November 1, 1944

No rain today, but still cloudy and rather cool. I don't know how far our part of the Philippines will be from the darned equator, but I hope far enough north to be cooler.

Our food is still good. The noon meal was roast beef, delicious steamed rice, gravy, peas, soup, and ice cream. In spite of this, one of the cooks told me the ship was lower on food supplies than in many months, after two quick trips to the Philippines without a chance to re-supply.

We have picked up the additional boats and now have nine LSDs and two destroyers. The destroyers travel ahead and to either side of the convoy, sometimes making trips here and there, hovering around their big flock. Once today one raced back toward the horizon, and the dull thud of depth charges was heard, but we never learned what was up. Apparently the destroyer thought it had picked up a sub.

November 2, 1944

Late this afternoon we suddenly turned about and headed east. Everyone was curious and soon the news came out. Our convoy had received a radio message that we were heading right into a unit of the Japanese fleet, and a mere seventy-five miles in front of us were three battleships, two cruisers, and six destroyers—all a part of the fleet that had slipped out after the pounding they received from our navy.[1]

Maybe they were attempting to reinforce the dwindling garrison on Leyte. Maybe they were simply running away. But even the five-inch guns and all the others we carry couldn't hope to compete with a Japanese warship. So away we went at increased speed, calculated to keep us out of range of any Japanese ship for at least ten hours, by which time we would be under the protection of our planes based at the newly won airfield at Palau Island.[2]

November 3, 1944

Dawn found us off Palau, but we did not anchor, just circled around. A plane or two passed overhead. There was a long line of ships anchored up the way. The sea was very quiet. Later we headed due west for several hours, then turned, and soon were again off Palau; so we concluded that we were merely killing time. Late this afternoon we headed west again and were still on that course when the moon came sailing up behind us out of the black horizon of the sea.

November 4, 1944

We have traveled all day westward and hear we are supposed to land tomorrow, making a full week aboard the boat.

November 5, 1944

Early morning found us heading up Surigao Strait with land to be seen dimly on either side. There was no excitement aboard the *Gunston Hall*. Things went on as usual, in spite of the fact that the last convoy through was fiercely attacked by large numbers of enemy planes. At breakfast the radio was on. Radio Tokyo was blaring out the astonishing story of our forces in the Philippines being completely isolated with rations for only two weeks, after which time they will be completely annihilated. At that instant we were sailing out of Surigao Strait into Leyte Gulf. When I came on deck, we were in the inner harbor, and things were far from being out-of-hand. I have never seen so many ships of all shapes and sizes before in my life! A fleet of P-38s flew like silver gulls against white summer clouds. The place was definitely unsafe for Japanese on land or sea or air.

The country is different, with low-lying hills and little of the languid, tropical look we have come to know in Guinea. The hills are less green, less wooded. Gone are the vine-matted shores. Coconut trees line the shores, but they seem to grow to themselves instead of melting into the surrounding country. We could see the town of Basey on Samar Island to the north as we turned off into a small bay off Tacloban on Leyte Island.

Fifteen days ago one of the landings had been made at this beach,[3] and it was now pitted with foxholes and littered with cans and the usual debris of battle. A battery of long 90mm anti-aircraft guns pointed skyward. They had been smack in the middle of what evidently had been a small park, and one tall, whitewashed, concrete statue still stood oddly in the midst of the guns. Later I found it to be in memory of a World War I hero born on this island. He had not found rest in his sacrifice in the "war to make the world safe for democracy."

We learned that air raids were frequent up until a few days ago. Then they slacked off. We are not too far from the airfield, which is an uncomfortable position in a raid, for the Japanese are sure to overshoot their target. The airstrip is along the shore, and we got a good look at it as we came in. It presented a sight of wreckage that is seldom found on one field.

Twisted and smashed planes lay all along the water's edge. Two P-38s lay half-submerged. Zeros were wingless in battered heaps, but the majority of the planes were our own navy planes that were forced to land when the two small carriers and one large carrier were sunk in the naval battle. The field was not ready, and many planes cracked up in the landings. All of the wreckage had merely been pulled off the field to make room for the planes that came and went all day.

Our tents are up, it is twilight, and—for the first time in nearly fourteen months—I can stand on the road and see the lighted windows of houses. The people here are somewhat like ourselves. They have houses that we are familiar with. They speak English. They are happy that we have come.

November 6, 1944

The air raids came last night, announced by the banshee wail of the siren at the radar station on the small hill nearby. It is guaranteed to wake all the tired soldiers in the vicinity. Several enemy planes went by very high, but dropped nothing. The 90s spat at them several times, but seemed more intent on keeping them high than anything else. We had not dug any foxholes, as the whole place is one mass of them already. Dotson insisted on not even getting out of bed for the occasion and lay there making remarks about people "who are so damned anxious to get in a foxhole."

Today was spent in getting camp set up—an old routine by now. We have learned to take it a little easier, for what isn't done today can well be done tomorrow. Late this afternoon Charles Wilson and I walked over to the town of Tacloban only a few blocks distance from here. We found it a far cry from the American cities we know. Even discounting the wear and tear of nearly three years of Japanese occupation, Tacloban is still a sleepy settlement of Filipinos housed in thatched-roof houses in somewhat of a "shanty town" fashion.

The largest building is a concrete, three-story capitol which was at one time painted white and is now windowless and gray. But it still wears the proud gold lettering high on its front—"PROVINCIAL CAPITOL OF LEYTE." It is now used as the headquarters of the provisional Philippines government and the administration of all Filipino affairs.

Near it is the long, solid-looking building used as a prison, wherein now reside the Japanese and pro-Japanese Filipinos arrested after our occupation of the town. I saw the courtyard inside filled with men, mostly Japanese in pajamas. Outside waited a cluster of women and children and some men, each carrying a bag of food of some sort, waiting until the hour when they would be allowed to give it to those inside.

As usual, the tragedy of war follows victory or defeat alike, and it is difficult to determine just which Filipinos willingly cooperated with the enemy and which did so merely to stay alive. The streets are narrow and dirty, but some have been oiled a little, and the whole town has the strange look of a ghost town that has suddenly been filled with people. Old women stood in the doors of paintless and neglected buildings; weeds grew high in yards; the few remaining store windows were covered with dirt. On one corner stood three or four busses, stripped of tires and parts. There was no moving transportation in Tacloban except army jeeps.

We wandered down into what had been the "residential section" of town—people were moving back. One yard had half-a-dozen chickens (each staked out with a piece of string). Food is scarce—too scarce to allow your chickens to stray. Practically all of the Filipinos were ragged. All wanted clothes instead of money for anything they attempted to sell. One said that occasionally they could buy trousers at 800 pesos[4] a pair, a shirt for 450, and bread for three. The Japanese paid them one to three pesos of Japanese invasion money for a day's work, if they worked for the Japanese army. Naturally trousers were patched and re-patched until they were just a group of patches held together by more patches, and so were shirts.

The girls looked neat in clean, but worn, dresses. Their long, dark hair is a pleasure to see after so many months of seeing only women with kinky wool. These girls are pretty and shapely too, sending the G.I. wolves into whistles and goo-goo eyes. Already those hopeful men are planning great conquests.

None of the population looks starved, although it was most likely a big job getting enough to eat. Many of the people went into the hills to farm in order to stay alive and, also, to get away from the Japanese. We saw only two stores open—both shoe shops operated by families, but they had little to sell. One had a number of leather dispatch cases of the kind I have seen captured on the battlefield, evidently made on order of the Japanese. Also there were several pairs of excellent wooden-soled sandals with tooled leather straps—a pair of which I would have bought Marie, but all my money was in Dutch guilders about which the Filipinos know nothing. (We left Dutch Guinea without putting any money into money orders and have not yet found the army exchange here.)

On a building side were several posters or notices connected with the liberation of the town and others yet to be re-taken. MacArthur's signature was large and conspicuous on the proclamations in which the people were told—in no uncertain terms—that now the United States of America was boss, that all Japanese laws, etc., were null and void, etc., etc., etc. One was an open letter to General Humma, Japanese General of the Philippines, telling him what he can expect when he is captured. Humma was responsible for the now famous (or infamous) "Death March of Bataan" and is one of our prime targets for revenge. All of these notices were in English, and I noticed that practically all of the signs on the streets and stores were in English; some, in Spanish.

A press photographer told us of the occupation of Tacloban, as he was covering the story for his paper (or whatever war correspondents cover a story for). His story was a rare bit of the truth that never gets back to the States and will never be known. Having photographed MacArthur all over the Pacific, this photographer was familiar with the general's stupid ego and the fact that the face angle must be just so, and the movies must reflect a certain personality or out they go. (Can our Mac be building for a real try at the presidency some day?) On the day that MacArthur came to Tacloban he planned a big "press campaign" for himself and summoned all the photographers known to have come with the army. He was going to "give back Tacloban" to the Filipinos in a grand fanfare of cheering Filipinos with movie cameras grinding and the MacArthur jaw jutting out over his loyal subjects. But the Filipinos were busy, and no one came!

However, dauntless Mac would not be put off. He merely re-set the time for later, sent out people to "beat the bushes" for Filipinos, and held the session in the afternoon. Just how successful it was the photographer seemed doubtful of, but he was honest enough to tell the truth, probably because he was not an army man and had nothing to lose by it. Only one of the illustrations of the way some heroes are made—in the good old Hollywood fashion!

About the time we decided that we had "done the town" and were trying to find our way out, a jeep came along, and an M.P. bellowed, "The town is off limits to all troops!" and rode on. Maybe he was fulfilling an order to clear the town of troops, but if so, he wasn't putting the usual M.P. punch into it. Maybe he looked at the number of soldiers in town and the number of M.P.'s in town and decided on a soft pedal for the time being. As soldiers are quartered in various buildings over the town, I can't see how any M.P. is to know who belongs and who doesn't.

November 7, 1944

The night was broken by a number of air warnings, and once the battery of 90s opened up unexpectedly before the siren sounded, causing "Iron Nerves" Dotson to bolt from his cot stark naked and dive into his foxhole before any of us had time to even move. That ended his self-made reputation as one who doesn't bother to get up during an air raid.

We have been lucky in not having any bombs fall near, nor any strafing. Between the battery of 90s and the quartermaster ration dump, we have expected some such thing anytime.

29 Typhoons and Turkey Time

November 9, 1944

Our first typhoon struck yesterday, after a telephone warning from the weather station on the hill in time to tie things down. No day could have looked less likely to develop a storm. It was quiet and bright—maybe too quiet—and the water too glassy. Soon the horizon showed smokey, black clouds. At noon the typhoon struck with full fury, driving rain before it in a fierce, torrential downpour. Once begun, the wind held its velocity for fifteen hours. There was no lull—no slacking of wind or rain—and the weather station later said that the wind maintained a sixty-five mile per hour strength for the duration of the typhoon.

Tents danced crazily in the air, straining at their ropes, and each minute you expected them to take off like balloons. There was nothing to do but wait it out. Any activity was absolutely impossible. It was a maddening game. During the night we dropped off to sleep, but I had weird dreams and woke often. About 3:00 the wind died as suddenly as it had come. The rain stopped; the crazy tents went limp; the typhoon was over.

Estadt came over from regimental headquarters with Lieutenant Williams, who was with this company for more than a year, so we know him well. Lately he was transferred to brigade to be an aide to General Heavey—"A-Fighting-Man-If-There-Ever-Was-One" Heavey. Williams was with Fighting Bill when the landing was made and told us that now Bill was doing his fighting in Brisbane. He had taken "nervous exhaustion," and demanded to be evacuated to the States, but finally compromised on Brisbane. I doubt that he will be back with the brigade. I guess it just took one landing to knock out Bill. This was his first real one.

November 12, 1944

Last night was a hot one with raids and raids! We didn't get a whole lot of sleep either. I have never seen such intense ack-ack fire before. The sky was ablaze with every type under the sun. Some small bombs were dropped near the unloading port down the bay, mostly the type bombs that are called "daisy cutters" because they burst off the ground and are intended for soldiers only—not destruction of installations. Our 90s fired and fired until our eardrums ached, but I don't think any of them ever came close to a plane.

Just before dark, a Zero "buzzed" our camp and was so low we could see the pilot plainly. The 20s opened up, but he was gone so quickly that no one hit him. Today one did the same thing about noon and ran right through ack-ack fire all the way down; but apparently none of it got him, for he headed back west and kept going. My guess is that they are taking photographs, or else they would not risk that dangerous business in broad daylight. Now they can map the gun battery and ration dump with us between and figure out how to do away with it—pleasant thought.

November 13, 1944

More raids yesterday afternoon with a number of planes over the bay. Several were shot down, but one dived into a liberty ship and released his bomb (the small planes usually carry one bomb) at the same time. The bomb went into the hold of the ship and exploded; the plane crashed into the bridge of the ship and exploded into flame. The ship did not sink and will be repaired. No other ships were hit or planes of ours destroyed, in spite of the extravagant claims by Radio Tokyo of fantastic destruction in this raid.

The captain of the ship was killed, but sadder still, more than 140 soldiers were lost—all of them on the ship to go home on furlough and rotation after more than thirty months of hell in the Pacific. Thirty months of longing, work, suffering, and looking forward to this trip! We never know, even after we have surmounted the unbelievable obstacles placed in our path by the army red tape, whether we will arrive home. Each of these thought he would spend Christmas at home, and, no doubt, there were joyful preparations in many homes to receive them.

Last night the ack-ack was unusually intense, filling the air with a display of beautiful destruction, but apparently hitting nothing.

November 14, 1933

The enemy slipped in for a dawn raid, but got a hot reception of ack-ack and P-38s. About 8 a.m. several Zeros came in and were surely given the old "one-two" in no uncertain terms. Two of them fell—trailing smoke—from ack-ack fire, but the third seemed sure to get away as he came over us and headed west with streams of tracer bullets following him. Suddenly he dived almost straight downward (I thought to get away from the gunfire). But instead, he had seen a P-38 hot after him and was apparently more afraid of that than the guns—which he should have been. The guns were a mile off.

The P-38 executed a beautiful twist and dive, got on his tail, gave one burst of gunfire, and the Zero exploded in a ball of orange flame and plunged earthward. It all happened in a matter of seconds and was the briefest, smoothest, most thrilling, and perfect act I have ever seen put on in our troubled sky. The 38 sailed away like a victorious eagle. No movie ever conceived anything approaching that scene for making the hair stand up on your head. Although the air was full of bursting ack-ack and smaller lead, no one got into a foxhole, but all stood and cheered like wild Indians.

The rest of our boys arrived today from Hollandia, and a few of them got off the ships and came into camp. The rest are still awaiting the unloading signal. Ed is somewhere out there, and I am anxious to see what he thinks of all this, as he has never before been around the sound of a gun or dog fight. It will be good to have him back in camp again.

November 20, 1944

The raids continue, but irregularly, and whole nights go by without an alarm. We have witnessed some more thrilling dogfights, but nothing to equal the performance of the fourteenth. It seems the enemy is determined to do some damage, even if they destroy themselves at each attempt. It is becoming a common practice for them to dive into our ships in the harbor. Five or six have been hit that I know of, with varying degrees of damage done—the worst being the 140 furlough and rotation men killed. Some overshoot their mark and plunge into the sea. Some of our men who have been near and have examined the parts of the planes that came up say they seem to be largely plywood construction. Maybe they are right, or maybe only wooden parts came up. When recovered, the bodies of the pilots usually have little information and no personal effects of any value—a few notebooks, some maps, a cheap cigarette case.

Two of our boats off the harbor came upon six Japanese soldiers in aviation clothing in a group, probably a bomber crew shot down at sea. As the boats approached, one of them opened fire with a pistol while others began killing each other rather than fall into the hands of our men. Of course, the boys shot them quickly. Three of the bodies sank, but the other three had on life jackets so their bodies were searched. Some interesting-looking notebooks filled with writing were found, but little else. They appeared to be log books of a small boat, or possibly of a bomber.

November 22, 1944

We have weathered another typhoon, but it was a mild one this time. The wind never went wild. The whole thing only lasted a few hours, in spite of all the preparations for a real dinger. Probably the weather has helped, but we have had few raids, and the big guns have not fired a shot in a week. There have been alarms, but no planes here that we could see.

Radio Tokyo says Japan will hold Leyte at all costs, as it is the key to the Philippines—a rash promise indeed, as the only "toe hold" they now have on all of Leyte or Samar islands is a beachhead around Ormoc on the west coast about twenty miles due west of here. That is surrounded by Allied troops, constantly pounded from the air, shelled by our guns, and dominated by our ships on the sea side. In spite of all this, they manage to slip reinforcements in during bad weather and fight stubbornly for a break-through.

Reports say we have killed 45,000 to date. Things are definitely under control, but we will have more Americans killed before the battle is finished. The usual things are happening that have happened all over the Pacific. Some of our boats were fired on recently up the strait, and at one place it is difficult to unload on the beaches because of enemy machine guns that are hidden cleverly. These Japanese are outside their lines—miles outside—and couldn't be part of a force of any size, but they will stay right there until they are blown to bits one at a time. I hear some infantry is going up the strait to clean them out.

Radio Tokyo also says there is a dauntless force of "suicide" aviators destroying us around San Pedro Harbor. (They are the dive bombers.) Some of them are hitting high in the rigging of the ships with little damage done. None of the planes that deliberately make these dives carry any explosives, and all seem to be obsolete models sent especially for this purpose. Why don't they fill the planes with TNT in order to do the greatest damage possible? Again the old story of Japanese failure to press home the greatest advantage.

The mail has come in with letters from all—Mother, Dad (it was so nice to hear from Dad himself!), several from Marie, Mae, Melody,[5] and Roy. They are all so faithful.

Again the old blues seem to surely overtake me with the usual lost and alone feeling of stale nothingness. I threaten to give up the journal, as I feel it has dropped into an uninteresting repetition of dull days. Seemingly Dotson still retains a fresh viewpoint and is able to write an interesting "My Day," as I see him busy every night.

The usual people seem so usual, the unusual ones so disinterested in things in general. Ed is his retiring self and never comes around for a chat. His intangible personality still puzzles me. Someday I will be happier when I just accept people and quit trying to "figure them out." In our tent we have only Dotson, Wilson, and myself, ever trying to find points of discussion—on people, education, art, or even cabbages. Bill Flint, the Kentucky Mountain "homespun" boy, never takes part in any of our discussions, but reads his Bible and little else. I am sure he is shocked by our frank discussions on life and religion.

Dotson just received a copy of *Sun Chief,* the autobiography of a Hopi Indian, which we all three plan to read and discuss together. It should break the dull evenings. I know many things of the Hopi and Hopi country from firsthand experience, and Dotson has the sociological data well salted away in his mind. Wilson will, no doubt, come up with something to contribute to a better understanding of *Sun Chief.*

In a "slump" like this I find myself thinking: "What sort of person am I now, compared with the 'me' of two years ago?" I realize my horizons have widened. Two years away from home and friends and country have given me a chance to look back and re-value the past, and things that once were a puzzle, fall into place. I can look from a far distance without the influence of people and things around me.

My ideas are my own, and some of them startle me. Now I can never go back to narrower places that enclosed me. There is less of the old conventional hedge. It is not a freedom of "doing things I wouldn't dare do before," but a freedom of thought and a freedom from thoughts of other people. I can face things today that I could not face two years ago. What will people see in me that will be different? How different will I appear to those who love me and for whom I have tried to stay the same? The old ideals are still present, but they are hung to a new star on a finer horizon of freer space.

Have I found the independence for which I have searched? Can I attend the New York Art Institute and get the training I missed earlier? Can I go to New Mexico when that training is completed and use it in building a full life in the only land that warms my heart twenty-four hours a day? Am I still selfish enough to forget obligations in other places to accomplish this? Will I succeed even after surmounting all these? What about marriage? What about a home? Hope springs eternal. . .

And there is the wail of the siren, and there is an air raid alert. I reach for my steel helmet and shake my dreams and come back to Leyte and a war as devoid of feeling as the steel of the guns. The blues are the weary sameness of day after day of war, war, war that drains me of everything good, bad, or indifferent.

November 23, 1944

Tonight we had roast turkey, and the suddenness of the change from bully beef shook me into the realization that today is Thanksgiving. I had not thought of it before. Last year it was Thanksgiving at Hervey Bay, Australia. Year before that at Fort Ord, California, and the one before that at Gallup, New Mexico. That one at Gallup was the last one before the storm. The last "free" one.

Of course, the old Thanksgiving days cross my memory—the ones at home with turkey, dressing, cranberry jelly, fruit salad—among a few of the major wonders of the day. The joy of it was wonderful! The smells, the excitement of the family gathering, the gusts of cold air as someone opened the door, the squeals of greeting.

Today I fell in at the end of the long mess line with my tin mess kit and tin cup. The mud was thin and ankle deep. There was a thin drizzle. Thin, tired soldiers from the boats filled up the line behind me. One had just returned from up the straits with a fresh red bandage on his shoulder.

There were dehydrated potatoes and peas—we have had them every day for weeks. There was bread with canned butter. There was canned fruit. Then came the turkey, which was good, in spite of the fact that Mother would have baked it juicier and used more seasoning.

When we were kids, we used to be asked, "What have you to be thankful for this year?" I thought of that tonight and wondered what I could answer for November 23, 1944. Surely I have something, if I have not allowed bitterness to crowd it out! Maybe just being alive, but sometimes the unlucky are the live ones, for they still can see and feel and plod on in the mud with a tin mess kit. The dead aren't tired anymore or hurt or discouraged, and their friends know at last that they are safe beyond the reach of war. No, I'll pass it up this year and leave "what I have to be thankful for" statements to someone who really knows. I don't.

30 War Shows Its Real Face

November 24, 1944

Beginning last night with a good show, the enemy took advantage of the bright moon. We had several alerts early in the night, and the ack-ack put up a terrific curtain at one time. Along about 10:30 a plane slipped over and scattered bombs across the bay right to our shore, then skipped over and dumped one or two in Tacloban. Bob Young and I were standing by the foxhole at battalion headquarters tent when the first bombs fell out in the bay, scattering fiery circles where they hit. Then there was a whistle like the hiss of fast-flying geese, and we both dived into the hole and beat the explosion by a second. Two bombs had landed just off shore, leaving a pall of smoke hanging over the beach.

This morning we again had alarms, and one Zero was shot down by three P-38s which executed a beautiful maneuver and circled the plane "Indian" style; he plunged in a mass of flames. (Later an airman came in to use the phone and said the plane was being dug from six feet of mud, as it was an unusual model, and our intelligence group wanted to study the motor—or whatever was left of it.)

About an hour later the sky was suddenly filled with two-motored Japanese bombers. I counted six myself at one time. Later I learned that sixteen had come in, and fourteen of them were destroyed. One started burning high up and cut a fiery arc to the ground. Bombs were dropping in the bay with huge columns of water and smoke. The bombers were mostly hitting wide of the mark, if the airfield was the mark. None of our fighters challenged the planes, but I do not doubt that plenty of 38s and 47s were outside the hills waiting to tear into the bombers that got away. In fact our boys had most likely given them a going-over long before the Japs got here, and we only had the lucky survivors to worry about.

There will surely be big news of the damage done and the number of planes shot down. We, here on the spot, find it difficult to estimate what really happened, but the news writers at home aren't handicapped by seeing the thing and generally manage a thrilling story that may fall short—or overshoot—the truth. Their account usually leaves our civilians breathless; maybe that is the duty of the newspapers.

All day the wounded have been coming in from up the straits—part of the infantry that has been cleaning out the enemy presence there. I thought I had become accustomed to the sight of pain and misery and death long ago, but today got me. Maybe I'll never be able to look upon it calmly. The first boatload of men stumbled up the beach, limped up, were helped up, and were carried up on litters.

They had been nineteen days in the thick of it, digging enemy soldiers out of their cleverly concealed machine gun posts along the straits. They were dirty—unimaginably dirty! Their clothes were muddy, their bearded faces were muddy, and some even had their hair caked with mud. Most of their faces wore a strained and empty look. Few smiled. These are the men who are carrying the war, and I felt guilty sitting here in clean, dry khakis.

This afternoon some more seriously wounded came in, most on stretchers. Our doctor met the boat and administered plasma to several. One was failing fast, and probably wouldn't last until he got to the hospital. It began to rain, and the stretchers were hurried into the various tents along the beach—ours getting about eight. The boys lie so quietly. One with a bloody bandage on the side of his head asked for a cigarette. I gave him one and lighted it for him.

Another was brought in sitting up. He was entirely naked except for a blanket over his shoulders. It had rained a cold, muddy puddle in the litter he was sitting on. Someone offered to put him on a dry one, but he refused, preferring the water to being moved, as he was shot in the chest and every breath was a trial. He asked for a drink, and I got it. Then he talked, but his mouth twitched with pain. I couldn't go away, but stayed and talked, finding out it isn't easy to sit beside such a man and talk of trivial things. The doctor came and gave him a shot of morphine, but apparently it didn't take effect, at least not while the boy was here.

Finally the ambulances came. They had been called three hours earlier and had only a mile to drive, but even life isn't important it seems. We carried the litters across the knee-deep mud of the road and sent them on their way to the hospital.

November 25, 1944

More wounded are coming in by boat, and we will most likely have another day of seeing the war at "rock bottom." You can't go any deeper into it than the wounded and the dead—that is the ultimate goal of each side. "Send to the glut of the guns, bravest and best of your sons . . . pile up pyramid high your dead to the anguished sky . . ."

November 26, 1944

Beginning early last night, again taking the bright moonlight as an asset, the yellow devils decided to send bombers over. I actually saw five, but don't know how many really came over. The searchlights were cooperating beautifully and caught the first pair of bombers and held them while the guns poured fire. The two planes flew wing tip to wing tip across the heavy fire; and if they were hit, it surely wasn't in a vital spot, for they kept going.

About twenty minutes later, a single bomber flew low directly over our area. The gunfire was terrific, but we were fascinated by the sight of the big plane caught in the shafts of light, and we stayed above ground. When the aircraft was almost directly overhead, the red of the wing markings shining in the light, a shell lifted the plane up with a jolt, like some giant hand had pulled a string, and white smoke trailed for a minute from the middle of the fuselage. I am sure the shell tore completely through, for the smoke came from both sides. Again it wasn't a vital hit, and the bomber disappeared into a cloud to the west.

I wondered why, after all the bombs had dropped (we saw them drop in the searchlight beams like silver eggs), the plane did not climb out of the gunfire. Another bomber fell in dull flames on the hill, and still another smaller plane was shot down by the naval fire from the harbor and fell flaming into the water.

At well past 1:00 we finally heard the "all clear" and climbed into bed. This morning there are a lot of red-eyed, sleepy-looking people around. I notice, too, that some aren't too tired to dig in foxholes they thought were deep enough before.

November 29, 1944

The past days and nights the planes have stayed high and done no damage. Something—likely the fact that so few returned from the last raid—put the fear of American guns in their hearts. Yesterday a bomber came over, but stayed so high it looked like a silver gnat, and the 90s couldn't reach it. Their ack-ack burst in black puffs underneath the humming gnat.

Last night it was the same story. Each night the harbor and airfield have been covered with a smokescreen to hide them during the nights of bright moonlight. A boat scoots around gushing heavy white smoke that soon thins and settles like fog over the land and water. But instead of having the irritating quality of smoke, the screen simply has a slight odor, and that is all.

Their pilots are flustered for the time being, but will most likely recover and, again, send their "suicide" squads over the harbor after our shipping and airfield.

In the mail is a letter from Mother with clippings about the death of Mr. Stallings. Only three days ago I received a long letter from his wife, but she did not mention his being ill, although for some time he has had serious heart trouble. His passing will not leave her in financial need, for together they were thrifty and exceedingly well off. She can live in comfort, or in luxury if she chooses, but Pearl is a real person on whom luxury makes little impression. She worked just as hard after they had plenty as before, and here again we find the old, old thing—people criticize where they lack knowledge or foundation for what they do. Pearl's newsy letters have kept me informed on the art happenings in and around Brownwood ever since I came overseas. She has sent goodies and made repeated offers to send anything I need or care for. At present a box containing her wonderful melon-rind pickles is on its way for Christmas. No, Pearl is far from the pinchpenny she is accused of being, and, where others would fail, she has the strength of character to carry on in the community and manage her affairs, even though Mr. Stallings is gone.

November 30, 1944

The last day of November is the beginning of the end of the old year.

Although last night the moon was full and exceedingly bright, we had alerts but no planes overhead, and we slept the greater part of the night. The alerts get somewhat wearing on us and some men show the strain more than others. There are all kinds of extremes such as those who dash into their foxholes at the first sound of a siren and stay there until the "all clear," and those who practically won't get in until a bomb hits and knocks them in. I take precautions and get in at actual bombing or heavy ack-ack overhead, but don't break a leg every time the sound of a truck or jeep is heard. I like to visit the various tents during an alert and do a lot of wandering around. Usually I call the boys I know to be "foxhole happy" and generally get a smothered reply from underground. They prefer to endure the cramps and bites of the vicious, foxhole mosquitoes to the imagined dangers above ground.

Most of us sit around and talk, as letter writing and reading are impossible, and even listening for planes is well nigh impossible, as the trucks and jeeps and bulldozers seem to wait until an alert to start their snorting and bellowing. I often wish a good bomb would fall on the middle of each one and give us some quiet. Soon the moon will wane, and dark nights will cover us again.

Looks like we are losing Callaway for good this time. An order came through suddenly, transferring him to one of the branches of Sixth Army. He and five other officers, who have been dissatisfied and generally unsatisfactory in their jobs, are transferred. Callaway has been uneasy since the "suggestion box incident" at Maffin Bay. Brigade sent an order out for boxes to be put up in each company for "suggestions on improving the morale of the companies, etc." The first day the box was up, our men filled it with their suggestions—all having the same theme, namely, "Callaway, we want a new company commander!" Many of those notes were masterpieces of subtle, razor-edged sarcasm. Others were blunt to the point of cruelty to dumb animals. As Callaway read the stack of notes, his thick neck reddened, then purpled, as each suggestion unfolded surpassed the other in cutting criticism. He was hit in the solar plexus, all right, and his ego underwent a good deflation. The men under him thought him a complete failure at his job and were willing to tell him so.

At the time I accused him of being too little to pass the information up the line unless forced to. Maybe now he has taken a way out, or maybe someone else who never heard of our suggestions had ideas. Sanders will be ideal, shoot square, and be popular with the men, and he isn't completely dominated by his stomach.

The boys who sat around, baked, cooked, and went out in search of delicacies for Callaway will now find themselves with work to do. The sergeant who got his rating for his ability to find the most pork chops will be in an embarrassing position and likely to be transferred or reduced, as there is no possible excuse for his presence in the company now. The whole place will be a good deal happier I am sure.

December 1, 1944

First day of the last month of the damned year of 1944, and me sick as a horse tonight for the second time in two weeks. Somebody just said I looked green around the gills, and I said I felt green around the stomach, and they had better not stand in front of me. Maybe if I lost the pork chops that Company B's mess hall crew half cooked for dinner, I would be a well man, but right now it's no fun, and I wish my stomach and the pork chops were in the middle of the bay.

I suppose the noise is no worse tonight than usual, but it hurts my stomach more. Of all the noisy places on the various planets, this war on this world has them all beat! Noise, noise, noise twenty-four hours a day, seven days a week—trucks roaring, bulldozers snorting, jeeps rattling and blowing, boats leaving the shore, guns firing, planes roaring overhead, generators running, and most of these all at one time. If one thing stops, there is a new sound to take its place. Every nerve in your body screams for quiet, and, even in sleep, you are aware of noise. No wonder General "Fighting Bill" Heavey ended up with "nervous exhaustion." Right now I could do with a good case of the same, but all I'll get will be the same old bellyache!

December 3, 1944

After a day in bed, I am again adjusting the nose to the stone, but with a light head and a stomach that still protests slightly.

Only two short alerts last night. This morning I find a copy of the publication "Map Talk" giving reasons for feeble air attacks over Leyte as follows:

"Toward the week's end, Japanese raiders were fewer and more irregular. The simple reason was that carrier-based strikes on Manila and land-based attacks on every other important airfield in the archipelago were destroying Japanese aircraft in the Philippines faster than they could be replaced."

Just what I thought! And if we can keep it up, maybe the war will be over in five or six years.

December 5, 1944

We seem to have settled into one of our "day after day" camp periods, the ones where the days just go by without incident. Now that the air raids have virtually ceased, it is dull, but pleasantly so. Last night we had one alert, but no planes, and about the only excitement I heard was Dotson and Wilson in a violent argument as we went to bed.

Wilson had accompanied Dotson to the home of the Boneuses, a family of educated Filipinos who do our company laundry. Dotson is the official laundry man and makes the deliveries and contacts with the Boneus family. Dotson accused Wilson of insulting his Filipino friends by his language. "Every other word you used was 'bullshit' or something of the kind!" says Dotson. "Also, you bragged and told all those lies about your war experiences. Don't you know these Filipinos have seen more of war than you will ever see?"

"Maybe I did say 'bullshit' too often," says Wilson, "but any man who has kept his family with him for three years of war and still managed to increase that family by three hasn't had a very hard time!"

I went to sleep with them still at it. Sergeant Young's father showed up on a liberty boat, and, of course, Bob rushed out and has spent the past three days with him. Mr. Young has some sort of supply job on board, and it was quite a surprise to Bob to hear his Dad was here. Yesterday they came in for a while, and Mr. Young offered to take this journal back with him, thus cheating the censors out of the greatest scissors job of their whole life. I will get the whole thing together and send it with him, trusting it will eventually find its way home. Too bad the Australian part isn't here for the ride too.[6]

December 6, 1944

The 90s woke me up at 2:00 this morning firing at a high-flying plane that was going like a bat out of hell. By the time the 90s shells got to the height of the plane and burst, the plane was out of hearing. As I was sleeping in the battalion office right across the road from the guns, they nearly knocked me out of bed. It was very dark, and I watched the four big guns moving silently like stalking animals. They would point their long snoots into the air; then slowly move in a half circle and back again, following the directions of the radar guide on the hill behind.

All the men manning them were in the pits, and no humans could be seen or heard, which gave the scene an eerie appearance. A couple more of the fast planes came over very high. One dropped a small bomb down the way somewhere, evidently a "daisy cutter," as its noise was a sharp, metallic sound rather than the deep "WUUMP" of a large bomb striking the ground. That ended the "raid," and we went back to bed.

31 Another Un-merry Christmas

December 8, 1944

Pearl Harbor Day seemed to have passed somewhat less eventfully than expected. If we made any bold strike at the Japanese, the news has not leaked out yet, and if they made any at us, we didn't hear. There was increased activity of some sort, for an enemy bomber or transport or something flew boldly among our planes down at the airport, circled around with them, waited for them to land safely on the strip, and then signalled in and asked for permission to land just as each plane is supposed to do. But he made the mistake of flying over the signal tower in the wrong direction—something our pilots would never have done, and he was at once spotted as an enemy plane.

However, he was told to circle and land, as if the ruse had succeeded. When about fifty feet off the ground coming in, every gun on the place let loose and blew the plane to bits—little bitty bits! It exploded and lighted the night sky for miles around, and there were many smaller explosions later. I have never learned the true story of what the plane contained, but heard that there were a number of Japanese in it, along with equipment that might have been used to blow up airfield equipment. Just what they really expected to accomplish by landing on the field may never be known, but Radio Tokyo did say last night that daring paratroopers had retaken the Leyte airstrip, and the lie could have had its origin in the fact that some suicide groups were sent with the purpose of doing any damage to the field possible. Why on earth lose the plane and men by trying to land when, if they got that close undetected, they could have loosed a whole load of bombs that would have done many times more damage than otherwise! The Japanese have a mind of their own, all right, but if they aren't careful, it is going to lose the war for them.

There has evidently been renewed activity across the island at the Ormoc pocket, too, for yesterday the planes from our field kept up a twenty-four-hour continuous bombing mission. I never before saw so many planes of so many different types, and even the little P-47s had a bomb under each wing as they headed for the west. The fact remains that we haven't cleared Leyte of the enemy presence in seventeen days as predicted.

We no doubt have enough troops here to push the Ormoc Japs into the sea, but don't consider it worth the sacrifice, as our bases are secure here. We have the harbor, the airfield, and—without a doubt—have some new fields open by now. The grip on Leyte is safe and secure, so any Japs killed at Ormoc will be that many more we won't have to chase up the other islands later.

I have written Mother a Christmas letter and sent her a money order, which—along with flowers—is about all I can hope to do for her Christmas. So many friends have written that they have sent me packages. They are all so faithful year after year, and there is so little I can do for them! So far, there has been no Christmas mail come in at all, and I wonder if we will get any of it, or, if it will be delivered in March. Most likely our Christmas will be just another day, and I expect no fancy food, as we have so many troops on the island to be supplied. Maybe this time though, I won't be eating a can of beans and getting ready to go on an invasion.

Last night Estadt came over and shocked me by his appearance. The strain has gotten him, sure enough, and he has lost pounds and gained five years in looks. He is now trying to get on the furlough list for a trip home and thinks with his connections at regimental headquarters he will be able to make it (although he is less entitled to it than most of the company).

December 9, 1944

The flocks of planes yesterday were supporting our landing in the middle of the Japanese Yamashita line—or rather in the rear of it—three miles south of Ormoc, splitting the enemy forces and spelling the end of the fighting on Leyte. Soon the two portions of their forces will be destroyed and Leyte cleared. General Yamashita has thrown in thousands of his troops in a vain effort to back up Radio Tokyo's announcement that Leyte would be held at all costs. We have destroyed convoy after convoy of their reinforcements off Ormoc, beaten them in naval combat, mauled their air force into nothingness. (Few planes ever get through to us here in Leyte Harbor.) I just wonder how long it will take to push them from all of the Philippines.

Looks like the journal will not go home, as Bob's dad has already reneged on the offer. He says he might have to go through customs, and—if so—he couldn't possibly get it through, which is most likely correct. Human nature is just human nature, and he isn't bothering himself with other people's worries.

War makes us more like that. Everyone feels that he has more worries than he can shoulder already, and so to hell with the other fellow's. Bob is still out on the ship with Mr. Young, and it is getting to be less of a joke here, as this is not a one-man job, and I am tied to it all day, every minute. Lieutenant Sanders is very considerate and asked today if I was able to keep up with everything or if I needed extra help. I am able to keep it all going nicely, but feel that as first sergeant, Bob should be here doing his part of it. I am not our first sergeant and don't intend to accept the responsibility of it for long periods. Sanders said he would send word to Bob that his vacation was about up and to get in the saddle again. You can depend on Sanders to see that one person doesn't impose on another if there is anything he can do about it.

December 11, 1944

Many planes are still headed west all the time. I suppose they are still giving the divided Jap troops a good lacing. There are alerts still, but few planes get through to the harbor here. Two nights ago there was a bad explosion down the island, which we hear now was a TNT dump. It flattened everything in the vicinity, but I have not heard how many, if any, men were killed. The first thought in such a thing is sabotage, but it just as easily could have been an accident of some sort.

Another fine letter from Mae in which she tells me some news concerning the price of land, etc., in New Mexico. I have about decided to buy myself a hunk of it, for there is nothing like having a place to call your own and a spot that belongs to you without strings. I mentioned to her once that I most likely wouldn't like to stay in one place, but she answers that by saying (of herself) that she might roam, but not far, because there is enough out there to keep her interested for a lifetime. Marie is still working hard, but Mae says she is getting very tired of it, so I expect her to give it up in the spring. Then all of them will go back home when Melody is out of school.

Wow! Just noticed an article or skit or something in the G.I. newspaper we get—to wit: "Brigadier General _____ has returned from a well-deserved rest on the mainland of Australia. This was the general's first rest in his twenty-two months of overseas duty. He looks very fit and ready to lead his Amphibians into further operations." My God! What next? Better it should have been left out entirely than to make that asinine statement and try so hard to have it sound casual.

Mmmmm...just a rest from duty—one he deserved after his hard twenty-two months. I suppose no one stopped to think that this is a hell of a time to "take a rest" right in the middle of the Philippines campaign! G.I.'s are dumb, but not that dumb, and the newspaper must be run by someone with the usual army ego if they think they passed that one off lightly.

December 13, 1944

Again thinking back over the past two years, I see that I have somewhat modified my opinion of the men around me. I thought them a worthless lot, and a sorry example of what an American should be, and still maintain that my opinion of the "average American" has been lowered considerably by my stretch in the army. But they are actually neither all good nor all bad, for there's good in the worst and, certainly, bad in the best. Many times I have received small kindnesses that were entirely unexpected from men I hardly knew, and again from men I knew well, but had never had any dealings with.

Smitty's gift of the carved pig from Kiriwina was a good example of an "almost stranger's" heart of gold. Recently Harry Chambers (mentioned long ago as the handsome Harry who always got himself in trouble by being fast with the women) brought me a large Filipino grass mat he had gotten on a boat trip to Samar. He cared little for such items, but remembered that I care a lot, and so brought it to me.

An unexpected friendship turned up in the person of Philip Maring, a kid from East Islip, New York. Phil is only about twenty-two, of an immigrant family, and has had small opportunity for education. However, his English is practically perfect without a trace of accent, and his manners leave little to be desired. He is instinctively a gentleman and one hundred percent American. He has the stocky, muscular build of his sturdy Czechoslovakian ancestors, with a body that is as hard and rhythmic as a bronze come to life. He hasn't had an ache or pain since he came into the army. I sense the fact that he missed in his childhood all the orindary things we Americans of generations back learn from one another—the small pleasantries that make life run smoothly—the "what to do" in this case or that.

He was confused as to what he would do for his mother for Christmas and how to accomplish anything from this distance. At that time I was writing an order for flowers for my mother and friends and offered to enclose one for his mother also. "I never sent flowers to her. She will wonder how I thought of that," he said. "All the more reason to send her some," I said. "That will be a bigger surprise than anything else." When you are twenty-two and have spent the past three years in the army, you have missed three years of life, and three years of the kindness friends and family would have shown you. So if I can do small things for kids that need them, I will make an effort to do so. Cigarettes are sometimes scarce, but I don't smoke and keep mine in my barracks bag, thus having smokes when none are available anywhere else. The boys appreciate it, and none has yet abused the custom by wanting them unless he was actually out.

Gradually and deliberately I have gotten acquainted with the various groups that make up our company—the boatmen, the radiomen, the truck drivers and repair men, the general workers around the camp. Some are bad, but none are ever bad enough to be completely ignored—a strange fact that took ages to soak into my thick head. I need not copy their thoughts or actions, but I can learn something valuable by making friends with them. In civilian life many of them and I would never have met, but in the army we are thrown together, and both may come out wiser if we make an effort to do so.

I am even astonished to find that I have somewhat modified my stand on drinking. I still intensely dislike it and am no nearer to taking it up myself than before, but, if another man insists on making a fool of himself, there is nothing I can do except leave him alone while he is a fool. He may be extremely interesting and worth knowing when he isn't drinking. Maybe I am learning—slowly—to get the good out of the moment and forget the day.

December 14, 1944

The Filipino guerillas come in often asking about boats to take them here and there, usually across the strait to Samar. They are very much alike, these small, brown, ragged men. Most all are barefooted, clad in tattered shirts and shorts, armed with old guns, new guns, Japanese guns, or only a knife. They look little like fighters, but I have learned that looks can be deceptive.

Across the half-mile stretch of water here in front of me lies the green shore of Samar Island. Samar, the core of guerilla activity in all the Philippines. The people on this island refused to surrender and took to the hills, organized their small government, printed their own money (backed by the U.S. with which they remained in contact).

Evidently the Japanese looked at the thing with a long-range eye and an assurance that the Philippines would be Japanese for all time to come. Sooner or later the Samar people would have to give up and recognize the fact that Japan had the place for keeps. Little thought was given to just what a vital part such a group could play if the Americans came back. Now the Samar faithfuls are receiving regular army pay and are digging out enemy soldiers that we would never find.

Today a group of these guerillas came in with sixteen soldiers they had captured. They had had a fight with some Japanese who were hiding on Samar, killed part of the lot, and brought in those sixteen to be turned over to us. The eight brown, tattered Filipino men squatted on their heels and smoked, while we phoned about the possibility of a boat to take them back to Samar. None of them mentioned the fight or the Japanese as I talked to them, nor did I question them about it.

One showed me some of the guerilla money he was carrying (which is recognized by us and is legal tender still). I asked him what he wanted for several of the notes, and he cheerfully replied, "That is up to you, señor." So I gave him a handful of Filipino coins, about eighty centavos.

Another had a fine, long, mean-looking bolo knife swung on his belt in a carved wooden case. I admired it, and he said politely, "Would you like to have that knife?" His offer was so lightly made and so cordial that it sounded like a gift, but I knew better. "Sure," I said. "What would you like in exchange?" He said with a smile, "Shoes! You see I need shoes."

I looked at his feet. They were not big feet, but practically square, and I wondered when, if ever, they had been encased in shoes. I was sorry I had no shoes to give him. "It is a good knife," he said. I pulled it from the scabbard. The long, keen blade was stained with dried, brown blood—yes, it was a good knife!

December 15, 1944

The only mail to arrive today was a cable from Mother. I knew at once that the red-bordered envelope marked "Urgent Telegram" was news of Dad, and not good news. It simply said, "Daddy much worse. Doctor says come." How helpless I feel about it! Mother knows I cannot get home, but she grasps a fragile thread of hope. Of course, there are supposed to be such things as emergency furloughs, but to date I have not heard of anyone getting one. One man applied, but the answer came back (two months later), "The Red Cross has examined the case and finds there is no necessity of this man getting an emergency furlough." Again, the offer of emergency furloughs is made, but never intended to be fulfilled. The army works that way. No amount of trouble would deter me if I could get home, but the fact remains that it is impossible. I have investigated far enough to find that out.

I've been reading Louise Dickenson Rich's *We Took to the Woods* and find it full of good things worth remembering; such as her feeling as she watched the annual log-drive down the swift river, with the golden wood tossing in the very blue water. "All the senses come alive, even that strange, rare sense that tells you—half-a-dozen times between birth and death, if you are lucky—that right now, right in this spot, you have fallen into the pattern of the universe." Yes, I had that feeling once or twice, no more, and it was in my Southwest. That is the reason I know beyond all doubt that I belong there. One of the times must have been when I looked over the Grand Canyon, for aside from my feeling awe and reverence, I knew that I belonged to this land—this and no other!

Louise Rich expresses a tinge of fear that someday she might lose her keen appreciation, "And then I repeated to myself something that I once learned in the hope that it would safeguard me from ever becoming hardened to beauty and wonder. I found it long ago when I had to study Emerson. 'If the stars should appear one night in a thousand years, how men would believe and adore; and preserve for many generations the remembrance of the City of God which had been shown!'"

December 18, 1944

The air raids have practically ceased. We have very short alerts now and no planes overhead at all. The new landing at Mindoro Island has taken even more of the enemy's attention. The rain has even held up somewhat; and some Negro soldiers are working the road in front of the office, grading it down, draining the grade, and making an all-weather spur to connect the beach with the main road for hauling supplies off the boats.

We must have a great many of the Negro soldiers. I see them so often working the roads, or hauling supplies with trucks or Amphibian "ducks." The magazines seem to make much of their serving in the army, and many groups are screaming long and loud, "The Negro wants equal rights and is fighting like anyone else in this war for them." All of which doesn't settle the Negro question by a long shot. We in the South expect things to go about as before when the Negro soldier returns home.

December 20, 1944

Since our arrival here, our boys have adapted themselves to the new surroundings with the usual ease, and the usual rash of pets has broken out. Whatever is available to be petted usually finds its way into our camps and onto our boats in a short time. Here, it is monkeys and parrots and the usual puppies.

Every man who could possibly want a monkey has one. The natives seemingly have an endless supply to sell and trade. I presume they come from the hills and are native to the Philippines, for all are of the same kind and seem to take to captivity with the same gusto that the soldiers take to them. One of our boys has a baby one, which acts like any baby in any family—cries to be held, screams for food, plays with the buttons on your clothes, pulls your hair, and refuses to sleep until the lights are out and all is quiet. Monkeys are interesting, but so much trouble that I surely don't want one around. On the boats they aren't so much trouble, I guess, as they are given the run of the craft. This solves a lot of problems except one—they throw things overboard when they get mad.

The parrots are all alike—small, green, with a blue head and a brilliant orange beak. Not a one I have yet seen has uttered a word or a whistle, and they seem to be content to sit dumbly on a perch. Pets in the army live a hard life, and I always feel sorry for them. We have a time getting proper food and care for ourselves, so naturally our pets suffer.

The Filipinos must have caught up to some extent on their clothes shortage, for today I bought some bananas for a quarter, instead of the usual price asked, "shirt," "pants," etc. Also some women came by, asking to do laundry for money. Apparently their situation is stabilizing, and the Filipinos realize their money is as valuable as it was before the war. One boy came by with some cakes or something of the sort—odd-looking balls of batter that had been rolled in seeds and baked until they were brown and cracked open. They looked delicious! Usually I will eat anything strange, but didn't buy any of these. Now I wish I had.

December 25, 1944

Of all days, this one should hold something, but, as I observed last Easter, I find all the joy of a holiday depends on being among friends and familiar surroundings, neither of which we have here. We are carrying on in the usual manner, and unless turkey shows up for dinner, the day will be like the last 365 in the army. Last night I lighted my Christmas candle and thought back over other years when I had done the same. Last year it was on the shore of New Guinea.

My reflections were short-lived. An alert sounded, and out went all lights. There was quite a display of ack-ack fire, and one Japanese plane burst into flames and fell into the bay. The alert lasted a long time, and finally I went to bed.

Sometime during the night Dotson and Wilson—somewhat drunk and noisy—came in from a spree of some sort in town, and woke up everyone in the tent. Then they decided I should be singled out for special annoyance and came over to pull at my mosquito bar. I suppose my voice carried a dangerous quality when I told them to get the hell away, for they soon went to bed and were quiet. If I have gained any new tolerance of drinkers—as I supposed I had—it doesn't extend to letting myself be bothered with their high-handed bullying. I am positive that, if they had persisted, I would have gotten up and knocked them off their liquored legs without hesitation, although I have never done such a thing. I can simply leave a place full of drunks anytime, but when they come to my tent with their liquor-inspired-courage and chips-on-the-shoulder, that is the end!

I have received the address of Ronald Johnson after a long time of not knowing where he was. Ronald and I have been friends for somewhere around sixteen years, having met in a Scout camp where he taught swimming, and I taught Indian lore. Ronald has always been an ideal pal with the patience of Job. (He would be much amused at the preceding paragraph and would say, "You haven't changed a bit!") I look back now and see that among the thousands of men and boys I have met in almost twenty years of work in camps over the country, he still remains the same friend—the same Ronald.

We see one another seldom, but if we meet after a couple of years, there is the same, sure friendship. His address tells me that he is in the Marine Hospital and, most likely, is in this general part of the world. I have written and should receive an answer soon.

For the second time, I visited Tacloban on a Christmas stroll, as I was determined this time to make the day different. The town is little changed from the first visit. Things are just as dirty, the houses are as shabby, and the stores as scarce. There are more government warehouses open to feed the people, however. All the life and color that is missing in the town proper I found down the bay where the streets play out and become irregular paths around the harbor. Here the houses straggle along the waterfront, and here is vitality and character entirely Filipino—no struggle here to "keep up with the Joneses."

Literally hundreds of canoes of all sizes were drawn up in a solid mass on the narrow beach or floated in the still water. A huge junk unfurled bamboo sails as it made ready to put to sea. Smaller ones with curved roofs housed whole families who seemed quite at home in their cramped quarters. On the beach an old woman with a face like a prune slept in a small canoe. Another lay on the sand in the shade of her craft. A small boy in an enormous coolie hat peered at me. Men came and went with their fighting roosters under their arms. Others came up with baskets of fish. An old woman turned her fish while they dried in the sun. A young girl washed clothes at the well, while another drew water from it with a long pole and a bamboo bucket. A boy went by with a huge stalk of bananas. In a yard a pig roasted, being turned over and over on a long pole above the glowing coals; he would be ready by Christmas night, as he was already getting deliciously brown. All was an endless stream of teeming life, of color and sound and odors, and I wondered if it would be so colorful at any time other than Christmas Day. No doubt many of these people had come long distances in their boats to attend Christmas mass, as the majority of Filipinos are Catholic.

Here was my corner of Tacloban Island, and I recorded as many scenes as possible with my camera and planned to return for sketches.

32 Coping, Remembering, Philosophizing

December 26, 1944

As the light of the moon increases, so do our visitors of the Japanese Air Force. Paying us a visit last night, they stayed high while our 90s pounded the heavens for the first time in a couple of weeks. We saw no planes fall, heard no bombs drop.

I have decided to catch up on my reading and have just finished Willa Cather's *My Antonia,* which is as beautiful and tender as only Cather can be. Her things were written years ago (she is in her seventies now) but are as timeless as earth and sky. Also did *No Life for a Lady*, the story of one of the cattle kingdoms of New Mexico. Now I am reading Lloyd C. Douglas's *The Robe* and planning to tackle *A Tree Grows in Brooklyn* next.

January 6, 1945

A new year—at least we can hope with the coming of each new one, until the new one becomes frayed and old, and we find it didn't turn out quite right. Then we can hope on another one.

Having received urgent letters from home and letters from the doctor and pastor concerning Dad's condition, I have been trying to get an emergency furlough. Efforts so far have been very discouraging. The army dislikes recognizing human need in any form. However, Sanders says that if the emergency request fails, he will see that I get on the earliest possible rotation or furlough of the regular quota. Things work so slow, slow, slow; and all I can do is wait.

Christmas boxes are still arriving. In fact, I have gotten only about three of mine so far. I have received a number of letters, but seem unable to answer them to my satisfaction. After reading them over, I keep tearing up my replies one after another.

Quirl writes, "Things here are more or less normal, in a material way. No sign of war, except on the faces of fathers and mothers whose sons have paid the price." How true that is, and I know I will be shocked to find everyone looking many more than the three years older. Where have the past three hectic years gone?

Our air alerts have dwindled to practically none, and whole days and nights go by without the sound of a plane. It is too quiet, for now we hear we are to move again, most likely to Luzon itself, but as yet we don't know. Some of our forces occupied the island of Martinduque, ninety miles from Manila, so it looks like we are closing in for the kill. Radio Tokyo seems alarmed and reports a huge convoy of ours heading toward Formosa, but, of course, if it is so, we are still in the dark about it.

January 8, 1945

A new friend popped up unexpectedly—Alexander Mozolic. I have seen him around in Company B ever since we came overseas, but never talked with him. Today he stood out by the headquarters tent here, waiting for his boat to come in. I went out and started a conversation and got the shock of my life. Alexander is a potter! The last person I would have picked as a creator of beautiful things from clay, he is around six feet, with the strength and grace of a panther and the body of a gladiator. One of those rare people who look as if they could tackle the world and win it single-handed, either by sheer weight of personality, or—if need be—by sheer strength. Usually you are fooled by splendid looks and find that too many of the people who have them are shallow and disappointing.

Although he was born in America, his parents came from Europe, the family having been potters for generations. The whole family works in the business in New Jersey, and Alexander's long association with the art is apparent when he talks fondly of the wonder of the glazes on his work as it comes from the firing; of his interest in color; of his definite plans to attend a school and specialize in glazes and color in ceramics; and then to create the finest pottery in the nation.

How refreshing to find someone with an art that they can love and have enough faith in still—after war has worn them thin—to be positive of returning to it for a lifetime of pleasant work. We talked for an hour and still had things unsaid when his boat arrived and he had to leave. I gave him a copy of a recent *American Artist*, which had a long article in it on the work of Wayland Gregory, a ceramic sculptor. Apparently Alexander had not, in his army career, encountered anyone really interested in pottery. We are a lonely lot who ignore so many things and dream of a day when we will be free to create beauty again.

January 12, 1945

We get more and more news of the Luzon landing. We didn't get there for the first one, but there will be plenty more, and we are busy planning for the expected move. Apparently it is about the same story—"landed with little resistance"—and we seem to be pushing on. Perhaps Count Juichi Terauchi, commander of all the Japanese army strength in the Philippines, will show some real strength on Luzon, for it is certain (according to Japanese tradition) that he will lose his position and most likely, his life, if he fails to make a good showing. I am just as certain that he will end up in "honorable disgrace" and be ready for honorable hari kari before long. We ain't foolin', Count!

Opened a can of pear preserves Mother sent me which were made from pears off the old tree in our yard. What memories they did bring back! That old tree was there—and had been for twenty or more years—when we moved into the property on Booker Street more than twenty years ago. An old man who had owned the place said there had been plenty of pears every year since he had known of the tree; and many seasons I have had to knock bushels of them off to keep the tree from being loaded to the breaking point on every limb. What big pears it has! But sometimes I think that, better than the pears, I always loved the snowy beauty of its blossoms in spring.

After the rattling blizzards of January, the tree would stir bravely on its old roots, and there would be the swelling of green buds; then that Mysterious Intangible which directs all things would say, "It is time!" Overnight there was beauty and fragrance and the humming of many bees, and a boy of ten worshipping at a white shrine that he couldn't explain any more than the geese flying north again. After twenty years, the boy finds he has never grown up and is no nearer explaining the fascination and the wonder of a faithful tree. He often wonders if anyone worships there now in spring, or if the tree misses people who love it.

January 16, 1945

The blue water of the strait between here and Samar Island is littered with floating boxes, as fifteen thousand six-foot-square pontoons of welded steel plate broke loose from their "corral" down the bay in last night's high wind. Now they are bobbing merrily as they continue on their way to Manila or wherever they are going "free lance," and our boats are trying to keep from smashing into them. It would be a super-human task to round up all these errant, stray dogies, so I guess those that do not take to the high seas will be washed up on beaches all over the Philippines.

A letter from Ruth telling me that Scrip[7] comes home to find himself minus a wife. Of course she trusted me enough to confide the information, for she knew that Scrip and I have shared a devoted friendship for more than twenty years. His English reserve was never a boon to intimate conversation, so I know little of the joys or sorrows he found in his married life, but he seemed quite happy and quite sure of the success of the venture undertaken over three years ago. After more than two years in the South Pacific as a lieutenant in the Navy, he returned just before Christmas with great expectations of renewing his home ties and perhaps making plans for the future with Pat. He wired her to meet him in California, which she did, with a request for immediate divorce, offering no reasons or excuses.

So apparently the thing stands; my first old pal to get the boot because he was too long in the "service of his country," instead of in the "service of his wife." Women are unreasonable wenches and expect the impossible of men, who are helpless to comply. We do all we can for the ones at home, but always there is a small feeling that we are, perhaps, capering around seeing the country while they suffer at home on rationed groceries and rationed gas with no one to love or fuss over them. Anyway, the rationed marriage just couldn't stand the strain, and it isn't an isolated example either. There will be literally thousands as time goes on, and more men return.

Well, Scrip, old pal, what say you we take a little of St. Vincent Millay's advice and quit building our houses on ugly rock that is supposed to endure. Come on, what about some castles in the shining sand? Yours is an unhappy incident, but I hope you don't let it get you down.

January 18, 1945

What do soldiers do who are sent to "rest camps" overseas? Of course, there isn't such a thing, but some places go by that name. Well, I talked with a person yesterday who is with a unit of about five hundred "rest camp" guys whose sole duty is guarding three hundred WAACs camped down the way. These WAACS are practically all hardened gals who could take care of themselves in a cage of gorillas. I have seen none who could—by any stretch of the imagination—pass for a sweet young thing. From reports the boys bring back (that is, those boys who have ventured out with the WAACS), they act the same way they look—tough. When the boys I'm talking about call a woman tough, she must be just that.

The fellow in the unlucky group of men "resting" says, "Now what can I tell people at home about my new job?" I stand guard at night in one section of the WAAC camp, and when a WAAC wants to go to the toilet, she yells, 'GUARD!' I go to her tent and escort her to the latrine. She stands outside while I go in and see that nothing is lurking inside that might make a pass at the gal. I come out. She goes in. I wait outside for her and escort her back to her tent. That's me—latrine escort for the WAACs!"

He was plenty disgusted, and so are all of us who have witnessed the needless and foolish work, waste, and expense of bringing women overseas. Evidently it is for effect only, as every group we have seen has tied up more men than they "released" for fighting. Never have there been more than three or four hundred of the women at any place, and even if they had actually released that many men—which they did not—the whole thing would have been an empty gesture. Three hundred men are a mere speck in the vast ocean of the army. We censor the Japanese for their army geisha girls but end up with a system much the same. Only we legalize it by making the WAACs a part of the army.

We are moving! Things are popping, and a day or two will see us again aboard a ship, starting out to grab another hunk of this damned Philippine soil back again. It looks like Luzon, of course, but we know very little.

I received an unusually nice letter from Mr. Maring, Phil's dad. I had written him a note telling him of Phil's promotion to corporal. His reply was a warmly grateful note expressing thanks for the family, extending me a welcome to their home anytime, and telling me how they loved their "kid." It was such a small thing; it took so little time; and that letter of reply was worth a million dollars to me. It is hard to realize just what each soldier means to someone until you read such a letter. That darned "kid" puts off writing letters, and I knew he had not written them about his promotion.

33 Into Subic Bay

January 19, 1945

The usual "moving rain" began last night and is still at it—one of those slow, deliberate, wet rains with thick gray sky and not the glimmer of a promise of ever raining itself out. Our beach looks drab and empty and lonesome with every boat gone. They are loaded aboard the various ships that are to carry them on the mission. Tomorrow the tents will come down, rain or no rain. What a soggy mess to pack!

January 22, 1945

The usual moving delay. Like always after things were packed, the day to move was put off—twice. Tomorrow?

January 24, 1945

Late yesterday we boarded an AP boat, the *Winged Arrow*. Just what the AP stands for, we are in doubt, but suppose it is "Assault Personnel." Anyway, it is one of those ships built to carry men and cargo into the invasion waters. It has guns, but is so loaded with cargo equipment that you couldn't possibly call it a fighting ship. It is also a U.S. Navy ship—the first we have sailed on so far. Others have been Merchant Marine with some Navy gunners and crew.

The Navy makes itself felt as much as possible on the ship—a thing noticeably absent on the Merchant Marine ships. I wondered how the poor little crew of 350 could possibly get the ship from place to place unless army troops were aboard for work details. The officers are separated in the mess hall, and you hear on the loud speaker system: "Officers of grade of captain and above are now being served." I suppose the lieutenants trail in to "second table" feeling hurt about the whole situation.

The food is good and well served, and the lines are not so long at meal time. At breakfast I had my first shipboard experience with the "democracy of the Army and Navy"—one of those things that strike you as a bit silly. After I had sat down and was eating, someone sat at my right and spoke in a pleasant voice. I looked up and it was Lew Ayres, famous as Dr. Kildare of the movies. He chatted in a friendly way. I was surprised, but of course gave no indication that I knew who he was, even though I had seen him a couple of times on deck.

Ayres has aged, his hair is grizzly, his face seamed; he is skinny to extreme. I doubted that the movies could ever again make him into the sleek, handsome man of the Dr. Kildare series. Only his rich, sure voice and his strong, sensitive hands were the same. Ayres has been through a lot of abuse for holding fast to his ideals and ideas. He must have boundless courage. He is a corporal and has refused a direct commission and other ratings offered him—which alone would set him apart as a man with higher ideals than the army could understand.

Someone sat down on my left. I looked around, not—of course—expecting a second movie star, but surely not expecting the big coal-black soldier who was there! He was one of the 150 who got on shipboard last night. Democracy at work! Me eating breakfast between a big, black man and Lew Ayres.

The noon meal again brought the "black versus white" question sharply into focus. A southern boy was standing at his guard post beside the door that leads down into the dining room, when the long line began to pass down for lunch. He had not seen Negroes eating with whites, so as the black soldiers came by, scattered up and down the line, he sorted them out and made them stand to one side. "You eat last," he was telling the group of them that he had backed up in the corner. Although they were mad, they couldn't do much about it. Evidently one of them got by, for soon a red-faced officer came puffing up the stairs and said, "Let these men eat as they come by!"

Tonight I noticed that most of them came to eat together instead of scattering themselves in with the whites, but a few still sat at tables full of white soldiers.

January 26, 1945

Our convoy got underway late on the afternoon of the twenty-fifth. We sailed down Surigao Strait, and last night late were in the Mindanao

Sea. Today we sailed most of the day in the Sulu Sea, heading into the Cuyo East Pass and Mindoro Strait. The ship's routine is ordinary, with a lot of time spent on the three meals each day. We have had our first guard for the company. Guard duty consists of sitting in some designated place on deck for four hours, off eight, and on four again.

During my eight hours nothing happened. I simply sat around from 8:00 a.m. to 12:00 noon, then again from 8:00 p.m. until midnight. There were plenty of people to talk with, and on shipboard talk is about all the exercise you can expect. It makes time go by faster. Usually we spend the cool hours of the evening talking, and when talk dulls, go below to our bunks, remove our clothes (against all regulations, which say you should sleep fully clothed in case of alerts, etc.), and read until the lights go out. My reading material consists of a dozen or so of the last letters I received from various people just before leaving, and a copy of *Bayous of Louisiana.*

January 28, 1945

Although I do not recognize the land to the east, I guess we must be sailing somewhere off Cape Calavite and Lubang Island this afternoon and will probably make a swing out to sea to clear Manila Harbor entrance tonight. Radio Tokyo says today, "The Americans are massing more ships for new blows at the Philippines." True for once, Tokyo.

February 1, 1945

On January 29, we did not wait until 8:30 a.m. for the landing. Long before dawn our boats were lowered from the big ships, and there was hustle and bustle all around the convoy. Only the earth and sky and sea remained calm. The water was still. The Southern Cross hung like a glittering jewel above the dark shapes of the mountains as we strained our eyes and wondered what was awaiting on the dark shoreline. Slowly—so slowly—the sky grayed for the coming of the day.

Not a shot was fired. Our troops moved ashore and poured inland. The ship's speaker boomed, "The naval barrage has been cancelled!" The Japanese had fled, if, indeed, any had been here.[8]

The village by the beach was La Paz, with the larger town of San Narisco located back a mile or less from the beach. Both towns were so different from the mud and filth of Tacloban that it was like coming out into sunshine after darkness. The houses are all constructed of bamboo, but are neatly and skillfully made. The yards are clean and planted with flowers. The streets are clean and dry. The towns were in a festive mood and displayed more genuine appreciation for the Americans' return than I had seen anywhere before.

By the second day you could hardly pass a house without seeing American soldiers inside. These people seemed superior to the Leyte islanders in appearance and intelligence; more spoke good English. One fellow said, "Manila is the heart and life of the Philippines. The nearer you get to it, the better conditions are."

The country looked inviting, so Dotson and I took our rifles and went for a walk across country a couple of miles. This is the dry season, so rice paddies are simply fields, and trails are dry and dusty. The whole lay of the land was surprisingly like California. Before us stretched a green valley of gardens with irrigation ditches flowing, while up behind rose a range of magnificent dun-colored mountains. Some tree much like our Texas redbud bloomed around the edges of the fields. Songbirds sang all around. (It has been more than a year since I have heard a songbird.) Farmers worked in the fields. Carabao[9] grazed beside the irrigation ditches. This was a smiling land practically untouched by war.

We came to a farm house in a grove and stopped to talk with the Filipino family there. They were bubbling over with genuine friendliness and insisted that we sit by the table under the fine old trees. The father of the family told us of the Japanese occupation. The rest listened with interest to our comments.

Evidently few Japanese had come into this section—only a patrol of a dozen or so occasionally, and once in a while a sentry was stationed in San Narisco. The patrols took food for themselves from the farmers along the route, but did no harm. The sentry forced all who passed him to bow, even if the person came by forty times a day, and failure to do so gave the sentry the privilege of beating the offender if he so chose. No goods had been brought in for three years, and these people had had no new clothes or equipment of any kind other than what they had made themselves. "We could have held out longer," the farmer said, "but we are glad you came when you did."

Evidently they improvised, invented, and fell back on primitive methods to accomplish the necessary things to carry on normal life. One of the younger men showed me his "balasoot" when I asked him how he made fire with no matches. The balasoot is the most ingenious of all primitive fire-making ideas and should prove embarrassing to the man who thinks he invented the idea on which the diesel engine works. A section of carabao horn about the size of a five-inch section of broomstick, with a hole drilled lengthwise nearly to the far end, and a plunger that fits the hold snugly—that is the balasoot complete.

The plunger has a hole in its end, into which is pressed a piece of soft, bark tinder; also, near its end it has a thin wrapping of wool thread which is greased with tallow when a fire is to be made. The plunger is simply slapped quickly into the hole, and when pulled out, the tinder is a glowing coal. I learned that this apparatus is peculiar to northern Luzon, and is found nowhere else in the world.[10]

Carabao were everywhere. Evidently the Japanese had not needed them for food. My opinion is that even they would have found these water buffalo rather tough eating. Even the tiny calf we saw didn't look like steaks to me!

The fourth day, February 1, we packed up, boarded our boats, and moved to our present location, Subic Bay, about fifty miles down the coast toward Manila Bay. From the sea the mountains were wonderful, all yellow and red ochers with patches and glazes of greens here and there. Some appeared to be covered with golden grass, which was an indication that we had hit one place in the dry season.

We entered Subic Bay past Grande Island, which guards the entrance to this excellent bay that prior to the war was a big naval base. Grande had been taken a day or so before and was now a smoking ruin, blasted to bits by naval gunfire. Evidently the Japanese had fortified it and had to be blown out. But they die hard, and as we passed the island, a shell from the hills landed on its southern tip, sending up clouds of smoke and dirt, indicating another Japanese gun to be located and destroyed. The battle all around the bay was hardly over. The town was a blackened ruin, but already our ack-ack guns, searchlights, and radar had moved in and set up in the wreckage.

February 2, 1945

Our campsite is a wonder. There is a good stretch of clean sand beach, with a fine palm grove on a slight rise. To the north a long valley stretches to a range of rugged and beautiful mountains. I took a good look when we came, for such a place is not cleanly beautiful after the army moves in with tents and machinery and wires strung from tree to tree.

Out beyond the grove stretches a gigantic "front lawn" of close cropped green sod (cropped by carabao and horses, no doubt), and at its outer edges grow some bushes blooming a misty pink, and a few gnarled old trees sporting bunches of flaming red blossoms. Yes, we are lucky that we came in our boats and could reach this ideal spot first, as—no doubt—a road will be built across the shallow river that separates us from access to the main highway.

February 5, 1945

Camp is established now, in by far the best location we have ever had. The Filipinos helped set it up, and today we have two working in our tent. These people are anxious to help and really work when you give them a job, asking nothing but their meals and what little we can find to give them in the way of food to carry home. Our two "boys" are a man and a boy of about fifteen.

They are skillful with bamboo and have made a large rack, mosquito bar frames, wash stand, table, etc. With only a knife they cut and fit bamboo and astonish you with their results. Bamboo, the standard building material here, is used for everything—houses, furniture, water buckets. Apparently, anything can be made from it.

Our palm grove is really a tuba plantation, I guess. Tuba is the national drink, and these natives around here must have it in gallons. The "tuba man" who tends the trees is busy going up and down all day. (Each tree is notched for climbing.) Small buckets made of bamboo joints are hung on the bloom stem of the tree. The stem is given a fresh cut each day, and the sap flows into the buckets. The man goes up the tree with a huge four-foot section of bamboo on his back, fitted out as a bucket for collecting the sap from the smaller buckets in the trees.

Naturally, when the bloom stems are continually ruined, no coconuts can mature, and our grove is practically bare of them. The sap, when fresh, has a not unpleasant odor and taste, but the Filipino isn't satisfied with that. He puts some sort of red bark in it, lets it set, and makes something with the potency of double strength TNT. Naturally the poor Filipinos get little of it now. The soldiers want it all and can get gloriously soused on it.

There seem to be a few Japanese left around here yet. Two nights ago shells fell down the coast around our boat-repair shops—no damage. Our officers, or most of them, have been rather nervous, and one lieutenant spent the night sitting with a lapful of grenades. Last night there was an air raid alert, and all lights went out. At that time I was going across the area to my tent, and the nervous lieutenant called out, "Who's there?"

"A Jap with a bayonet," I said.

"Don't you know that is a good way to get shot?" he asked.

"Just how do I get across the area without walking?" I replied.

No answer.

February 7, 1945

The military situation here seems to be that we are slowly cutting off Bataan Peninsula with the battle of Zig Zag Pass. The infantry is slugging on, but it is slow and bloody going. The artillery has moved off somewhat, so maybe they are making some progress, but we can still hear the big guns pounding the Japanese there.

February 9, 1945

Of all the complaints to acquire—a bad back! In the army it is a standard joke: "Oh my back!" Mine was acquired unloading ammunition from the ship at the landing, and after days of having to assume a "grandpa" stance, I went to the doctor. He seemed to think it more than just a sprain and sent me to the hospital for an x-ray. The hospital was crowded with wounded from the battle of Zig Zag Pass, and they were refusing all x-ray cases without large bullet holes. I had none, and, of course, got no x-ray taken. However, the men I saw there were so much worse off than I that I didn't feel it was unjust.

I was told to come back in a week or so, probably with the idea that I would be well by then anyway. When I returned to camp, the medics here decided to tape up the back, such a job consisting of applying large pieces of three-inch-wide adhesive tape from the outer edges of the stomach, around the hips, and across the back. My tape was applied by Philip Prejatel, and that gorilla doesn't know his own strength! He practically gave me a wasp waist, and I decided the idea was to make the tape so uncomfortable that I would forget the original ailment. After wearing this adhesive girdle all day, I couldn't stand it any longer and went over to get it removed. They removed it all right, along with patches of skin the size of a quarter and various blisters. "We usually treat patients for tape wounds after this," Philip said, and I believed him. The back isn't any better or worse, but the hide on it is lots worse!

February 15, 1945

We still have the older of the Filipino pair who worked for us the first few days—Max Kaai. He has made things easier in many little ways. He speaks good English and understands more than he speaks. He identified the odd noise in the coconut trees as a tree lizard called "Taco." I had supposed it was some sort of tree frog.

Today Max brought a nice woven mat to trade to me. I had shown him a piece of printed dress material and told him it was to trade for a mat. As a matter of conversation when he came in, I asked, "What do you want for the mat, Max?" "A pair of dress for woman," was his reply. I suppose if a man wore a pair of pants, Max surmised that the correct statement about a dress would be "a pair of dress."

Part of our company and others of the outfit boarded ships and barges today for a landing, most likely on the tip of Bataan and probably Corregidor, as we hear rumors of a push there. Evidently the Navy has been busy there already, because today we had an urgent request for a tug to tow in a damaged destroyer.

Subic Bay is a lovely spot! Every direction you look is natural beauty. Late yesterday I walked down the beach and climbed up onto a small hill point that juts out into the water—a pile of ancient, black lava rocks streaked with red, that once must have flowed into the sea from some long dead volcano. To the north I could see the range of blue rugged mountains, and across Subic the closer range of coastal hills hung with gold-dust atmosphere from the glory of a sunset that was all golds and oranges and yellows.

To the south over the Kalaklan Mountains, a buff cloud held the phenomenon of an upside-down section of rainbow across its mellow face. It was a quite satisfactory close to the day and gave me—for an instant—a feeling of contentment and rest in the midst of all this that is neither. Out beyond Grande Island lay the convoy ready for the strike again, but it was only a far distant group of shapes on the horizon. Its noise and guns and men were not evident. The guns had moved out of hearing in Zig Zag Pass. How long until guns and planes and ships move forever from our lives?

February 22, 1945

The past twelve days have been full of interesting things, but I hit one of those long, low slumps of lethargy in which nothing seems worthwhile, nothing seems to have its true value, and everybody around me is a bastard. I tried to pull out of it, but nothing seemed to do any good, though I hated myself for it. I have to hold up and hold on. It's too late in the game to go into a tailspin now.

I received twenty letters in the mail that finally caught up with us Sunday. So I took my twenty letters, went down to the point of beach by the black rocks, put my cloths on the rocks, lay down in the warm sand, and enjoyed each letter. It was quite peaceful there. No one was around to even talk. No one else wanted to lie in the sand and read letters.

News from home was bad, but I'm helpless as ever, with my request for emergency furlough either awaiting more information of the rotation or lying forgotten on some headquarters desk. I could easily become very bitter and give up the effort it takes to carry on in the army in a decent way; but I haven't. The whole thing has simply robbed me of interest in people and things and places and made the nights too long. The nights are beautiful here, though, and I don't have to go to bed until I get good and ready. The stars are good company.

34 Making Filipino Friends

February 23, 1945

Our boys made the landing on Corregidor and Bataan and report a thrilling time of it. We lost one man from Company A. Several were slightly wounded. The man lost was shot while steering his barge into the beach. A shell went through the half-inch of steel of the wheelhouse, through a two-by-four, through the man, and out through the other side of the wheelhouse. No doubt an armor piercing bullet of 50-caliber or less, judging from the hole it made. I am not so sure it was an enemy bullet even, for from all reports, there was a mess of crossfire from our own naval boats. Maybe I just doubt the ability of a Japanese bullet to travel like that.

Our boys watched the parachutists land on Corregidor, went in later, and brought out wounded through a hell of shellfire on the Corregidor beach. One man was bitten on the hand by a Japanese soldier he attempted to pull from the water. Unfortunately for the biter, the fellow who was bitten had been working with the boat and had a ramp crank in his other hand. (Japanese soldier wasn't much good when pulled in after encounter with crank!)

Other boats without time to pick up groups of swimming Japanese soldiers simply ran through them. Major Gudgeon arrived back from a trip there today (it is about fifty miles from here to Corregidor), and he reports that in spite of what radio and other commentators say, there is actually little of the rock in our hands yet. There seems to be long and bloody hand-to-hand fighting ahead. The major says the part of the island he was on is a veritable no man's land, pulverized by shells and bombs into a mass of rubble. He was fired on several times by hidden enemy soldiers.

Zig Zag Pass is finally cleared, and the road can now be used on into Manila. Only snipers are left to contend with.

Our Filipino "old man" works each day. We pay him a little canned food and give him his meals. I slip him small change sometimes, and he seems happy at his work. Max is not old, at least not by standards we have in America. He says he is fifty-five. Life here begins and ends sooner than in our society, and Max—at his age—has practically completed his life cycle. He has six grown children, numerous grandchildren, his wife is dead, and—in the eyes of the Filipinos—is indeed an "old man."

But he is good to have around. He is honest, works hard, and seems generally happy. He is my informer on nature lore of the Philippines and furnishes a wealth of information about things in general. It wouldn't be a good day unless his bare feet padded up and I heard the cheery "Good morning, Mr. Browning!" and saw his smiling brown face. He rowed up each morning in his outrigger canoe, until one of our careless boys backed over it with a big truck. Now I have the job of finding him another canoe and settling the thing satisfactorily with him and the truck driver, which won't be so unpleasant, for we will have to visit other Filipinos and that will make new contacts.

Last night was one of those rare nights when the moon reflected on white fluffs of clouds in a dark, starry sky; the wind was in the palm trees; the tide lapped at a wide, smooth beach. I walked down to the point and sat for a long time on the black rocks at the water's edge. It is good to sit and think sometimes, but I usually end up in a quandary and come no nearer to figuring things out. We humans are complex animals. So often our thoughts and actions don't jibe, and we wonder why. We want to be noble and fine, but such thoughts turn out to be just brainchildren which do not come to life . . . maybe next month or next year we will accomplish . . . and time laughs and goes his way.

March 15, 1945

The routine has been going along with little variation, and I have become thoroughly bored with life as lived in an army camp in the Philippines. Almost the only breaks have been some pleasant visits out to Tugboat 109, a ninety-six-foot boat manned by a civilian crew with a Filipino skipper. These boys are employed by the Army Transport Service, and this fact certainly has its advantages. The ordinary seamen get two hundred dollars per month and are not under the petty control of the army. Their morale is high; their attitude, superior to ours. They are free men working because they want to do the job.

At present the tugboat and crew have been gone a week on a trip to Manila. All of them wanted me to go along, but the situation summed up to my being in the damned army—I didn't go. Sanders was hesitant about granting permission, so I told him to skip it. One of the unfortunate things in our organization is the inability of any officer to look a man in the eye and say either, "yes" or "no." Contrary to popular opinion, the army does not build leaders; it appoints officers.

The laundry seems in a good way to vanish, as Bilger has decided there shall be no Filipinos coming into the area and has posted guards to keep them out. Rosita Baza has been picking up my laundry every day and bringing it back the following day—all neat and clean and pressed. She was not hesitant about informing me, "Mr. Browning, those trousers you are wearing, they are dirtee!" With the result that I have worn cleaner clothes here than at any time since coming overseas. Now I have to carry the clothes to Rosita, which is very inconvenient, and, of course, I can't do it every day. Yesterday I went over for the first time, crossing the river on the "Maboohi Ferry," as we call it. Maboohi is a Filipino word meaning a variety of things, such as "long live," much like our "hurray!" Also the Filipinos use it in departure, much like our "goodbye." But Maboohi has come to mean most anything Filipino to the American soldier. We call Filipinos "Maboohis" often, so the designation of the ferry is only natural. After all, Maboohi Ferry does sound pretty classy.

The ferry consists of a group of small outrigger canoes, each paddled by a boy or old man who has little else to do all day but wait to carry soldiers back and forth across the shallow river that runs into the sea. A few cigarettes or coins pays your fare, and the service is quick and efficient. Sometimes you are ferried over simply for good will, but I rather suspect that too many trips on good will would eventually cause strange accidents in midstream.

Directly across the stream is the barrio of Matain, one of a string of small villages that hover around from the upper end of Subic Bay to the town of Subic, which is little more than a tiny barrio itself. The streets are narrow, and the bamboo houses are scattered about in a somewhat haphazard fashion. Most of the people I met my first day there seemed familiar, and I realized they were the same people who had been coming to our camp ever since we arrived. They are our nearest neighbors, whose afternoon diversion was a visit to the camp to pick up laundry and gossip with the soldiers.

Parts of the village are rather smelly, reminding you of the overpowering odor of pig pens one minute and the enchanting fragrance of mango blossoms the next. Cashew trees present their odd fruit. The nut we are familiar with grows on the bottom of a bell-pepper-shaped fruit, and apparently the natives pay more attention to the fruit than the nut. The fruit smells like a delicious apple, but falls short of that in taste. The nuts have a greenish taste and little of the attraction of those we buy at home over the counter of the candy store.

The villagers lounge in the shade of coconut trees or look from the windows of their homes. Apparently they have little pressing business to attend to. Aside from the able men who are away in the service of the guerillas and other army work, life flows in an easy stream here. Fish dry in the sun. An old woman husks rice, the rhythmic "whish, whish, whish" of the pestle falling on the rice only adding to the quiet, domestic rhythm of the whole.

I found Rosita ironing clothes with a huge charcoal iron. Her round, brown face lighted up in a smile when she saw me, and I suspected that she had wondered if she was to lose all her laundry customers because of the ban on entering the camp. But, here was one who had stuck, and that would mean a little more food, a few more pesos for the family.

Rosita's mother was there—a gaunt, tall Filipino woman with large, gold rings in her ears. She spoke no English, but Rosita chatted back and forth between us, first in English, and then Tagalong.[11] I had brought the old lady a package of cigarettes, for Rosita had said her mother was the only one in the family who smoked. Pedro, Rosita's husband, was there too. I know him, for he had worked for a while here in camp. The two children were down at the river with the family canoe, running a unit of the Malboohi Ferry.

I wondered how they all lived, with rice scarce and expensive, fish selling for two pesos fifty centavos each, and even small watermelons the size of your head, six pesos; eggs, eighty centavos each or the equivalent of $4.80 a dozen.

March 23, 1945

Yesterday found me with two events on schedule—both unexpected. First, I have developed a rash that rises in welts and itches awfully, so I went to the regimental doctor to find out what ails me. He said hives, possibly from something I had eaten. I disagree with him and suspect that it could be something I *haven't* eaten, as the monotonous canned food has been the same for weeks, with positively nothing fresh, nothing green. Anyway, there had been five cases of the same rash in the past week.

Treatment consists of an injection of a rather large bottle of something-or-other into the arteries. I lay on the table, and the "operation" began. I didn't feel much when the needle was first put in my arm, but soon the something-or-other began to flow warmly over me like a hot bath, and I was a little dizzy. That was all until I opened my eyes, and someone was fanning ammonia under my nose to bring me around. Everyone seemed quite concerned, and the doctor was trying to figure if the treatment or my nervousness caused the fade out. I knew it must have been the something-or-other, for I don't faint while lying down. Definitely! Anyway, I gave the fellow who was standing by waiting for his treatment a good introduction as to what it was like, but how his came out I don't know, for I left as fast as possible.

After spending most of the day on my cot following my return from the hospital, I felt some better in the afternoon. After supper Arthur (Buddy) Lund came ashore and wanted to go to the town of Subic for the evening. He is a swell friend from the crew of Tug 109, hails from Minnesota, is twenty-two, was reared on a farm, did scout work, and is someone who enjoys the usual things that scouts and scouters are always interested in. He is a civilian and very proud of it; says he is going home when his contract is up in a few months.

First we met Salvador, the mess boy on the tug, who lives in Subic with his family. He is very fond of each and every one of the boys on the tug and was proud to introduce us to his Filipino friends. He ended up taking us to the town's best restaurant, recently opened and called "Victory

Club." "This is on me," he said. "These people, they owe me money anyway. I painted their sign. See?" (Salvador is a part time sign painter too.)

A neat Filipino girl appeared and greeted Salvador. "My cousin," he said, which I find is a usual greeting to anyone in your town. They all seem to be kin to the extent of being cousins anyway. When the girl reappeared, she carried a small bottle of whiskey. Salvador was treating us to twenty pesos worth of Manila whiskey, which he poured into small glasses with a flourish. Arthur looked at me, and I looked at him, and we both decided we were trapped like rats. We'd drink it if it knocked us loop-legged. It wasn't bad either, but fortunately there wasn't enough in that bottle to do much damage to three people. Arthur ended up drinking more than I, and when we left, he was maybe a slight bit jollier than before. If I was, I didn't notice it myself.

We all three went by the house of the skipper in Subic, who brought his family here from Manila, where they had been prisoners of war for a long time. We met his wife and little daughter and kindly old mother. The latter, unlike most Filipino women her age, spoke good English, so I chatted with her. She talked mostly about her four sons. Besides the skipper, she had one in New Guinea, one working with the Manila Philippines Government, and one in Chicago. Of all their better-than-average accomplishments, she seemed proudest of the fact that the son in Chicago had married an American girl. "I am proud of my American daughter-in-law," she said.

Some "cousins" were there, and I decided that a Filipino could go to the North Pole and discover a cousin. The man and woman had brought their two daughters, about the most attractive Filipino girls I had seen. They were clean, neat, wearing attractive white slippers and silk dresses, and had ginger blossoms in their coal-black hair. All in all, they were smart looking, which even extended to red nail polish.

They wanted to sing some American popular songs, so we all sang some of the things we knew with them. Arthur has a good voice, and Salvador's tonic had helped it along, so it wasn't hard to get him to sing. He also has a knack for knowing most of the latest music, and the girls were overjoyed.

Nobody had any idea of taking the girls anyplace at all, but if we had, it would have been the wrong thing, definitely. They had been reared under the old Spanish custom, which has a low estimate of humans in general, and young men in particular. Where the girls went, the old lady went. I doubt if they had ever sat alone with a young man three minutes in their lives. We left soon, as Arthur had heard some sort of celebration was going on at a home he had visited before. Salvador left us, and Arthur and I found our way to the corner of the main street and down to the home mentioned.

A crowd of people seemed to be there, mostly Filipinos, but also soldiers. More soldiers were on the porch than inside. We looked in and spotted one of the tug crew and went in to find out what was going on. It was a wake. The father of the family had died, and this was the last night of a nine-day wake for him.

An altar was set up in the first room, and a Filipino priest in a long white linen robe was there. The daughters and wife of the family were dressed in black dresses and wore black shawls over their heads.

But the solemnity of all this clashed terrifically with the fact that people were drinking mixed wine and whiskey, laughing, singing, and playing cards at tables. Also, the large table in the next room was set for about fifteen with huge platters of food of all kinds. As soon as we entered, we were practically seized and dragged to the table. We protested, but were firmly informed that it is "the Filipino custom" for all who come to eat. Seemingly, there was no way around it, short of murder.

We found ourselves seated at the large table along with thirteen Filipinos of various ages. It was rather an odd situation; we felt rather out of place. The priest sat at the head of the table, and I noticed that—in contrast to the other guests—he ate very little. Later I learned that he probably couldn't afford to, as he sat at every table all night, and the meal went on almost continually.

The food was excellent, mostly rice dishes with chicken, odd fried cakes of something I couldn't identify, bread that seemed half-way between wheat bread and corn bread, and custard pie made from the white Filipino sweet potatoes; also good coffee. All of it was well served, much in the style of any meal we were accustomed to. After the meal, we got away as soon as was polite and caught a ride back (which wasn't too difficult, although when we got on the truck, we found it was loaded with five-hundred-pound bombs). Arthur caught one of the night patrol boats and went back to his boat, and I took the path from the highway back to our area.

April 3, 1945

Again we move! And within an hour of the notice a nice shower swept across Subic Bay—our MOVING RAIN. The rainy season will begin soon, so I guess we are in for it. Our move seems to be below Manila Bay, near Luzon's second city, Batangas.

Again it is tear up and move—tear up tents, equipment and friendships that have been made here. So little time to make friends that you will never see again, and some of them you regret leaving so much. No two are exactly alike. They all sparkle with their own individual wealth.

BUDDY
I've watched him as he hauled the anchor in
And as he rested in a palm tree's shade.
He is all the clean design of youth,
The stuff from which all glad, free lands are made.

Where'er he goes he stands beside the best,
And plans to share the world he fights to free;
But should he go before his task is done,
He'd toss his unlived dream to you and me.
J.G.B.

35 Going Home

April 9, 1945

The move has been completed, but this April morning finds me still in the old coconut grove at Subic Bay. The grove is quiet now, only a few tents and a few men remaining of the once teeming camp. A bird sings in the bamboo; a native sings as he paddles his banco down the river—sounds you never heard above the roar of machinery and the noise of many men. Always I seem to come back to quiet places after adventure.

On April 5, I went on board Tug 109 to ride to our new location, Batangas. We found that we were not sailing until seven o'clock that night. I had left early expecting the boat to leave very shortly. Things sound confused, but really came about thusly.

Having missed two trips with the tug, I was determined to ride down with it when I learned it was due to tow our oil barge. Captain Pete had invited me, and Arthur had insisted. Various members of the crew had asked about the possibility. By riding the tug I would miss the uncomfortable trip aboard one of our boats, and, at the same time, have a last and pleasant visit with friends on the 109. As our company commander, Sanders, had left suddenly for the States four days before, I approached the new man on the subject of my trip by tug. As expected, he was hesitant; but later Sergeant Young came by and told me to go aboard 109 for the trip, so I supposed the company commander changed his mind. Anyway, I went.

On board 109 Arthur got me located; I had a bunk in the cabin with the chief engineer, Robert Russell. Arthur ransacked his laundry, which was just in, and brought me clean sheets and pillow case, and we made up the bunk. What style! The first sheet I had slept on in more than two years.

After I was properly stowed, bag and baggage, we went in the galley and talked with "Cookie," who immediately opened the big refrigerator and brought out two big pieces of Boston cream pie. Unconsciously the boys were giving me big slices of pure delight. They didn't realize it, for all along they had been sleeping on sheets and eating such pie.

Since we had all day, Buddy wanted to go to Subic for a few hours and take some photos of us with the Filipino girls he knew. We had several times visited a couple of them, and I can give Buddy credit for knowing the top layer of the Subic society. He was admired and trusted by them, which isn't unusual considering the kind of guy he is. You just feel that way about him instinctively. I could always go to Subic with Buddy and be sure of an afternoon of good clean fun, as neither of us rushed off for a bottle of rum and a visit to the local "cat houses," as is the custom with at least seventy-five percent of our boys.

We found Luming (Iluminada Ponco) at the small "shop" located in a corner of her home. The shop is merely what we would call a stand with board counter, bench, and some stools. It contained very little for sale—a few pots of cooked food, candied *camotes*, spaghetti, rice cakes, and a few bunches of *cincomas* or white turnip-like vegetables that are always eaten raw.

Luming brightened when she saw us, for she—like all Filipinos—is proud of her American friends. Luming is above ordinary in the town in appearance and family standing. Her skin is a clear coffee and cream, her dark eyes sparkling; her black hair curls in a long bob at her shoulders. Once she told me that she had Chinese blood, which accounts for her slanting eyes and slightly different appearance in stature and color. As she sold food to various women and children, she told us the native names of the dishes. When business slowed, we ate rice cakes. I took photos of Buddy talking at the stand; he did the same for me.

Then Nene (Gregoria Perea) came up, and we photographed the two girls together. Nene is a friend of Luming, and the sister of Salvador. She is rather homely and dark, and her command of English is less than Luming's, but she is friendly and another of the better people of the town. She invited us down to her aunt's house, where we were served melon and mangos—both delicious.

When we left we mentioned that we were going by to photograph the old church, and Nene said she would go along, as she had not been down for her prayers today. She entered the church with a wisp of black lace over her head. I photographed her at prayer in the big empty church, as the battered saints looked down from the time-worn walls.

At 7:00 p.m. we hauled anchor and got under way towing a ninety-foot fuel barge loaded with sixty thousand gallons of diesel fuel. The day was old, and the mellowness of twilight was settling over the hills as we headed out past Grande Island through the new submarine net and into the open sea. The mountains had taken on a new greenness since the recent showers, and Eddie commented on it as we stood on the very top of the ship admiring them. Eddie isn't someone who would be expected to make comments on the beauty of the hills, but he had real appreciation.

A word as to the crew of the 109. (I object to a boat going by a number, but apparently the army doesn't, as the tug has no other name.) The Filipino captain is gone and was replaced by the first officer, Peter Betts, an Australian. Peter is popular with the crew and is a fine fellow. We kid him about Australia. "Say, Pete, are you really going to live in that place after the war?" But he takes it fine.

The first officer is new, having only come on last week. His name is Ward—young, handsome, and well-liked. Norman Kettering or "Pappy" is the second officer. Pappy is only in his early thirties. His dry wit is something rare. Robert Russell or "Rus" is chief engineer. Barber is his assistant, and Messmer is second engineer. Messmer had taken a few drinks too many and had his broken ankle in a cast from foot to hip. "Messmer used to be the first man to the table before he got his leg in a cast. Now he can only make second place," they tease. The cook, Phil Steffen or "Cookie," spends all his working hours keeping excellent food available, and he is a fantastic cook.

There are three army gunners aboard, and one radio operator known as "Sparks," whose name is Horace Newell. Arthur Lund, Edward Jones, Micky Malo, and Floyd Lanier are the four seamen. Tuba is the dog—an awkward, half-grown pup of uncertain ancestory. Tuba was cute as a tiny puppy and found a home aboard; however, as usual with puppies, when they grow into dogs, they are lots of times decidedly not cute. Tuba has little sense, but the whole crew loves him and puts up with his gangling nonsense.

It was soon evident that the oil barge was a contrary piece of equipment to tow. To begin with, it had been too heavily loaded for such a trip, but Sergeant Greene had received orders from our new and green company commander to fill it up. Greene protested, as he had towed the old barge around for fourteen months, clear from Australia, but Edmunds' order was "Do as I tell you! Fill it up!" So it was filled up.

Greene stood on deck of the 109 shaking his head as the cable on the towing line was unrolled and the barge fell behind, but refused to be led gracefully. It dashed from side to side like a stubborn bull. Being very heavy, it refused to stop when headed to the right until jerked up by the cable. Then it swung to the left. There seemed to be no remedy for its capers, but by dark it seemed to be riding fairly well, although its decks were awash.

After dark settled over the ship and the usual duties were taken care of, the people who expected to be on watch later went to bed. Some of us stood on deck talking. Someone made coffee in the galley. The ship was blacked out, and the lighted galley became the focus of the life of the ship. About 10:00 we smelled oil and wondered if the oil barge was splitting a seam, but it seemed to still be coming along. The ship settled down for the night's run.

I awakened several times, the final time when the throb of the engine stopped abruptly. Someone ran by the porthole, and as I tried to get my fuzzy head together, Rus came in and said, "Get your life jacket. I think that damned barge is sinking!"

I lost no time in slipping on trousers and shoes, also, and stepped onto the port deck just as the 109 gave a mighty heave to port. The rail went down to meet the sea, and solid water rushed over, wetting me to the waist. Immediately I decided that was the wrong side and turned and made for the opposite door leading to the starboard deck. As I crossed the large iron grating to the engine room, I heard a mighty crashing and clanking below. Everything that was not tied down was "walking." On the starboard deck were most of the gang in life jackets; the starboard rail was high above the sea.

Someone was tying an extra life jacket on Messmer's rear. "That is to hold up the game leg," they told him. "Get a jacket for the dog!" "That water looks awful cold!" Somewhat of a surprise, but little fear was evident anywhere. Everyone seemed to be taking it as a matter of course.

There were loud chopping sounds from the stern deck, and in a moment the 109 righted herself, and a yell came, "All clear!" The cable had been chopped off with a fire axe, and we had been saved from a serious accident that could easily have cost us the ship and any number of lives.

It was 4:00 a.m. and we were off Corregidor, whose dim shape was sighted now and again by flares and gunfire. Men were still fighting there, although the place had been announced cleared of the enemy about February 20. I wondered if they were shooting at Santa Claus, or maybe MacArthur had made a mistake in the announcement.

As to the oil barge, she had been riding practically underwater for an hour, and the cable had been reeled in to see what the trouble was. Shortly thereafter, she simply dived for the bottom, which happened to be just four hundred fathoms deep, or twenty-five hundred feet. Evidently she did split a seam, or a lot of seams, from the heavy load. The towing cable had slipped to the port rail, which it cut through like butter when the barge went down, and the towing reel snarled. We headed back to Subic Bay at full speed.

At dawn we again went through the sub net and into the bay, passing our convoy of Ms[12] on their way out. We dropped anchor in the old spot, and Pete went into headquarters to report the accident. I was glad to miss the convoy, glad to be left behind for a few days of peace and quiet. This was the first move I had missed since joining the outfit on Cape Cod!

Suddenly I realized how I had had the old nose to the grindstone. There have been good times and a few breaks, yes, but no long stretches of detached service, no weeks in the hospital, no jobs taking me away from the old routine as others have had. No furlough, no trips to Manila. Yes, I had really been close at it, and I wondered why. Never again will I do the same in the same way. I will do my job, but take more rest and time away.

I stayed two more days on board the 109, helped Jones weave some rope fenders for the boat, read, slept, and visited with various members of the crew. I was surprised to find each of them anxious to talk, as they had been right on the ship seeing the same people, hearing the same things so long. Also, I photographed the ship from top to bottom—not the ship, actually, but the men working on it. Quirl had sent two rolls of black and white film, and I was glad to do this for these swell guys.

They had never had anyone who would spend two days photographing them in all the various phases of their work. All the shots were candid and should reflect the real spirit of the 109. It was all wonderful, living those few days with good quarters, good food, and men who do not have the defeated, worked-out, and tired look of our soldiers who have taken it all for more than two years in the tropics.

The night before I left, Jones made cocoa and brought it up to the table on the top deck for a sort of farewell chat. We talked and listened to the radio, and each wondered what we would be doing in future months. Again I felt the old and awful pang of friends slipping forever from my circle—my golden circle where I hold the highest and best of them. I wouldn't likely see any of these fellows again—ever—after I left in the morning.

I hope to look Buddy up in the States, but at the same time, I realize that we were here thrown together by the circumstances of war, and that perhaps traveling our own and different ways at home, we would be different people. Who knows? The whole pleasant event joined the beautiful and brief things that become a part of our distilled selves and add gold to the whole of us.

April 14, 1945

Arrived yesterday here at Batangas after a week of waiting at Subic for boats to come down. The week was one of rest and relaxation. I had nothing on my mind, no job to do, no one to tell me that anything needed doing. Finally a convoy of our boats formed up, and I boarded one of our large cabin boats, the P-19, and rode down. The trip down was over pleasant seas, with a stopover for the night half-way at WaWa.

At WaWa we traded for bananas and mangos and fresh eggs, and looked over the small town. Here again was evidence that the Filipinos can fall back on their knowledge of how to get along without civilization. Women and men were carrying bundles of what looked like bark, but when I examined it, I found it was cactus root, flattened and dried. Here was soap! The Navajos have used it for generations. The pueblo Indians wash their hair with it in sacred ceremonies. The Japanese had cut off the supply of soap, but they couldn't destroy the knowledge that would make more soap available from an old, old source.

Here in Batangas I find our camp not very complete. Only a few tent floors built, everyone more or less sitting around awaiting lumber to continue construction of the most "garrisoned" camp we have had since leaving the States. Rumor has it that we will train green troops for a long period; but again, that is only a rumor. Also rumor says I am to go home on furlough, but no one has told me anything official. Maybe the letter did bear fruit. Maybe not.

April 28, 1945

No action of any kind in the past days. We are still sitting here. Filipinos are building the camp—slowly. Only one tent has its bamboo floor; the rest of us are still on the ground. There is no camp activity. Battalion headquarters is again being separated from the combined company-battalion set-up, and I am doing absolutely nothing, awaiting the building of the battalion headquarters building.

We have hundreds of banana peddlers coming by—most of them colorful native women in bright dresses with huge trays of golden bananas on their heads and their familiar query, "Do you like banana?" We "like banana" and keep a lot of them all the time. They are the most delicious bananas I have ever eaten, and there are several varieties. The cost is about five cents a dozen, or rather, you can get a dozen with a small five-cent bar of soap.

Although the camp is restricted because of the killing of four Negro soldiers by "unknown persons," I have visited the old church a couple of times. Built 150 years ago by the Spanish, it stands practically intact, except for the front, which crumbled in an earthquake the day before Bataan fell. Inside it is very pleasing and restful, beautifully designed. The bell tower still stands, and each morning the bells toll out at daybreak as they have for a century and a half.

We walked into the courtyard behind the church, and strikingly framed in a huge archway was a nun, immaculate in her white and black habit. I determined to come back later and photograph her there. She seemed anxious to talk, and I supposed she was tired of the company of other sisters exclusively. She had not been interned by the Japanese in Manila, but ran an orphanage with other sisters. However, not being interned was small comfort, as food was practically nonexistent, and the Japanese were as annoying as possible to them. The nuns were slapped and insulted on the slightest provocation because the Japanese tried to show their contempt for an "inferior" people and religion.

But I suppose that the sisters got even in the end, for they made trips (after the Americans started driving the Japanese out) to our intelligence headquarters and pointed out Japanese strong points. When they fortified themselves in the lower floor and basement of the orphanage, the nuns slipped out with the children, informed the artillery, and saw the whole place flattened. "But we were glad," she said. Evidently even a nun can revel in sweet revenge.

A pleasant surprise was the reappearance of my pals of the 109. The army is full of anticlimaxes. You leave a place forever and—presto—you find you are transferred back again the next week. You leave some friends, never expecting to see them again. Presto! They show up from nowhere. Anyway I was awfully glad to see the 109 boys again. They are here for quite a stay, so we will resume our pleasant visits.

Buddy is looking fit as ever, but worries because he has received his A-1 classification for the army. I am positive his B-? something-or-other classification is on its way though, for anyone now in service as he is wouldn't be called home.

May 13, 1945

Today I was called to the medical headquarters to have my medical record checked, vaccinations brought up to date, etc., in preparation for the trip home. It was the first real knowledge I had received that my furlough had gone through. So long the waiting, but all the bitter days are now behind! I don't know what is ahead, but there will be days at home, days with friends, days to rest, days to paint, and days in which to plan for a normal life again.

Today I received a letter from Dot in which she said, "When I read that you were sure you would get a furlough, I just blubbered." Well, Dot, dear, we'll probably have a big blubbering spree when I get back, for I almost blubber just thinking of it myself!

I have met a very nice Filipino family, living down near the waterfront. One day I was going by when I met the girl with the beautiful hair, and the meeting resulted in my photographing her later and meeting her three sisters, brother, and mother. Few women on earth are ever crowned with anything approaching hair that comes to their ankles when they are standing upright, but hers does—an amazing mane of lustrous black. She washes it with the same type of cactus-root soap I have seen the Filipinos selling. She says that is better for it, and she is right.

I was somewhat annoyed that she plans to enter a convent, and, of course, clip her head. I can't see God giving a woman such a head of hair and then expecting her to cut it as a "sacrifice" to gain favor with Him. This family plans a Filipino party the twenty-fourth, and I am very anxious to go—if I am still here at that time.

June 22, 1945

The waiting ended, and on May 20, I boarded ship in Manila Harbor bound for home. It was high time! I had ceased to have the will to write or hope or care what happened, and the memories of overseas living had crowded close. The voyage was uncomfortable, and we worked eight hours a day on guard shifts, but our boat was bound for home! There was a twenty-four-hour stop at Pearl Harbor on June 5, and a brief glimpse of that shining land held all the romantic ideas associated with it. The green hills were misted with a late shower that evening, and a rainbow arched over Diamond Head. We tied up to a pier very near to shore, and once the fragrance of many flowers wafted across as I stood on the ship's bridge—as I stood within a stone's throw of my long-cherished desire, never to be accomplished, to stand on Hawaii's shore with a flower lei.

On June 16, we reached the Panama Canal, and on the 17th went through this amazing engineering feat to the Pacific Ocean.

On June 20, we arrived at Newport News, Virginia, two years, four months, and two days after bidding goodbye to America. Here was all we had been away for, and I found my hard bitterness slipping, slipping away.

Here was America—big and rich and throbbing with activity and love and all things dear. Here was a smiling woman with lemonade and doughnuts, and she looked so wonderful!

All the people looked wonderful, and they did feel the war and work for it as hard as we had done; we were just out in front doing our part in a different place. As the train rolled out to the reception center for overseas veterans (we were veterans—funny!), I watched the people who lined the tracks, the poor people, the ones in big cars, the Negroes by their shanties. They all smiled and cheered so sincerely that big tears welled up, and I was glad of my big sunglasses, but am sure others had eye trouble too.

Arrangements at the camp were fit for a king, altogether the finest equipped and managed army place I ever stayed in. Soft mattresses, sheets and pillows, wonderful food—served by German prisoners of war. There were telegraph booths and stores and movies and service clubs. But best of all, everyone was so damned nice to every soldier. Nothing was good enough for us.

Early the first morning I strolled through the grove to the Chapel in the Woods. The door was open, but it looked closed and dark at this early hour; so I turned back through the grove and lingered there to give thanks to my God for a return to a land so wonderful, and I'm sure He understood.

The chapel sign said "Protestant Services, 11:00; Catholic Services, 7:00; Jewish Services, Friday," but I wanted to talk with a God who listened without a specified day or hour. And He was here this morning as the early sun slanted through the pines and sweetgums and touched the jewelled grass with a million lights.

A graceful, gray squirrel played at the base of a tall tree. Birds sang, and a redheaded woodpecker beat a tattoo on a dead limb. It was a magic hour made for talking with God, and I resolved again to seek Him outside of man-made churches. Always it would be awkward to try to explain so unconventional a thing to anyone, so I won't try. If they are people who care enough, they will ask no explanation. If they aren't, they don't deserve to have one.

The future is, indeed, uncertain, but with sufficient points for a discharge, I anticipate at least re-assignment in the States. I hope my war is over. I am tired of it all—tired clean through—and long for a permanent place among people I love, and a chance to begin again.

Epilogue

Although the Browning Journal ended when Gaitha returned to the States in June 1945, the real story of his life as an artist was just beginning. Since he had taken no leave during his years in the South Pacific, he had accumulated enough "points" to be discharged from the army. He arrived in Brownwood in time to be with his father for a short time before the elder Browning's death. Typical of his unselfishness and filial devotion, he remained to care for his mother, who also suffered from heart disease.

Following her death at the age of seventy-four, he began to put into action plans he had made during his army years. He studied at the Brooklyn Museum of Art in New York for two years and went to a portrait school in Phoenix, Arizona, on a G.I. scholarship for about a year. Although he was anxious to return to his beloved New Mexico, again family illness intervened. His sister, Elizabeth Giddens, was diagnosed with breast cancer. Once more Gaitha returned to Brownwood to care for a loved one until her death. He began teaching art classes in the area, and before long had groups of students in towns all over Central Texas—Brownwood, Coleman, Comanche, Breckenridge, San Saba, Dublin, and others.

Although he spent three years as an artist and trader in Zuni, New Mexico, and six years in Taos during the decade of the fifties, he periodically returned to Brownwood to complete paintings from the sketches he had done on site. Many of his works sold before they were even completed.

Area art students pleaded for him to teach "just one more course" before leaving Texas until, finally, he bought a brick house and adjacent lot in Brownwood with the intention of building a studio there. Five years after returning from New York, he sold the lot and designed and built a studio behind his house, which he maintained until his death on November 10, 1992.

His flare for artistic design was never more evident than in this studio, a wonderland of antique ceiling beams hung with Indian artifacts and priceless colonial copper pieces, an array of collectors' item books, many of the

Australian aboriginal and New Guinea items sent home during the war, lush tropical plants, stacks of paintings to be framed or in progress, sketches for planned works, a self-designed giant coffee table in the form of an artist's palette with paints, and a tangible ambiance of peacefulness and contentment, all cheerfully lighted by an expanse of skylight windows. Tacked to a closet door is the original flag which he was commissioned by Colonel Cecil Bilger to design for their LCM (Landing Craft Mechanized). Indicative of the esteem in which the artist-soldier was held by his commanding officers, Bilger gave the flag to Browning when they both left the South Pacific theater. Only an artist of incredible talent could have brought all of these parts into such a complete and fulfilled whole. The big easel at which he works belonged to his beloved teacher, Harry Anthony DeYoung, and was given to Gaitha by Mrs. DeYoung on the death of her husband.

Other than DeYoung, numbered among Gaitha's artist friends have been Joseph H. Sharp of Taos, New Mexico; Richard Goetz of Oklahoma and New York; Peter Hurd, and Norman Rockwell.

Although he spent as much time as he could in New Mexico, Colorado, Arizona, and Montana, sketching and painting, living and dancing with the Indians, learning their languages, designing jewelry, working in trading posts, and absorbing the atmosphere which fed his soul, Gaitha never moved from Texas. From his time in the larger Southwest came a legacy of hundreds of paintings which grace the walls of friends and art collectors all over the nation. Every Gaitha Browning work is a one-of-a-kind, because he never had prints made. Any framed print to be found was taken from one of the magazines which featured his life and work in earlier years.

One of the regrets expressed by this gentle man concerning his war experiences is that he once shot a cockatoo during target practice. He never again shot at wildlife, after seeing the beautifully marked, dead New Guinea parrot, and he retained his compassion for and delight in nature's creatures up until the day he died.

He also maintained a vital interest in preserving the culture of the North American Indians. He was active in thc Texas Indian Hobbyist Association, of which he was a charter member.

In each of our memorable conversations, he talked of subjects he still wanted to paint and places he still intended to visit, including the rugged western part of Australia he didn't have a chance to see during his service years, and a return to Canyon de Chelly in Arizona which he characterized as the "most beautiful spot on earth." Surrounding his studio painting area were photographs of Indian friends of whom he wanted to do additional portraits.

Though limited by the confines of his health, Gaitha sat at his easel and spanned the globe by brushing bursts of beauty from palm groves in Cairns, Australia, or New England seascapes, or his mesa lands of Arizona and New Mexico, or Saint Elena Canyon in his well-loved Texas. One of his last works in oil was a series of three panels depicting the Río Grande at the mouth of the Big Bend canyon.

Once when I asked him to paint me a verbal portrait of his mother, he concluded by saying, "and if I painted her, it would be with a book in her hand." I like to think that *this* is the book she would have wanted in her hand.

O.S.T.

NOTES FOR PART III

[1] The battle for Leyte Gulf cost the Japanese heavily. The core of their Navy was demolished and was no longer a significant factor in the Pacific war.—*Ed.*

[2] Admiral Nimitz's forces moved into the Palau Islands in the western Carolines in mid-September 1944. Not until late October was organized resistence overcome where airfields were to be constructed for air access to the Philippines. Heavy fighting continued until November 25, in what proved to be among the bloodiest battles of the war. With the southern Palaus and Ulithi in Allied hands, the rest of the Palaus were neutralized by air action. The western Pacific was safe for Allied air and naval forces, and the road to the Philippines was open from both the south and the east.—*Ed.*

[3] In October 1944 the Japanese made an all-out effort to defeat Allied forces at Leyte. The battle cost them keenly.—*Ed.*

[4] The value of a peso there in 1944 was fifty cents.—*Ed.*

[5] Melody McCay was Marie's younger sister, and the daughter of Mae and Roy McCay of Gallup, New Mexico.—*Ed.*

[6] The first part of the journal, which had been left in the Commonwealth Bank of Australia at Cairns, Queensland, was mailed to Gaitha by his request after the war ended. His journal entries from New Guinea and the Philippines remained in his possession until he returned home. Mr. Young decided not to try to take the journal through customs and declined to take it back to the States with him.—*Ed.*

[7] Stewart "Scrip" Painter, a long-time scouting friend whom Gaitha remembered with affection and kept in touch with after their return to civilian life.—*Ed.*

[8] Later we found that, along that long stretch of beach, there had never been a Japanese pillbox or gun of any kind. —*G.B.*

[9] Carabao, the water buffalo of the Philippine Islands, are commonly domesticated.—*Ed.*

[10] I later learned that the balasoot could not be found even fifty or a hundred miles south of La Paz, which seemed to be the southernmost limit of its use. For instance, natives around Subic Bay never heard of it.—*G.B.*

[11] The Indonesian language of the chief Malay people in the Philippines.—*Ed.*

[12] Convoy of Ms refers to the combined group of LCMs and LSMs forming the convoy. LC designates Landing Craft and LS, Landing Ship. While many Amphibians used Mechanized for the letter M in the acronyms, the M more commonly stood for Medium, the general size of the crafts and ships described.—*Ed.*

Index